Applications in Intelligence-Led Policing: Where Theory Meets Reality

Marilyn B. Peterson, Paula Carter and Jennifer Johnstone, editors

Published by The International Association of Law Enforcement Intelligence Analysts (IALEIA)

P.O. Box 13857, Richmond, VA 23225

Technical editors: Robert Fahlman and Karen Aumond
Cover Design: Matthew Fegley

ISBN-13: 978-1720476542

ISBN-10: 1720476543

Contents

Section I. An Overview

Chapter 1: History of Intelligence-Led Policing – *David Creagh, U.S. Department of Justice, Federal Bureau of Investigation*…..p. 9

Chapter 2: From a posteriori to a priori analysis: a new paradigm (in France) against crime – *Clément De Maillard, Ph.D., Captain, Gendarmerie Nationale (France), Project Manager for INTERPOL (seconded officer) and Patrick Perrot, Colonel , Ph.D, Criminal Intelligence Service, Gendarmerie Nationale (France)*…..p. 21

Chapter 3: ILP : A View From the United Kingdom – *Jonathan Larkin, Th.D., Surrey (UK) Police Force*…..p. 37

Chapter 4: ILP and Privacy Issues – *Gregory Thomas, Ph.D., Pennsylvania State University; Kerri Salata, J.D., Bank of Montreal ; and Linda Randby, J.D. Pennsylvania State Police*…..p. 59

Section II. Applications

Chapter 5: Strategically Combating Organized Crime – *Andrew Wright, Interpol, Zimbawe, and Lt. (N). Lee Heard, Canadian Armed Forces* …..p. 77

Chapter 6: Proactive Approaches to White Collar Crime – *Marilyn B. Peterson, Peterson Analytic Associates, LLC*…..p. 111

Chapter 7: Cyber Crime Applications – *Navid Sobbi, National Intelligence and Surveillance Pty Ltd and Melissa Vives, Ph.D., U.S. Government*…..p. 127

Chapter 8: Financial Intelligence Applications – *Alison Callery, State of New Jersey and Anne Walton, K2 Intelligence* …..p. 137

Chapter 9: Gang Crime and ILP – *David Creagh, Federal Bureau of Investigation and Alyssa Ryder, Lake Superior Drug and Crime Task Force*.....p. 159

 Chapter 10: National Security and Intelligence – *Maj. David Gervais, U.S. Army*......p. 175

Section III. Appendices

1. *Glossary – Marilyn Peterson*.....*p. 195*
2. *Software – Paula Carter and Sean Tolbert*.....*p. 201*
3. *Biographies*.....*p. 221*
4. *References*.....*p. 229*
5. *Index*.....*p. 245*

Preface

The aftermath of the September 2001 terrorist attacks against the United States included a call for "intelligence-led policing" across the country. Several attempts to encourage this shift in policing strategy were mounted, among them was a paper I wrote for the International Association of Police Chiefs (IACP) that was published by the Bureau of Justice Assistance in 2005, *Intelligence Led Policing: The New Intelligence Architecture.* Since then, there have been numerous articles, chapters and books written on intelligence led policing. Nonetheless, the intervening twelve years have not brought about wholesale change in this direction.

This book is a look at how law enforcement efforts in intelligence-led policing are progressing in Europe (Great Britain and France), Australia and North America (U.S. and Canada). Thus, about eighteen intelligence professionals add their experience in ILP and their expertise in analysis to demystifying the role that analysis and intelligence should play in preventative policing. The contributions of several IALEIA Board and Executive Advisory Board members must also be acknowledged. We hope this book supports the progress of ILP around the world.

- **Marilyn B. Peterson, CICA, CFE**

Chapter 1: History of Intelligence-Led Policing

By David Creagh

Introduction

While intelligence-led policing may seem like a new concept in law enforcement, it is not. Thanks to the efforts of Great Britain in using intelligence to thwart property crime during 1994, American law enforcement saw the benefit of using it to standardize intelligence collection throughout the law enforcement community. Every attempt, however, was plagued by different versions of definitions. To combat this discrepancy, working groups attempted to fix the standardization problem. The unfortunate events of September 11, 2001 caused the nation and the entire law enforcement community to rethink intelligence collection and analysis, albeit at much faster pace than normal.

Definition of ILP

Intelligence-led policing (ILP) has been defined by every author who has written about it. Richard Anderson, of the Kent Constabulary, referred to it as: "the collection and analysis of information to produce an intelligence end product designed to inform police decision-making at both the tactical and strategic levels" (Anderson, in Smith, 1997, 1).

Ratcliffe and Guidetti defined it as "a business model and an information-organizing process that allows police agencies to better understand their crime problems and take measure of the resources available to be able to decide on an enforcement tactic or prevention strategy best designed to control crime" (2008, p. 109).

Other authors suggested multiple definitions for ILP. In addition to quoting Anderson, Townsend et al., provided other definitions for ILP:

- "A business process for systematically collecting, organizing, analyzing, and utilizing intelligence to guide law enforcement operational and tactical decisions."
- "The application of criminal intelligence analysis as an objective decision making tool in order to facilitate crime reduction and prevention through effective policing strategies and external partnership projects drawn from an evidential base."
- "A collaborative philosophy that starts with information, gathered at all levels of the organization that is analyzed to create useful intelligence and an improved understanding of the operational environment" (Townsend, 2010, p. 1-2).

The Virginia Department of Criminal Justice Services also found no single definition of ILP (2013, p.2).

If ILP resists a singular definition, is that a bad thing? According to Ratcliffe, the world of ILP is always changing; however, it is possible to have one definition. After reviewing the Kent Policing Model of ILP, it was apparent there were central ideas in which a definition can be established. Those included:

- Target prolific and serious criminals. By doing so, a law enforcement agency has the opportunity to become proactive by targeting those individuals who are responsible for violence in an area.
- Triage out most crime. It was believed that creating a crime desk would be helpful in handling all initial calls. This is important because the crime desks can determine which calls required investigations. Additionally, it was important to limit the number of visits to a crime scene.
- Make greater strategic use of surveillance and informants. Informants have the greatest access to a criminal enterprise and have vital information pertaining to the areas in which they live. While these individuals are used for operational objectives, it is equally important to remember they harness strategic intelligence.
- Position intelligence next to decision-making. For ILP to be successful, it is important to keep the intelligence mission at the center of operations. Law enforcement agencies expecting to become successful in managing an ILP model must always run their investigations synchronously with the intelligence cycle (2016, p. 63).

Although ILP can be defined in a number of ways, it is still possible for a law enforcement organization to apply this model to varied crime problems within different organizations. Ultimately, ILP, regardless of definition, attempts to achieve the same results since each definition has similar drivers. As law enforcement agencies progress in their use of the ILP model, they should begin to answer the question of why certain events are taking place within their jurisdiction and not just flood the streets with patrol officers as a mere show of force. In the next section, we will examine how the Kent Model allowed an agency to prioritize how calls were handled in order to tackle property crime.

Tactical and Strategic Intelligence

As if defining intelligence-led policing is not difficult enough, oftentimes analysts have trouble providing analytical support to their customers because information their customers sought does not meet their expectations. In their effort trying to become intelligence-led, analysts should be looking at methods to predict and thwart crime problems before they occur. Law enforcement officers, with their traditional mindset, are more or less likely to remain in their reactive comfort zones. Much of this can be attributed to the different types of intelligence: strategic versus tactical.

To provide an accurate picture to law enforcement decision-makers, analysts rely on providing the most accurate strategic intelligence. Strategic intelligence is more concerned with providing "the big picture." Tactical intelligence on the other hand requires immediate action. This information is time-sensitive and highly perishable. This intelligence "contributes to the success of specific investigations" (Peterson, 2005, p. 3).

Since the role of the analyst is to provide a proactive approach to get ahead of crime, law enforcement officers' needs do not often match that of the analysts. Analysts are trained to provide decision-makers with crime trends, forecasts, and early warning and analysis. Unfortunately traditional mindset police officers find this intelligence less rewarding since they are focused on their investigations. To understand this better, the following example from the Kent Constabulary provides an immediate response (tactical) to mitigate the problem and a plan to sustain that process (strategic) to stay ahead of any crime problems.

The Kent Model

In the Kent Constabulary ILP model, a strategy was devised to mitigate a single type of crime problem within a single geographic district. Following its lead, several other agencies in Great Britain also adopted the method.

Originally called the Kent Policing Model, ILP helped the Kent Constabulary answer the question on how best to run an effective police force with a limited amount of resources. The Constabulary found its answer by prioritizing calls for service. In order to utilize its police force more effectively, non-serious calls for service were assigned to other personnel while serious calls were assigned to the officers (Anderson, in Smith, 1997, pp. 5-9).

According to Anderson , the Kent Constabulary established a committee to review its intelligence mission and provide recommendations on maximizing its police effectiveness while increasing public safety. The results of the committee contributed to one of its biggest advancements since the Constabulary's founding (Smith, 1997, pp. 5-9)

As a result of this overhaul, the Kent Policing Model allowed the Constabulary to be successful in reducing the effects of property crime by the late 1990s. In 1996, crime throughout Kent's jurisdiction fell by 6.5 percent (143,000 offenses). In 1997, Kent continued to see a drastic reduction when crime fell by 16.3 percent (119,000 offenses) (Anderson, in Smith, 1997, pp. 5-9).

While it seems the ILP process in the 1990s was successful, the process would prove time and time again to be an effective strategy. However, the Constabulary may have overlooked one important component. Instead of saturating the streets with constables as a show of force, the department may have missed the opportunity to use the intelligence and analyze why the problem was occurring in the first place. Alternatively, the Kent Constabulary (2012), formed partnerships with the Essex Police and the South East Region Group. Their intended goal for this time frame was to reduce crime one percent or 100,775 offenses.

United States Intelligence-Led Policing

Intelligence was used in the United States in varied forms from the turn of the 20th century. The New York Police Department, for example, had a squad that worked for several decades against a form of an Italian Mafia during the late 1890s and early 1900s. In the 1930s and 1940s, "Red Squads" were present and targeted anarchists and bombers (Bouza, 1976). In 1956, the Law Enforcement Intelligence Unit (LEIU) was formed to support the sharing of data on organized criminals across the country. LEIU created *File Guidelines* that were adopted by all its members and ensured appropriate standards were met (www.leiu.org). Those *Guidelines* were updated in 2002.

In 1967, the President's Commission on Law Enforcement and the Administration of Justice noted the importance of collecting and using intelligence. Then during the early 1970s, major steps were taken to get enforcement to use intelligence. A book, *The Basic Elements of Intelligence*, was published by the Department of Justice (Godfrey and Harris, 1971). It defined intelligence and established standards for setting up intelligence units in departments. In 1973, the National Advisory Commission on Criminal Justice Standards and Goals stated that law enforcement agencies should develop a system to acquire, analyze, and disseminate intelligence to combat organized crime. While the intention was to target organized crime, it was vital that the commission ensure that individual rights would still be protected.

While the concept of integrating intelligence into law enforcement may be seen as an enhancement to traditional policing, some agencies contributions hindered its implementation. Some law enforcement agencies abused individuals' civil liberties. Because of this, several law enforcement agencies were ordered to abandon their intelligence programs. It would not be until 1976 that new guidelines would require law enforcement agencies to have predication when conducting intelligence on a person or a criminal enterprise (Peterson, 2005, p. 5)

To accomplish this, law enforcement agencies adopted a means to effectively manage an intelligence operation, regardless of an agency's size. The official recommendation suggested that agencies make an effort to adopt a "minimum standard" for implementing the use of intelligence. While the suggested minimum standard included various administrative processes, it also included the management of disseminating intelligence products and safeguarding an individual's privacy (Virginia Department of Criminal Justice Services, 2013, p. 2). In 1976, the *Basic Elements of Intelligence* was re-published with multiple authors (Harris, et al).

The intelligence movement gained further momentum with the formation of the Regional Information Sharing System (RISS) projects (ROCIC, RMIN, MAGLOCLEN, NESPIN, MOCIC and WSIN) [1] between 1973 and 1980. These were funded by the Department of Justice and provided analytic services, surveillance equipment on loan, pointer data bases, and intelligence training.

To help govern the Regional Information Sharing System projects, the Bureau of Justice Assistance, in 1979, created 28 *Code of Federal Regulations* 23.20, the "Criminal Information System Operating Policies". These policies were the first U.S. regulations on criminal intelligence and remain the only national guidelines on the topic. Law enforcement agency members of the Regional Information Sharing System projects were required to agree to follow these regulations as condition of their membership in the project. The policies covered any federal criminal justice grant recipient whose funding included an intelligence database.

In 1980, the International Association of Law Enforcement Intelligence Analysts (IALEIA) was created at the International Association of Chiefs of Police (IACP) conference in New Orleans (www.ialeia.org). This organization gave a voice to civilian intelligence analysts found in federal, state, county and municipal agencies and became instrumental in the development of intelligence-led policing.

---

[1] The Regional Organized Crime Information Center (ROCIC), serving the Southeast U.S. was created in 1978, with the Rocky Mountain Information Network (Southeast U.S.) following, along with the Middle Atlantic-Great Lakes Organized Crime Law Enforcement Network (MAGLOCLEN), serving eight states in the midwest and mid-Atlatic; the New England State Police Information Network (NESPIN), the Mid-States Organized Crime Information Center (MOCIC), serving the Midwest; and the Western States Information Network (WSIN). See www.iir.org for additional information on the projects.

The role of the International Association of Chiefs of Police in the acceptance of intelligence in law enforcement was also significant. In 1985 the IACP *Enforcement Policy on the Management of Criminal Intelligence* was developed by IACP, giving its thousands of members' guidance on the use of intelligence.

In 2000, the National Criminal Intelligence Service (NCIS) of the United Kingdom launched the National Intelligence Model (NIM). It was adopted by the Association of Chief Police Officers (ACPO) and the government placed the NIM at the center of its police reform platform (https://ict.police.uk/national-standards/intel/).

The National Intelligence Model is used for:

- Setting strategic direction
- Making prioritized and defendable resourcing decisions
- Allocating resources intelligently
- Formulating tactical plans and tasking and coordinating resulting activity
- Managing the associated risks (https://ict.police.uk/national-standards/intel/)

The IACP Information Sharing Summit

During the fall of 2001, law enforcement officials realized the need to standardize the way intelligence was collected and disseminated throughout the law enforcement community. It was envisioned all participants could form a strategy aligned with that of President George Bush even before the terrorist attacks of September 11th, 2001. The unfortunate events of that tragic day would catapult the law enforcement community into a drastic transformation (U.S Department of Justice, 2003, p. 1). The International Association of Chiefs of Police met in October, 2001, in Toronto, Canada and several groups represented agreed that it should hold a Criminal Justice Intelligence Sharing Summit in March, 2002.

That Summit included over 120 participants from varied groups including Federal agencies, state and local law enforcement and intelligence associations such as IALEIA and LEIU. The UK *National Intelligence Model* was highlighted, as was the Drug Enforcement Administration's *General Counterdrug Intelligence Plan* (GCIP) (https://www.dea.gov/pubs/pressrel/pr022602_01.html) which had also been completed in 2000. This plan included 73 action items in areas including: national counterdrug intelligence coordination; national centers; regional, state and local cooperation; analytic personnel development and training; and information technology. The plan provided for a three-tiered mechanism to ensure effective counterdrug intelligence and continuing coordination (https://www.ncjrs.gov/App/Publications/abstract.aspx?ID=180750).

The IACP Intelligence Summit included working groups on critical areas which arrived at recommendations for action. It resulted in the publication of *Criminal Intelligence Sharing: A National Plan for Intelligence-Led Policing at the Local, State and Federal Levels* (http://www.theiacp.org/portals/0/pdfs/CriminalIntelligenceSharingReport.pdf).

The *Sharing* report core recommendation was to "promote intelligence-led policing through a common understanding of criminal intelligence and its usefulness" (U.S. Department of Justice, 2002, p. v). Additionally, the report said the following steps must be taken:

- Provide the critical balance of civil rights;
- Increase opportunities for trust building;
- Remedy analytic deficits;
- Remedy information deficits;
- Address training issues; and
- Address technology issues (U.S. Department of Justice, 2002, p. v-vi).

National Criminal Intelligence Sharing Plan

As a result of the Criminal Intelligence Sharing Summit, the U.S. Department of Justice's Office of Justice Programs paved the way for the creation of the Global Justice Information Sharing Initiative (Global) Intelligence Working Group (GIWG) during the Fall of 2002. Law enforcement professionals from all levels of government developed a mission statement which would allow them to devise the following strategy to standardize how law enforcement agencies would integrate intelligence with operations. Those included:

- Creation of an intelligence sharing plan;
- Promotion of ILP;
- Development process for an intelligence system;
- Guidelines to ensure an individual's civil liberties and rights are safeguarded;;
- A model for intelligence process principles and policies;
- Technological infrastructure that would allow for seamless information sharing;
- A national model for intelligence training; and
- An outreach program to promoted intelligence sharing (U.S Department of Justice, 2003, p. 2).

To facilitate the above recommendations, the GIWG understood that certain barriers would exist for law enforcement agencies attempting to adopt this new method of policing. These barriers included:

- Development of management standards for an intelligence function;
- Establishment of the Criminal Intelligence Council;
- Institutionalizing the *National Criminal Intelligence Sharing Plan;*
- Protection of individuals' constitutional and civil rights as well as their privacy;
- Development of standards for intelligence collection and analysis;
- Increase flow of classified information to state and local law enforcement;
- Creation of standardized criminal intelligence training; and
- Creation of an intelligence sharing platform accessible by all levels of law enforcement (U.S. Department of Justice, 2003).

The above list may seem like an overwhelming feat to accomplish; however, the GIWG did provide numerous recommendations on how law enforcement agencies could transform their agencies to conform to these new standards. For the purposes of this publication, only those recommendations involving operations were included. First, it was necessary for law enforcement agencies to adopt the minimum standards of ILP and implement the intelligence function as outlined by the *National Criminal Intelligence Sharing Plan* (U.S Department of Justice, 2003, p. 10).

Second, it was imperative to establish a Criminal Intelligence Coordinating Council (CICC) to ensure appropriate law enforcement followed proper oversight when it came to implementing ILP. To do this, the CICC would provide a regular report to Congress, the U.S. Attorney General, and the Department of Homeland Security to maximize the effectiveness of criminal intelligence. The CICC observed the implementation of the *National Criminal Intelligence Sharing Plan* in order to monitor its success. To ensure the implementation was followed appropriately, the OJP was provided an annual report to monitor the implementation (U.S Department of Justice, 2003, p. 11).

One of the most vital recommendations involved adequate funding. Many law enforcement departments do not have the financial ability to implement these new measures. Therefore, it was crucial federal funding be provided to aid law enforcement agencies in implementing these changes. At the time of its publication, however, *The National Criminal Intelligence Sharing Plan* did not have an estimate of the funding level needed to implement these changes (U.S. Department of Justice, 2003, p.11-12).

During this time frame, other activities in support of intelligence-led policing occurred. In 2003, the IACP released its *Criminal Intelligence Model Policy* (June). This provided a blueprint to agencies looking to establish a criminal intelligence function. The IACP also published a *Criminal Intelligence Concepts and Issues Paper* that year.

The Criminal Intelligence Coordinating Council asked IALEIA to work with all parties to develop the first edition of *Law Enforcement Analytic Standards* and that was completed and published in 2004 (a 2nd edition was published in 2012).

In 2005, the DOJ and IACP published *Intelligence-Led Policing: the New Intelligence Architecture*, which gave examples of how ILP was being used in various locations in the U.S. (Peterson). This was followed in 2008 by *Reducing Crime Through Intelligence Led Policing* which highlighted reports from a dozen municipalities that had received grants to implement ILP in their areas (Bureau of Justice Assistance).

In 2008, *Fusion Center Guidelines* were published and provided insight on how the various fusion centers would operate and disseminate intelligence (Department of Justice). Much like the *Basic Elements of Intelligence*, these guidelines focused on safeguarding individuals' civil rights, disseminating intelligence, and security. Additionally, the guidelines provided information on how the fusion centers would receive funding.

In 2013, Chernak, et al. reported results from a study that showed only 13 percent of those state, local and tribal (SLT) law enforcement agencies surveyed thought their agencies had developed a robust intelligence function. In fact, it stated;

> "The results…illustrate that there is widespread agreement that the law
> enforcement community has a long way to go in building an intelligence capacity—a

conclusion indicated by the respondents from both survey samples. Less than 10 percent of the SLT respondents thought their agency was far along in developing and maintaining a law enforcement intelligence capacity, 13 percent strongly agreed they had the capacity to identify the characteristics of events that represent the indicators or precursors of threats, and only 17 percent thought their agency provides actionable intelligence in a timely manner" (Chernak, Carter, Carter, McGarrell and Drew, 2013, p. 226).

Within "traditional" policing, information was gathered and stored in files, but the agencies had no capability to analyze the data. In order for a law enforcement organization to become proactive, it is important to step out of the role of traditional policing. Throughout time, however, it has been very difficult for law enforcement agencies to break away from their traditional mindset. The traditional model worked for them and it is that model which these seasoned officers were comfortable. One of the biggest issues facing ILPs adaptation in U.S. law enforcement is the entrance of intelligence analysts into daily operations. According to Cope, many police officers felt uncomfortable taking guidance from their intelligence analysis counterparts (2004, p. 191).

It is not an easy task to incorporate analysis into daily operations. Surely, the typical patrol officer knows more about their job and their community than an intelligence analyst. What may not have been emphasized enough is the fact it was never the intention of analysis to take the place of traditional policing. While policing will frequently have to be reactive, intelligence attempts to enhance operations by recommending different strategies to mitigate criminal threats (Cope, 2004, p. 191).

If the purpose of intelligence analysis is to enhance criminal investigations, then why is much of this ignored? Cope believes the patrol officer is a primary source of the information. What could analysis provide the officer that he or she does not already know? The biggest contributing factor to the reception of analysis rests solely with the officers understanding of what intelligence analysis provides (Cope, 2004, p.194).

If law enforcement insists on using ILP in its daily operations, then it is imperative for mid-level management to understand the purpose it plays and provide proper training for the law enforcement officer. Criminal intelligence training is a must not only for the patrol officer, but also managers. In one study, only four percent of law enforcement officers received training which would make them more comfortable working with intelligence and instill confidence with intelligence analysis. Approximately 50 percent of supervisors believed they received sufficient training to implement it. Phillips argues if training was increased, support for ILP could increase (2012, p.16).

Confidence in ILP

While intelligence appears to show law enforcement the advantages to utilizing an unorthodox approach to examine different crime problems, many law enforcement officers were still hesitant in accepting such a drastic transformation. One of the main reasons why ILP was not graciously accepted by law enforcement as outlined by Cope could be due to confidence. Ratcliffe noted that the current ILP model challenges the traditional mindset of policing. This challenge, if not overcome, can be damaging to an organization's attempt to create an ILP model. The operational component will not establish the confidence necessary to put their faith in the intelligence process or their analysts (Ratcliffe, 2016, p. 64).

In 2011, Dr. Ernie Scott, a visiting professor of criminology at the University of South Florida Sarasota-Manatee, claimed that because ILP was still new, not much research has been conducted on ILP. It appears that between the late 1970s and the time Dr. Scott was interviewed, it could be posited that law enforcement agencies reverted back to their normal techniques of reactive investigations due to their lack of trust for this new tool (Sullivan, 2011).

The fact there were not enough data to support, or negate, the effectiveness of ILP may very well be due to the lack of willingness due to confidence in this new model. Since mid-level managers are key to this process, the reason there is no data to show the effectiveness of ILP must be due to the process being abandoned at some point. Not only did mid-level managers not put their faith into ILP, but this would send a message to those officers under them. Surely, they too would reject this new intelligence model, allowing the cycle of shifting priorities to continue. This cycle would prove devastating for ILP since there would never be sufficient positive data to examine like there was in the Kent Constabulary case.

In order to build up trust within an agency, it is vitally important to include the operational component during the planning phase. Because mid-level managers were excluded from the planning phase for ILP's implementation, ILP runs the risk of being improperly implemented. Mid-level managers are vital during this phase. Without their confidence in the strategy, the operational units will almost certainly ignore the benefits of ILP. This oversight would ultimately result in failure before the model can be given a chance (Phillips, 2012, p. 15).

According to Toch, the best way for an organization to achieve a successful reorganization is to allow participation of those individuals who will be affected by an organizational change. Toch said the following to Scottish prison wardens: "the premise of this approach is that people work more effectively when they are involved in making decisions that govern their work, and that organizations are more effective when they deploy the intelligence, wisdom, and judgment of all their members—particularly those on the front line of the organization" (2012, p.27).

The cases for the Kent Constabulary and the United States are completely different. While Kent had to worry about its department tackling a single issue, the United States tried to implement ILP across the entire law enforcement community with numerous issues at hand. All of this was done in the midst of a national tragedy.

FBI Following 9/11

In the United States, there is no centralized police force; however, the Federal Bureau of Investigation (FBI) has filled some parts of that role as a leader in the law enforcement field. Following September 11, 2001, many in the Intelligence Community were forced to answer the question of how such a devastating attack could occur. One of the biggest criticisms the Intelligence Community was forced to admit to: its failure to disseminate intelligence which could have prevented the attack. For its part in this intelligence failure, the Federal Bureau of Investigation (FBI) was widely criticized (Cumming & Masse, 2004, p. 2).

Many believed the FBI had to improve its intelligence corps in order to assist Federal, state, and local law enforcement agencies to combat terrorism. While the idea seemed plausible on paper, it would not be long until it was realized the agency had to break away from its traditional policing role. Like most law enforcement agencies, the FBI was focused on investigating and solving crimes after the fact. It would be imperative, however, that the FBI re-examine its reactive posture if they were to become successful in thwarting future terrorist attacks (Cumming & Masse, 2004, p. 2).

Regardless of what the FBI did to reinvent itself, many believed the efforts were moot given traditional policing would trump any proactive approach. Forcing the FBI—or any law enforcement agency deeply rooted in traditional policing—to change could cause a rift between intelligence analysts and their sworn law enforcement counterparts. To fix this problem, the 9/11 Commission recommended that the FBI integrate its cadre of intelligence professionals with that of the special agents. By doing so, the analysts could work alongside the special agent and be in a better position to ask the right questions and mitigate intelligence gaps. If this were successful, many would hope that the FBI could retain specialists with expertise in intelligence and national security (Cumming & Masse, 2004, pp. 2-4).

In response to the 9/11 Commission Report's recommendation, the FBI established "field intelligence groups," or FIGs, in each of the FBI's 56 field offices. The FIGs were tasked with helping operational squads prioritize intelligence needs while driving investigations. It would not be long, however, until skeptics pointed out that traditional policing would hinder any progress the FBI made due to this mindset (Cumming & Masse, 2004, pp. 8-9, 18).

No matter what the FBI did to rectify their intelligence failures, why were so many still doubting the premier law enforcement agency's ability to conform to a new approach to policing? The problem may rest with buy-in from mid-level managers. As the law enforcement community sought to reinvent itself, many changes to their policing style were decisions made by senior management.

Because mid-level managers and their sworn officers were not included in the planning phase, both groups would certainly experience a major rift. Not only did a rift occur between operations and senior management, but this would carry over into the operations and intelligence realm making intelligence collection difficult. According to Phillips, one major implementation problem occurred when senior leadership excluded officers during the planning phase who would execute this new strategy. Because of this, senior leadership ran the risk of their new policy becoming distorted (2012, p.13).

While many in the law enforcement community made strides to become intelligence-led, those changes were not enough. What did occur that administrators did not foresee was a division between intelligence and operations, as well as senior managers and their sworn officers. How would administrators tackle this major rift?

Integrating the FBI

In order for ILP to be successful, administrators knew they had to bridge the gap between operations and intelligence analysis. The FBI led the charge. In 2015, it established a new training curriculum that combined new agent trainees (NATs) with their new intelligence analyst trainees (NIAT) counterparts (Federal Bureau of Investigation, 2016).

Prior to this change, the FBI Academy at Quantico, VA segregated the training for NATs and their NIATs. Because of this, when these candidates graduated from their respective academy classes, they would have a skewed idea of each other's roles. Under this new model, the Basic Field Training Course (BFTC), NIATs sit alongside with their NAT counterparts. Not only did this new curriculum instill agents with instruction on the intelligence cycle and identifying emerging threats, but both the NATs and NIATs did something that was rarely seen in the past—they developed team cohesion. Although NIAT training lasts approximately 10 weeks, NATs still attend their colleagues' graduations. Many NIATs who remain in the area of Quantico make every attempt to attend their NAT class' graduation (Federal Bureau of Investigation, 2016).

Because this new integrated model was employed at the FBI Academy, the FBI has the ability to flood many of the field offices with special agents who are more open to the intelligence cycle, the role of the intelligence analysts, and how best to answer intelligence gaps affecting their area of responsibility. As more agents and analysts graduate from BFTC, it may be more difficult for traditional policing mindsets to continue in the FBI.

By integrating the NIATs and their NAT counterparts, the FBI is effectively using the "Medici Effect" to maximize the full potential of both proactive and reactive policing. While traditional managers still exist in the FBI, by filling the FBI's 56 field offices with new breed employees, it may only be a matter of time before the idea of ILP cannot be ignored. Eventually, managers may not be able to avoid the countless number of special agents trained in ILP. What exactly is the "Medici Effect" the FBI employed?

The "Medici Effect" is considered a phenomenon when two different specialties or disciplines intersect—or in this context, are merged—and the outcome is a new range of ideas than can enhance either field. This is what led to the Renaissance. Between the 13th and 16th century of Florence, Italy, the Medici's found a way to maximize their economy. In order to do so, they found that if they were to find a way to converge different specialties, they could enhance their society (Johannson, 2006).

That being said, the Medici's acquired sculptors, poets, artists, philosophers, and financiers to help in this venture. As a result, the city became the focal point or innovation resulting in the Renaissance era. By combining different ideologies, a society could enhance and maximize their effectiveness. Within the FBI Academy, and much of law enforcement community altogether, two unrelated fields would collide. Harnessing the benefits of intelligence with operational law enforcement could open up a new "renaissance" for policing (Johannson, 2006).

Ends Justify the Means?
While many Federal law enforcement agencies and metropolitan police departments have budgets to support an ILP model, smaller organizations may not be in the position to achieve a major overhaul, especially in today's economy. While the cost at the start may be troubling to some administrators, the pay-off in the end may allow for them to see the benefits of incorporating ILP into their daily operations. With any success, law enforcement agencies may end up streamlining processes and maximizing their workforce more efficiently. Therefore, is it worth all the trouble to force change and begin to think proactively?

According to the International Association of Law Enforcement Intelligence Analysts (IALEIA), law enforcement managers learned that an analyst's contribution to an operational mission is crucial. Because of this, many law enforcement organizations saw the wide range of salaries for intelligence analysts during an IALEIA survey conducted in 1998. During this time, it was reported that analysts expected to receive an annual salary anywhere between $16,000 to approximately $118,000 for new analysts to supervisory analysts, respectively (2001, p.7).

At the time the Kent Constabulary established its approach, the department was experiencing its own strain of budget cuts. Regardless of the budget constraints Kent faced, they were still able to reduce the threat of property crime in their area. The claim by administrators that they were concerned they could not sustain an intelligence mission due to funding may be false. At the time of its publication, the IALEIA (2001) stressed that any law enforcement agency willing to adopt an intelligence component could receive funding through various sources that supported priority police initiatives (Peterson, 2005, pg.9; IALEIA, 2001, p.6)

The IALEIA recognized the importance of intelligence analysts and worked to ensure that agencies have an analytical component before receiving funding. This funding originated from grants issued by the U.S. Department of Justice, Bureau of Justice Assistance. Analysts allow for law enforcement agencies to investigate and prosecute their cases more effectively. Additionally, many of these agencies found that by using analysts in the face of budgetary constraints allowed for a more effective allocation of resources (2001, p.7).

So while it may be difficult for a law enforcement agency to stand up an analytical component, it may actually be more fiscally beneficial. Using intelligence analysts to help achieve mission success can allow many of these agencies to free up more resources—much like the Kent Constabulary did.

Conclusions

For some in law enforcement, ILP is nothing more than an enhancement tool. Its design fosters the integration of intelligence with operations. While those with a traditional mindset fear that ILP is going to replace their comfortable norm, ILP harnesses the strength analytical support can bring to an investigation; not to replace the investigation; but to enhance its effectiveness. ILP can allow analysts and investigators to think about issues plaguing their area of responsibility and target those areas more effectively. By ignoring ILP, investigators will ultimately miss out on the chance to embrace a force multiplier.

For others, it is a "smart policing" strategy that will help face the ever-changing challenges of crime across the country. The history of ILP, in many ways, is yet to be lived and recorded. The next few decades will be needed to more fully determine what impact it has on policing.

Chapter 2. From *a posteriori* to *a priori* analysis: a new paradigm (in France) against crime

By Clément de Maillard, Captain, Ph.D., and Patrick Perrot, Colonel, PhD.

Nowadays, crime can no longer be considered a simple expression of social marginality or accidental abnormality of society, as it used to be considered over decades. Instead, it is now a mirror (barely) distorting our own society following all its contemporary forms: complex and intangible, open and uncertain. It is based both on this new perspective on the societal place of crime and its new forms of expression, and on a lucid observation about traditional police and the judicial system's difficulty to deal with it, that intelligence-led policing ILP - ultimate model of policing strategies - has emerged over time among researchers, as in many modern police forces. Abandoning the study of the offender and the underlying reasons for his/her motive –whether psychological, socio-economic, cultural, etc.- this criminological trend is more focused on how to address new threats' complexities with a holistic approach. Indeed, the ILP model prescribes to reverse the traditional police operation modes. As part of this vein of policing, ILP recommends substituting a global and proactive police approach focused on the detection and anticipation of insecurity upstream, to reactive policing attitudes that merely solve problems downstream, isolated and with a case by case approach.

Thus, in the 1990s and 2000s, many countries have turned - sometimes painfully - towards new solutions as a way to counter criticism regarding their ineffectiveness. Yet, also facing the exhaustion of traditional solutions in the fight against crime and strict budget restrictions, the French police institutions must reinvent today. Indeed, France tirelessly repeating old recipes, has long remained ostensibly far from these thoughts that have gone through contemporary criminology, as an allegory of the French criminology's inability to think differently. The reasons for this hermetic are multiple; one of them is probably due to the fact that criminology is not an academic discipline recognized as such, and removes *de facto* any major thinking on these issues. However, the uniqueness of the French police organization unquestionably plays a major role as well.

Facing such objective limitations, the French police system is now seeking new solutions. Disregarded completely two years ago, the concept of criminal intelligence is now entering into the French police lexicon and emerges as a key issue in the fight against crime. As proof of this new ambition, an innovative initiative is being started by the *Gendarmerie nationale* to produce a new type of analysis based on an original criterion: crime predictability. This analysis represents a new approach in several respects: it symbolizes (however small) the transition towards a new policing philosophy, with an innovative method differing from all the other predictive analytical initiatives already implemented.

Knowledge management and the stakes for a modern police

As highlighted by Jobard & de Maillard, (2015) the fight against crime has been marked by three major changes in the past five decades; "general expansion of criminality, extension of human rights in criminal procedures and appetite for information technology." France is not a stranger to these changes, although many lessons have yet to be learned.

In 1950, France had 200,000 burglaries per year in which over a third of those were solved. Today, more than 2.5 million burglaries are recorded annually in the country, of which only a quarter of those are solved. The increase of burglaries illustrates the constant, widespread and irreversible growth of criminality in our modern society. This general expansion of crime is part of a global evolution that has accelerated in the last decades. Today, in addition to its more polysemous nature, criminality now has the technical means to leverage its nuisance capacity with a lower risk, and its mobility combined with a continuous growing portability. The face of crime has metamorphosed and has not met its transformation, revealing both a total destructure of criminal groups, and an increasing hybridization from massive and low-level-crimes to high-level crimes like terrorism.

In France, the current restructuring of crime groups poses difficulties for law enforcement entities as traditional groups were based on an organized and pyramidal structure. Today, crime groups work more and more in disjointed, autonomous cells with a geographic reach. These groups slip through the police net and justice system, taking advantage of the opportunities to spread its action through time and space. Now both the "*gendarme*" and the police are less familiar with how the criminal population operates on the territory of which they are in charge. Therefore, classic police intelligence mechanisms based on proximity are undermined.

The concept of hybridization relates significantly to the increasing porosity between different forms of crime. Therefore, criminals specializing in burglaries are no longer limited to armed robbery, physical assaults or drug trafficking. Considering criminal diversity, this hybridization can be described as horizontal rather than a vertical hybridization when referring to criminality gradation (serious or low-level crime). Certainly, the link between mass crime, specialized crime, and organized crime appears to be increasingly narrowing. In France, members of organized crime groups are committed to low-intensity crimes such as burglary, on a broad scale.

A second notable phenomenon in France emerged, driven by both international norms (in particular the European Convention on Human Rights) and an increasing demand from the public on transparency of police action. Criminal procedure has broadened principally due to the offenders' rights strengthening. This has increasingly complicated the investigator's task and consequently jolted the work of the judicial chain.

Finally, another factor also marks our era: the evolution of crime-solving science in regards to the emergence of new information technologies. From the birth of forensic science and the first police databases in the 19th century to the so-called digitization of multiple databases today, crime information management (telephone traces, evidence, anthropomorphic data, DNA, criminal records, etc.) has become a major issue for modern criminal investigation. Fueled by the systematization of forensic capacity, data search, collation, collection, classification, and sharing are now predominant factors in crimes solving. In a traditional policing approach, collated and collected data such as traces, DNA, wiretapping, surveillance, etc., all consist of a broad mass of information that an officer can use in solving crimes. The development of technology and information science is a social phenomenon whose influences extend far beyond mere policing. However, its generalization became nonetheless a permanent feature in basic police work over the time.

The transformation of crime, the strengthening of rights, and the modernization of technological tools have become triggers for a sustainable and irreversible movement that draws the contours of a new paradigm in which the police must now take into consideration. The combination of these three factors has transformed the police approach in the fight against crime. Faced with the challenges of a rapid increase in crime and the increasing constraints related to the strengthening of criminal legal procedures, the French police entities are now seeking solutions. However, it is the development of information technology, the third key element of this recent evolution that a new police approach is being built upon. In the context of policing strategies initiated by criminology researchers and applied by police chiefs, ILP was theorized and implemented in the 1990s. ILP requires the police to reverse its traditional management, focusing less on a crime solving and a case-by-case approach to downstream their findings, and undertaking a proactive approach, which combines every type of knowledge to identify, figure out, and deal with criminality.

Ratcliffe defines ILP as "a business model and managerial philosophy where data analysis and crime intelligence are pivotal to an objective, decision-making framework that facilitates crime and problem reduction, disruption and prevention through both strategic management and effective enforcement strategies that target prolific and serious offenders" (Ratcliffe, 2008, p. 109). Such an approach is made possible through new knowledge-management technologies described above, as they should not only be handled in an investigative framework, but also in an intelligence framework (de Maillard, 2014).

In reality, the intelligence-led model is less about the use of information. Rather, it is about the capability to bring in this information into a clearly defined enhancement process in order to determine the understanding and consequently, the management of security issues at all levels. Thus, ILP is a comprehensive and structured methodology for all police activities: public safety for criminal investigations, from minor disorders to organized crime.

An archetypal model led by intelligence is based on a threefold level of analysis: operational analysis, tactical analysis, and strategic analysis[2]. Operational analysis is defined as an investigation support. It works with criminal investigators through appropriate case data management.

---

[2] Other terminology does exist to describe the different levels of analysis: tactical analysis, operational analysis and strategic analysis. Tactical and operational analysis are interchangeable in reference to the referring literature. The choice has been made to respect the one used within the French *Gendarmerie nationale.*

Tactical analysis should be seen as a decision support: "[It] follows the evolution of crime in using situational statistics, crime-mapping and detection of patterns in a real-time process. [Tactical] analysis assists decision-makers to drive and allocate police resources" (de Maillard, 2014, p. 51).

Finally, strategic analysis can be considered as an aid to understanding. With a qualitative macroscopic study on crime, strategic analysis is able to describe the criminal landscape, its trends and issues, and remains a true instrument of knowledge.

In addition to this threefold structure, the criminal intelligence model is also based on a threefold approach: geographical analysis, crime-patterns analysis (detection of trends and series), and a focus on prolific offenders and groups of offenders (de Maillard, 2014).

Criminologists have always understood how inseparable crime and territory are at an early stage. In criminal science, the geographical dimension of a territory is taken into account to determine how men and women interact in and with their space through the prism of their criminal activities. Criminality, in addition to the police response, rarely evolves out of context: it complies with a multitude of evolving exogenous and more or less, decisive variables (Besson, 2004). Therefore, geographic crime analysis is based on a multitude of criteria: population density, demographic composition, mobility, socio-cultural and economic context, the degree of urbanization, modes and motion vectors (roads, access, transport, distances), etc.

The second essential thematic: crime-patterns analysis is based on the fact that offenders mimic a *modus operandi* that has proven its efficiency either by themselves (series) or with others (phenomenon). The interest for the detection of phenomena and series was mainly highlighted by the environmental criminology: the theory of routine activities (Cohen & Felson, 1979), the theory of opportunities (Felson & Clarke, 1998), and the theory of patterns (Brantingham & Brantingham, 1993). From a police perspective, the detection of crimes phenomena and series is based on search and identification of traces. Forensic/ crime scenes experts traditionally seek the trace during investigations. However, when inserted in an iterative process of criminal intelligence, the trace can highlight patterns, allowing the correlation of different cases previously seen as isolated to reveal a criminal trend undetected (series of burglaries carried out by a single team) or underestimated (low-value goods stolen at an industrial scale, in order to supply a parallel/ foreign market).

Ratcliffe said that approximately six percent of the population accounts for 60 percent of criminality (2008). Consequently, the focus on the offenders and groups of offenders is the third pillar of criminal intelligence. Usual crime and its ability to operate in networks are a reality in the criminal world, and represent key elements of the underground economy. An in-depth examination of criminal networks' operations reveal essential information: the type of criminal structure (family, ethnic, neighborhood, opportunistic networks, gangs, mafias, etc.), members, organization and degrees of acquaintance, signature criminal activities and the usual modus operandi, roles played within the network (money collector, drug dealer, money-launderer, etc.) distinctive signs (tattoos, dress codes, etc.), territories, well-known links with other criminals (belonging to the same structure, business links, conflicts), etc. These pieces of information are crucial to understanding the stakes of their networks, activities, influence, dimension, or threat dangerousness, and therefore provide them with tailored police and judicial responses.

Geographic crime analysis, pattern analysis, and prolific criminal analysis: these three key elements determine a list of variables that, while observed with a holistic perspective, draws general features of criminality. At the light of this triptych, police approach consists of identifying and containing the causes and consequences of the crime on a social area. Modern police becomes capable of surpassing its action's gravity (gravitational pull) to be transformed into "knowledge workers."

This holistic approach opens the way towards a new paradigm. If investigation and case-by-case approach is no longer the *alpha & omega* of policing philosophy, then by analogy, the criminologist's attention should be less focused on the offender *intuitu personae,* i.e. his/her personality and possible motivations. In criminological terms, this new perspective is reflected in a decreasing interest on the offender per se, through an "individualizing" approach. The debates that stirred the research on knowing whether the criminal is purely rational, free and mindful of his/her actions, or are the opposite--the result of a social marginality expressed through a transgressive act--then become irrelevant. Now, criminology considers crime more with a comprehensive and holistic approach: its typology, its variables, and its consequences. This approach combines theory: the environmental criminology, and practice: the strategy of ILP. Big data analysis associated with the observation of criminal behaviors theorized by environmental criminology, outlines the perspectives for a new dimension: once crime can be understood, explained and anticipated; and then highlighting the prevalence of a new criterion specific to this paradigm: crime predictability (de Maillard, 2014).

The intelligence-led model arises in the field of contemporary criminology as a suitable solution – perhaps sometimes idealized- for modern societies' requirements. France has long ignored the notion of criminal intelligence. However, today, this vocabulary becomes more and more familiar in the police glossary. Despite persistent obstacles, several initiatives demonstrate that changes are currently moving forward. Predictive analysis of crime implemented by the French *Gendarmerie* embodies this change (Perrot & Kader, 2015).

Police & Gendarmerie nationales : The French Law Enforcement system and the challenges of ILP

Heritage of its history and its uniqueness, the French police system is based on two distinct and equivalent forces: the *Police nationale* a civil status force, and *Gendarmerie nationale,* a military status force; administrations are in charge of public safety and criminal investigations. Competences-sharing is based on a geographical criterion, each operating on predefined territories: predominantly urban areas for the *Police,* mainly rural areas for the *Gendarmerie.* Thus the *Police nationale* is active on about two percent of territory, 50 percent of population and 60 percent of criminality recorded in the national territory; the *Gendarmerie* is responsible for about 98 percent of the territory, 50 percent of the population and 40 percent of recorded crimes.

On 14 May 2013, a Parliamentary commission report pointed out the "deficiencies of French criminal intelligence" and emphasized the delay of law enforcement forces in the matter (Assemblée nationale, 2013). In *Police* or *Gendarmerie*, criminal intelligence is an underappreciated and underrated concept. Other countries such as in the Anglo-Saxons region, have already conceptualized, applied, copied, and even criticized and readapted the concept. However, France has long been incredibly apart of these debates. The main reasons are primarily cultural. First, the question of whether or not criminology should be considered as a science still shakes the French academia today. While supporters and critics affront, global thinking on crime and police remains desperately silent. Moreover, the notion of intelligence drains an irreversibly negative image in the French collective imagination, and arouses basic apprehensions of fear and phantasm. This negative tropism does not favor the emergence of a peaceful scientific debate; even less the establishment of an ostensible strategy inspired by intelligence-led policing. The cultural environment is undeniably an obstacle to the adoption of an intelligence-led model in France. However, it is not the only one: the organization of the French law enforcement system by nature does not fit in an intelligence-led model. Two major obstacles have long hindered the emergence of an intelligence-led strategy: the highly centralized management of the police system, and the duality of the legal conception of police missions.

The French law enforcement system, like the French administration as a whole, remains nationally centralized. Both the *Police nationale* and *Gendarmerie nationale* have a *Direction Générale* at the top, and in each territorial level the system is organized in a uniformed and hierarchical way[3]. This centralized and unified system differs from the federal system, which is more popular in Common-Law countries. In a federal system, the head of the local police has a high-level of flexibility: he/she is in charge of public safety, resources allocation (human, logistical, financial), and anti-crime strategy. This kind of sovereignty provides considerable autonomy and flexibility. It is precisely this autonomy and flexibility that enables the ILP model to grow (as well as policing strategies in general). In a context of mutual influence and interests, researchers, together with local police chiefs were able to set up--or be inspired by--intelligence-led strategies, through subtle partnerships gathering both theory and practice.

However, the federal system's flexibility and autonomy compatible to ILP's development remain out of reach for a centralized system such as the one in France. Each reform requires changing the course at the national level, from top to bottom, which can be a long process and at times painful. Additionally, the cost of such a uniform system is the loss of its flexibility.

A second feature characterizing the lack of a French appetite for ILP, is that police organization in France is based on a strictly dual legal conception of policing. Indeed, from a legal point of view, the exercise of police missions is based on strictly separating police action in two categories: administrative police mission–*police administrative*--and judiciary police mission–*police judiciaire*. This distinction is

---

[3] Nevertheless, it is important to specify the fact that *Police nationale* and *Gendarmerie nationale* do not have the same organizational structure. *Gendarmerie* is essentially subdivided into territorial divisions, while *Police nationale* is mainly subdivided into types of police missions (public safety, criminal investigations, intelligence, etc.).

important because it determines the relevant legal framework for the police officer such as jurisdiction, powers, duties, and the type of judge who will control the validity of the act.

Basically, the discriminant criterion is the nature of the aim pursued by the police action. To sum it up, if the purpose of police action is the prevention of crime, then it must be considered as an act of *police administrative*. Conversely, if the purpose of the police act is repressive, it will be an act of *police judiciaire*. "So *Police* or *Gendarmerie* patrol agents walking down the streets are dedicated to a crime prevention mission, therefore they act in the framework of a *police administrative* mission. When the same patrol agents are required to intercept the perpetrators of a robbery taking place, they legally switch to [a repression crime] mission, in a *police judiciaire* framework " (Maillard, 2014). In the first example, their police powers are limited by the *police administrative* framework: identity check, car check or house-search are very restricted (almost forbidden). Police action is restricted and submitted to an administrative judge. In the second example, the purpose of police action is to stop an ongoing crime, or to find out offenders of a crime that occurred; thus they are acting in the *police judiciaire* legal framework: they have more powers (identity-checks, car checks, etc.), and their action is controlled by the judiciary judge.

Applying to simple *Police* or *Gendarmerie* patrol agents, this distinction also applies to all police activities: competences and powers of each type of police department, police databases, rules information-exchanges, etc. This *police administrative/police judiciaire* distinction is so deeply rooted that it also encompasses the whole philosophy of French policing. French policing has long utilized this crime prevention/repression dichotomy, emphasizing either one or the other, according to the current political sensitivity.

If this legal approach can make sense in the daily exercise of police missions, it can also cause issues within intelligence matters. On one hand, 'administrative intelligence' identifies and attempts to prevent public, economic, social and even terrorist threats[4]. It encompasses prevention of social troubles, major disorders, sects, extreme political movements monitoring, etc. It is conducted by specialized services with no judiciary competencies, and the intelligence they produce is only delivered to the administrative and governing authorities (local or national).

On the other hand, the "judiciary intelligence" is shaped by information gathered by law enforcement services in the framework of the investigations: location of offense, victim's and/or offender's name, criminal records, etc. "Judiciary intelligence" management is conducted by police services and mainly dedicated to law enforcement entities (both investigation services and prosecutors). "Administrative" and "judiciary" intelligence are not addressed by the same services; they do not use the same tools (including databases) and are subjected to separate legal frameworks. However, criminal intelligence does not fit in such a distinction. Indeed, its nature requires a holistic approach to problems,

---

[4] In France, counter-terrorism is conducted in the framework a specific derogating legislation offering a continuum between intelligence and criminal investigations.

and separating *a priori* information regarding their nature encompasses the understanding of crime phenomenon, with a biased and partial scope.

However, stating that nothing exists would not be fair. Driven by governing authorities, one thought has been recently initiated in this regard. Several initiatives tend to demonstrate a willingness of both the *Police nationale* and *Gendarmerie* to develop tools or dedicated structures to criminal intelligence, each of them in regard to their own culture and constraints. Mostly deployed in urban areas, the *Police nationale* is historically and culturally familiar with organized crime issues. In 2009, it created the SIRASCO[5], a strategic intelligence analysis service on organized crime in France. Since 2013, the SIRASCO relies on a network of regional offices. Because of the large expanse of territory the *Gendarmerie* is in charge of, and the geographical dispersion of its units, in-house information sharing has always been thought as a challenge. For a long time, the *Gendarmerie* has been developing and implementing tools and practices in order to identify and analyze emerging crimes in its territory. Still in this perspective, the *Gendarmerie* created the Central Service for Criminal Intelligence -SCRC[6] in 2014. This service is the national level of a local chain of criminal analysis units. One of the most outstanding initiatives this new direction reflects is currently being developed within the SCRC: a criminal risk management method based on predictable crime analysis. (Perrot, 2014).

Between necessity and urgency: Predictive Analysis

Considering on the one hand, the current constraints on crime (crime evolution, crime extension, crime destructure and hybridization) and the changing context where the French police forces remain-- extension of human rights in criminal procedures, appetite for information technology, and the specificity of the French police system on the other hand--new methods to tackling crime appears both as a necessity and an urgency. In other words, the mutation of the criminal landscape requires law enforcement entities to appropriate new methods based on the development of proactive capabilities and overtake traditional divisions such as administrative/ judiciary police or petty/organized crime.

The urgency relates to law enforcement ability to remain as the core stakeholder in the fight against crime. Today, who can predict the risk of an epidemic flu with big data collected on the Internet? Who is now able to transmit this information to the entire world through simple smartphones? Tomorrow, who will be able to estimate the criminal potentiality of a neighborhood, the offender's risk of recurrence with big data collected on the Internet? Who could disseminate this information through smartphones? The answer appears increasingly obvious: GAFA (Google, Apple, Facebook, Amazon) but also TIM (Twitter, Instagram, Microsoft) or NATU (Netflix, Airbnb, Tesla, Uber). In the age of collaborative web and while individuals and goods interact and generate data, should we not pay attention to the possibility of an "uberization of security"?

This risk is real and the stakes are obvious for police forces who must urgently make the shift towards big data analysis and artificial intelligence. Otherwise, it can be expected that security issues will

---

[5] *Service d'information, de renseignement et d'analyse sur la criminalité organisé (Police nationale).*
[6] *Service central de renseignement criminel (Gendarmerie nationale).*

be managed by GAFA's emanations. Those entities will be capable of producing risk analysis -as relevant as it can be- which will be partial, emphasizing less on criminal concerns rather than economic ones, and with few considerations for individual rights protection.

The challenge police forces have to face now -both a changing criminal world, and stakeholders' capability to compete their exclusive legitimacy- is considerable. It requires the implementation of new methods complementary with the reactive approach, and a better pro-action methodology based on mathematics. However, these new methods are neither in the Police nor the *Gendarmerie's* DNA. There is no shortage of criticism (Ferguson, 2012, 2015). Some would see crime prediction as a free-pass for *a priori* and baseless police action. Others see it as confirmation of banality or as a simple curves' extension.

These criticisms are not meaningless. It reflects a societal fear for an unconstrained police world, while police action would meet the preemptive criteria; while an individual known for burglaries could no longer walk in a high-risk area for burglary, without being arrested and where the machine would guide police action with no human sensibility. Nevertheless, these criticisms are often based on a misunderstanding about real police action and its scientific potential in regards to decision support. In terms of mathematics, prediction is neither a crystal ball, nor is it the result of a spontaneous generation born from nothing.

Of course, prediction is based on elements of the past; it is also what human does in terms of thinking, either with an inductive or deductive rationale. Prediction is a curves extension, how could it not be, considering that time is continuous? Prediction highlights banalities, which illustrates how conforming the model is in reality. Nevertheless, even banalities, while considered from a broad perspective, appear extremely difficult for the human mind to figure out.

Predicting not only when the next burglaries will take place, but also sexual assaults, muggings, car robberies, or anticipating the evolution of economic crimes, is an outstanding asset for law enforcement. Therefore, prediction answers the question of "when." Moreover, spatial scale should also be taken into account (Rohard & Perrot, 2015). Providing decision-makers a multi-scale vision from the local to the national level answers the question of "where." Moreover, because crime is neither a deterministic signal, nor a random process, it meets a number of explanatory factors. The analysis of these factors, often exogenous of crime, offers a better understanding of crime. The three questions of where, when, and why, are what predictive analytics try to answer.

Based on this observation, multi-vision scale of predictive analysis from temporal, space and law enforcement perspectives is being developed in France through a criminal intelligence approach. Indeed, restricting to operational activities on burglary only eludes the need to anticipate medium and long term crime phenomena, and to dispense with a capacity to act in tactical and strategic levels including non-police partners into the fight against crime. The majority of business tools and devices developed as PredPol (Predictive Policing) (Brantingham & Brantingham, 1993) or PreCobs (Pre crime observation system) deal with an orientation focusing on a veryshort-term approach for police patrols in hotspots and generally in megacities. These tools are based on a "crime repeatability in space" concept. The *Gendarmerie nationale* is committed in a different way: rather than a predictive analytics software, it focuses on the development of mathematical methods applied to predictive analysis of crime. The nuance is not insignificant. It is based on the rejection of the "black box" effects, and the willingness to keep a real decision-making capacity. Indeed, using analytical software without understanding the different stages is undoubtedly a prerequisite for multiple interpretation errors in addition to the gradual loss of decision-making independence. However, the innovative and original approach that is being developed by the *Gendarmerie nationale* also raises a number of practical questions on data interpretation methodology and on the application (the roles of both the analyst and the decision-maker, for instance), as well as theoretical ones, in particular what it would mean for criminology.

Conceived ten years ago, the concept of Big Data (Chen, Mao, & Liu, 2014) (Madden, 2012) has been a fruitful foundation for a better comprehension for criminality causes. Thanks to this new concept, data now offers new perspectives on many disciplines in regard to its availability, its capability to be used easily, and its potential for improvement on decision-making. The term "massive data" emerged over the past few years to encompass the flow of information collected in our daily activities, social interactions, research papers, and other connected items. Besides this ability to collect a great volume of data, it is also possible to analyze this data and quickly sort through it.

Perspectives offered by big data allow the dealing of a huge, heterogeneous and non-structured volume of data in near real-time processing. Data offers the possibility to take into account developments in a short-, medium-, and long-terms. It allows the gap to be filled between globalization and individualization. Indeed, it is both possible to follow and anticipate major epidemics on a global scale, and analyze the individual behavior of Mr. X compared to his actions or purchases. The fight against crime is deeply related to what data can deliver in terms of crime evolution, crime predictability, and criminal behavior.

Contrary to widespread thinking, prediction is not based on a single magic algorithm, but is the result of the combination of different methods. It deals with time series, regression methods, machine learning, and now Artificial Intelligence (AI). The context has rarely been so favorable to developments in mathematics dedicated to the fight against crime. Knowing what will occur tomorrow, this philosophical myth, illustrated by Cassandra in the Greek mythology, is becoming a scientific reality today.

The temporal approach based on time series analysis is particularly relevant. Indeed, widely used areas such as economy, insurance, marketing or finance, time series are relevant as far as characterizing a chronology by a seasonal, an irregular component, and/or a growing or declining trend, makes sense. This is obvious for instance regarding many common offenses such as burglaries for instance. These methods are not new, but illustrate how efficient they can be in terms of time prediction either on a weekly or monthly scale. The main limit still remains depth of the data available for analysis. Thus, a monthly prediction on homicides at a district level will not be so relevant due to a low volume of registered data. However, burglaries or car thefts can be considered as a time series analysis due of the volume of data (Perrot & Kader, 2015).

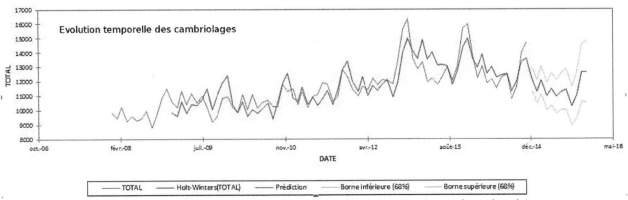

Fig 2.1: Prediction model process based on time series (Source: Gendarmerie nationale)

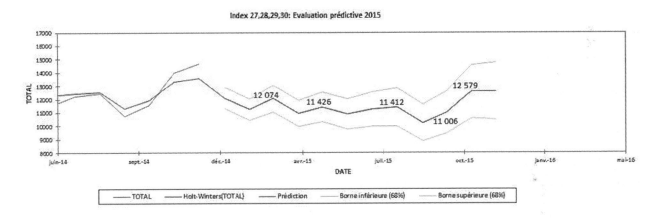

Fig 2.2 : Predictive evolution (Source: Gendarmerie nationale)

Figures 2.1 and 2.2 illustrate the prediction process based on time series analysis. Between 2009 and 2013 is used as a model, and the year 2014 is used for test and validation. Once the model is validated, predictive projection is carried out for the year 2015. Beyond the estimated quantitative value, prediction offers the potential to assess and anticipate the increasing and decreasing rate of certain types of crimes. Used for several different types of offenses, this method can prioritize police actions and determine a strategy in regards to the temporal evolution of crime, for instance in optimizing police patrols to specific targets. Usable at an operational scale, this method can also have an added value at a strategic level in prioritizing the allocation of human or material resources for a long-term perspective. Thus, law enforcement agencies improve their flexibility at a different scale in dedicating the most appropriate action to tackle crime.

Alongside temporal analysis, a spatial evolution of crime can also be carried out. A long-term estimation on potential crime hotspots offers an opportunity to highlight a specific issue, and consequently reinforce specific areas, for example during summer time (holidays). Figure 2.3 illustrates the spatial predictive evolution of crimes against properties during the summer months within a French *departement*[7].

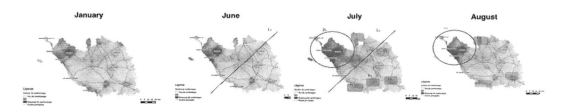

Fig 2.3 : Spatial crime prediction (Source: Gendarmerie nationale)

In regards to the regressive analyses, exogenous variables of crime can be taken into consideration to provide relevant information to figure out offenses. For instance, the multiple linear regression stands out as the most suitable technique to understand basic and widespread crimes. The aim is to describe the variation of an endogenous variable associated with variations of several exogenous variables. For example, burglary trends (endogenous variables) can be explained from socio-economic variables such as, the age of the population, household income, the level of education, etc. (exogenous variables). The regression model can be written as follows:

$$y = \beta_0 + \beta_1 x_1 + \beta_2 x_2 \dots \beta_n x_n + \varepsilon$$

where Y is the endogenous variable (number of burglaries), x_i, are the exogenous variables (socio-economic), β_i, the regression coefficients and ε represents the residue. The regression coefficients correspond to the relative contribution of the explanatory variable (exogenous) on the variable to explain (endogenous). The regression model can be evaluated by the coefficient of determination: R^2. It indicates how suitable the proportion of the endogenous variable's variance is vis-à-vis the exogenous variable in terms of predictability.

The understanding of crime based on regressive analysis opens new perspectives for crime prevention. The influence of social factors allows, for example, to measure the impact of the evolution (increase or decrease) of social housing, commercial areas or residential areas. It is then possible to consider preventive solutions beyond the law enforcement framework taking into consideration new housing and territory planning. Only then are solutions against crime more orientated towards a societal and comprehensive dimension rather than only law enforcement.

Currently, another field of mathematics also has a potential to renew law enforcement methods: artificial intelligence (A.I.). The development of AI provides many perspectives, which are not necessarily opposed to the protection of individual rights, as is sometimes assessed. Through machine learning techniques, the objective of AI is to model some specific behaviors or patterns in classifying them. Considering crime as a non-random process, criminal behavior as characteristic of its targets is perfect for modeling.

---

[7] In France, the *Departement* corresponds to an administrative and governing local district. France is divided in 101 *departements*.

To model an offender behavior, the main interest of machine learning is to destroy nominal data in an irreversible way after used, and to protect privacy. Mirroring advertisements on the internet which target our main interests, a similar behavioral modeling process can be used for a certain type of offender, such as a serial rapist for instance, and forecast probabilities and conditions of new potential occurrences. While dealing with data collection, it is necessary to look at nominal data as those nominal data disappear in an irreversible way in data modeling.

Regarding criminal target modeling, the same techniques can be used. For example, it is possible to characterize an ATM machine targeted by criminals with a number of variables. These variables can be: the type of bank, the geographical location, the characteristics of this location (close to a road with strong flow of circulation, localization in a city center, etc.). Once a large volume of ATM machines has been listed and related-data configured to fit in the database matrix, a risk assessment of each ATM machine reported can be determined for the future. This risk is based on the Bayesian decision theory in measuring the probability of belonging to the category of "risky ATM".

Amongst AI methods currently being developed, Deep Learning (Bengio, 2013) (Bengio, Goodfellow, & Courville, 2015) based on neural networks, is now emerging. The main interest of these approaches remains the capacity to avoid the curve of dimensionality as defined by Bellman in 1961 (Bellman, 1961) (Giraud, 2014). Neural networks offer better results in dealing with large volumes of data, in terms of discrimination and swiftness of analysis. The neural network principle is to mimic the operation of the biological neurons of the human brain. Like any learning process, they are based on empirical data, which are improved in an iterative way by their volume and their heterogeneity.

A decision-making process based on a business intelligence model consists in privileging an optimal and objective solution amongst a large number of options. Nevertheless when dealing with crime, the most objective or likely solution is not the only explore options. The police decision-maker must be able to take into account the "most likely", but also the "most unlikely" scenario encompassing the political or local consequences. AI methods have revealed a sufficient maturity to provide computational assistance to humans in practical situation. It is not so easy for a decision-maker to drive his/her action based on an analysis that differs from the result provided by a machine. This last one reveals the most likely and objective option. How difficult might it be to not take a decision confirmed by the result of the machine, when this machine favors a specific option to 95 percent, to 99.99 percent or even 51 percent? This is the challenge for the future of police decision-makers; of when to keep their own autonomy and decision-capacity. We cannot answer this question now, but this issue will in the very near future and will reflect the capacity of law enforcement agencies to retain their autonomy of action.

AI involvement in the decision-making process is becoming a growing cause for concern. In providing relevant and quick information through machine learning, deep learning and tomorrow quantum learning techniques, AI tools exceed our understanding of reality and leads to results which overtake our human abilities more and more. Algorithm-based predictability becomes more and more-- perhaps too much–complex to be accessible for human understanding. Therefore, how can human autonomy of decision-making be maintained, and not become a simple validation of a machine process?

A risk could be to substitute human interpretation with relentless decision-making logic. A machine is able to read better, to hear better, to see better, to detect better than humans; but emotions, and subjective consequences are not in the spectrum of the machine decision process.

The solution can be found with the association of prediction and "prospective". Prediction is only the heritage of the past, which means a way to forecast the most likely event. The prediction is an extrapolation of the past and represents just one part of the anticipation (Perrot, 2014). Prospective consists in considering the future, and not only as a continuation of the past, but also as the outcome of different scenarios. Those scenarios result from the analysis of various actors as well as the constraints of the environment. In such a way, it is possible to plan the most unlikely event by creating alternative options. Therefore, the methodology is to identify the anomalies, the ruptures, and the discontinuities that may affect the future. Those different concepts include the societal and economic changes, innovations and of course human imagination, which in term of criminal activities,always remains active.

Prospective opens the flow of potentialities, while prediction narrows and targets priorities. Prospective is generally considered more as an art than a science. It can be categorized with different scales. On the strategic level, prospective will consist of detecting gaps in legislation, or a change in the allocation of police resources, etc. At the operational level, prospective will consist of identifying new phenomenon such as the introduction of new types of shops, the arrest of a prolific offender, or even a change of roads infrastructure. Those new phenomena may have direct or indirect impact for law enforcement activity. Therefore only the analyst can determine how certain types of phenomena, their diversity and their magnitude may influence crime, and which ones must be looked after.

While prediction can be largely fulfilled and even optimized by artificial intelligence, a prospective approach remains appropriate as a human decision-making sanctuary in regards to security.

Thus, because the future is not only a continuation of the past or a set of predetermined potentialities, the criminal analyst must take into account effects led by uncertainty, indeterminacy, and unpredictability. Attention should be paid to this aspect, since it can bring about further questions.

Conclusion

The added value of the predictive approach--and especially the model developed by the French Gendarmerie--are twofold: theoretical and practical.

In conceptual terms, crime predictive analysis empirically confirms the prevalence of crime's predictability, which would replace the traditional criterion of the offender's rationality.

Indeed, the hypothesis of the "rational offender" still reigns in most major schools of thought in criminology such as the neo-classics Gary Becker and Isaac Ehrlich, or the architects of environmental criminology: Brantingham, Felson Cohen, and Clarke. Taken from economic sciences to describe how economic agents behave, the criterion of rationality is now jeopardized by the Behavioral Economics. The work of Dan Ariely (Ariely, 2009) (Bengio, 2013) (Bengio, Goodfellow, & Courville, 2015) (Bellman, 1961) (Chen, Mao, & Liu, 2014) (Giraud, 2014) (Ferguson, 2012) (Ferguson, 2015) (Madden,

2012) (Perrot, 2014) (Perrot & Kader, 2015) (Rohard & Perrot, 2015), Amos Tversky, and Daniel Kahneman (Nobel Prize for Economics in 2002) show that economic agents cannot be considered as rational from an economic perspective.

Rather, they prefer a more relevant criterion: predictability. In criminal sciences, such an analogy is now possible thanks to predictive analysis. In focusing on the crime rather than the criminal, predictive analysis favors an inductive approach inspired by the holistic and neutral observation of crime phenomenon. This is contrary to a deductive approach, which tends to explain the addition of individual behaviors in light of their characteristics, theorized and determined by a priori. Moreover, in implementing the criterion of crime predictability (instead of rationality offender's criterion) within the range of environmental theories: routine activities theory, opportunities theory and pattern theory, predictive analysis becomes a bridge, which embodies the filiation between criminological theories and theorized proactive policing models such as intelligence-led policing.

In practice, predictive analytics is an indisputable asset for any criminal intelligence police system. Understanding that criminal phenomenon characterizes the essence of criminal intelligence and its ultimate objective still remains at the forefront to better anticipate causes and consequences for society. Despite the obstacles predictive analysis fully contributes to the development of the French criminal intelligence model.

While the strong centralization characterizing the French police system, this can now appear as a break for the innovation and the development of new strategies such as ILP, whose centralization may be a key factor for engaging in structural reforms. French police system homogeneity offers both a unique police and crime data management capacity, policing geographical continuity at all scales, and a bottom-up operations management. The delay accumulated by French authorities in criminal intelligence although consubstantial with its nature, is not inevitable. Recent developments prove that the growing interest in criminal analysis reflects this desire for change at both local and national levels. Moreover, the predictive analysis model herein described remains the most significant initiative in this regard. Firstly, because it differs from any other similar initiatives already developed in other countries. Secondly, because it fits perfectly with the specificities offered by the French police system.

As it remains original by its ambition, its conception and its implementation, predictive analysis developed by the Gendarmerie foreshadows the fulfillment of an effective, comprehensive and suitable criminal intelligence model, which undoubtedly constitutes the base for a future ILP model "*à la française*".

Chapter 3: A View of ILP from the U.K.

By Jonathan Larkin, Th.D. [8]

> Intelligence products support Senior Investigating Officers and Senior Intelligence Professionals in managing police operations and working effectively within their community. Effective strategies and solutions are found through intelligence analysis of crime problems.

Introduction

In being asked to contribute a chapter for a text book with a global target audience, I have had to bear in mind that I as the author, and every reader, will have come from various professional backgrounds, all of which have their own unique approach to Intelligence and more specifically Intelligence Analysis. Additionally, each country has its own core doctrines, techniques, practices and local policies.

Each reader will be at different stage in their analytical careers. This could range from an academic pursuing intelligence studies at undergraduate or post graduate level, a newly appointed junior analyst, seasoned higher analyst or senior analyst looking to keep their skills relevant, an intelligence researcher looking to become an intelligence analyst, or an intelligence manager who is seeking a greater understanding of the skills that analytical staff can offer within a team. With this in mind it is important to establish a common ground on which to build, allowing a reader to adapt the material to fit within different working environments.

Common Ground

An organisation's purpose and culture will ultimately determine the function of its intelligence analysis arm. Broadly speaking, intelligence agencies such as the Secret Intelligence Service[9], Security Services[10], Central Intelligence Agency or Mossad[11] are primarily proactive and keep intelligence analysis at the core of their business. In contrast, law enforcement agencies are predominantly reactive and their Intelligence Analysis functions form part of a wider intelligence apparatus that plays a key part in the organisation as a whole. That is not to say that law enforcement agencies don't conduct proactive operations, far from it, and this is something that will be discussed at length in this chapter. However, there is a need for an intelligence analyst to often be "all things to all men"[12] or at least to all customers.

As this chapter is concerned with the application of intelligence analysis in the management of police operations, the focus will be on law enforcement and specifically intelligence analysis within Surrey

---

[8] Disclaimer: Although I have referenced my organisation the views mentioned in this chapter are my own and may not necessary reflect those of the Surrey Police Force.

[9] More commonly known as MI6

[10] More commonly known as MI5

[11] National Intelligence agency of Israel which translates as "The Institute for Intelligence and Special Operations"

[12] The Apostle Paul 1.Cor.9.22 discussing how he adapts his methods to the intended target audience.

Police (UK) and will be discussed from this context. To begin with, it is helpful to define the following pieces of terminology to assist the reader:

- **Senior Investigating Officers:** A Senior Investigating Officer (SIO) is an officer of considerable experience, typically holding the rank of Detective Chief Inspector or above. In the course of an investigation, the SIO has overall responsibility and sets the investigative strategy.
- **Senior Intelligence Professionals:** This is a broad term and is used to encompass those Intelligence Professionals who have responsibility for managing a team and who oversee the development of intelligence packages, such as Intelligence Managers or Senior Analysts, Principal Analysts or Heads of Intelligence Analysis and Heads of Intelligence (SIP).
- **Intelligence:** It is important to define this term. The Police, in common with many organisations, are bombarded with information but this is not 'intelligence'. Intelligence is defined by the National Intelligence Model as "Information that has been subject to a defined evaluation and risk assessment process in order to assist with police decision making" (National Centre for Policing Excellence, 2005, p. 13).
  In more simplistic terms, information becomes Intelligence when it has been subjected to a series of checks to ascertain its veracity, evaluating both its reliability and its usefulness. After which, the intelligence can be actioned and have any risk associated with it managed.
- **Analysis:** This is a very common term but the *Oxford Dictionary* defines 'Analysis' as a: "Detailed examination of the structure or elements of something" (Oxford Dictionaries, 2014)

The State of Intelligence Analysis in the UK

The world of intelligence is ever-changing. Over the last decade the Surrey Police has undergone various changes and its Intelligence apparatus has adapted in support of the organisation's needs. As a result of budget cuts there is the continued drive to do more with less, something that is generic to all public service organisations globally. Budget cuts have resulted in a more stringent focus, ensuring that resources are allocated based on:

1. Risk
2. Harm
3. Opportunity
4. Threat
5. Intent

In reality, this means that some of the products that intelligence analysts routinely produced in the past, such as Drug Market Profiles, are no longer done as a matter of course. Instead, the services of an intelligence analyst are usually requested in support of a specific problem.

These changes are reflected in the wider Intelligence culture. Eight years ago the National Intelligence Model[13] (NIM) was more closely adhered to than today. NIM stipulates that there are four Intelligence Products:

---

[13] It is not possible to provide an exhaustive discussion around NIM. Suffice it to say the simplest working definition is that of a business model within Policing that has Intelligence at its heart.

1. **Strategic Assessments:** These provide an overview of the current and long term issues affecting a Region, Police Force or Division. They drive the business of the Strategic Tasking and Coordination Group. It is used to set the control strategy and intelligence requirements.
2. **Tactical Assessments:** These identify the shorter term issues affecting a Region, Force or Division. The Tactical Tasking and Coordination Group uses the assessment to amend the intelligence requirement where necessary.
3. **Target Profiles:** These are written to provide a greater understanding of either a person or a group (victim or suspect).
4. **Problem Profiles:** These are written to provide a greater understanding of an established issue, an emerging crime series or an area of high risk (National Centre for Policing Excellence, 2005, p. 64).

As departments and individuals became more aware of what analysts could contribute, a progressive trend started, particularly in the world of proactive investigation, whereby officers or staff would request what is classified as an 'Analytical Technique'. In the UK, there are ten recognized techniques:

1. Crime Pattern Analysis
2. Social Demographic and Trends Analysis
3. Network Analysis
4. Market Analysis
5. Criminal Business Analysis
6. Risk Analysis
7. Subject Analysis
8. Results Analysis
9. Operation Intelligence Assessments
10. Case Analysis (National Policing Improvement Agency, 2008, p. 2)

In addition, there is the "Analysis of Specialist Data". This is an umbrella term initially used to cover Communications, Financial and Automatic Number Plate Analysis (ANPR) data. In a world of continuous technological advancement, this area of analysis will certainly increase. It is also important to note that within the UK, Intelligence Analysts are aware of and utilise methodologies that originate in other countries. Analysts may also supplement techniques from other disciplines, for example utilising Force Field Analysis[14] from business intelligence to examine the sustaining factors that support an organised crime group's activities.

A recent development is the "Five Product Family". This has come into vogue in a number of organisations and seeks to provide a product tailored to the customers' requirements ensuring that it is timely, relevant and of appropriate depth. Although this hasn't been formally adopted at a national level the Five Products are generally described as:

1. **Studies:** A comprehensive piece of Intelligence Analysis on a subject.

---

[14] Force Field Analysis looks at the supporting and detracting forces that maintain the status quo of a situation.

2. **Assessments:** Writing which seeks to answer a question or series of questions posed by the customer through Intelligence Analysis.
3. **Bulletins:** Highlight new developments or trends from Intelligence Analysis.
4. **Notes**: Informs the customer or relevant team of developments from Intelligence Analysis being undertaken.
5. **Memos:** Provide key information from Intelligence Analysis to the customer.

Although not formally adopted, having an awareness of the scope that each product is trying to cover encourages the Intelligence Analyst to consider the appropriate length and audience at which their product is being directed.

One important aside to note at this juncture, particularly for international readers, is that the current state of intelligence analysis in the UK is reflected in staffing. When I first started in intelligence, some forces had separate crime analysts in addition to their intelligence analysts. This is no longer the case and the function of Crime Analyst has been amalgamated into that of intelligence analyst. There is however clear delineation in Surrey Police and a number of other organisations between that of an intelligence analyst and a performance analyst. The chapter does not have time to discuss performance analysis in-depth; however, in short, a performance analyst evaluates the performance and outcomes for a company and therefore in policing is a way of assessing overall business success against organisational and national targets.

Despite the numerous changes seen in the world of intelligence, and specifically intelligence analysis, there are numerous aspects that are a constant in this arena. Although job descriptions for intelligence analysts vary in some details according to the organisation's requirements there are typically two key purposes to the role:

1. Advise and assist in all aspects of investigations by providing strategic and tactical analysis of intelligence, crime, evidence and disorder to Senior Officers.

2. Produce and disseminate analytical products that inform the decision making process and contribute to an intelligence led culture.

Products created in support of the above can vary greatly in length and to a degree will be determined by the scope of the work according to the negotiated Terms of Reference (this will be explored in the next section) however every product has four things that it attempts to do:

1. Create an intelligence picture or answer a question put to them by answering the "5WH"; Who, What, When, Where, Why and How.

2. Where any of the 5WH's is not answered create inferences in an attempt to do so.

3. Identify any intelligence gaps that exist.

4. Make recommendations in order to fill the gaps and identify additional analytical opportunities.

After establishing the foundations upon which to build, we can now explore how intelligence analysis supports senior investigating officers and senior intelligence professionals in managing police operations.

Managing Operations

Good intelligence analysts will always seek to be creative, however the best will be polymorphic adapting themselves to the needs of the individual customer, departments and organisation that they support and find solutions to the problems at hand. One of the most important pieces of advice I've been given in my career regarding how to take my analysis to the next level was from a then Detective Chief Inspector for Intelligence:

"Treat each problem as a unique challenge that requires a tailored product in order to offer the most effective solution"

This is excellent advice. It helps the analyst remain objective and avoids the fallacy of "it worked on the last job". This is also true in the case of a requesting customer who is familiar with what intelligence analysis can offer him/her, he/she may approach you wanting a product that was extremely successful on a previous operation and so request it again. As the analyst it is your job to select the most effective technique(s) for the product in order to assist the customer. As an important aside, it is not that we don't learn from experience, far from it; we draw on this as we go and it aids our creative thinking. Experience is a well of knowledge to draw upon after we have considered the problem, not before.

Intelligence analysis helps senior investigating officers and senior intelligence professionals manage operations at every stage of an investigation. This somewhat mirrors the intelligence cycle and so will be explored under the headings found within it.

Planning and Directing

As an intelligence analyst you will be approached by your customers who are looking for your help to assist them in solving the problem that they have. At this stage it is important to frame the question; this will allow you to understand what they are asking or requesting of you, consider its feasibility and allow the requester to consider if they've asked the right question. The clearest way to achieve this is through a Terms of Reference, this is a way for the Analyst to record the tasking that is required of them, define the scope of the work being undertaken and the Analytic techniques that will be employed in the creation of the product.

The now defunct National Policing Improvement Agency [15] stated the Terms of Reference should:

• Set clear direction leading to a focused piece of analysis.
• Ensure the analytical tasking is in line with current priorities.
• Focus the questions that need to be answered by analysis.
• Be agreed to by the analyst and the customer (National Police Improvement Agency, 2008, p. 18).

---

[15] It has been replaced by the College of Policing

The terms of reference should be centered on the questions that need to be answered by the analysis, typically part of the 5WH. This will result in the creation of an intelligence picture. The product however will include relevant supporting material such as i2 charts, call schedules and maps, etc.

The terms of reference will be negotiated between the Intelligence analyst and the customer. This is an opportunity for the customer to pose their problem and why they require assistance. In turn the analyst can discuss the most effective way in which they can assist. Key skills for the analyst are to be able to negotiate effectively, confidently and listen attentively.

This allows the analyst to:
1. Ensure that the customer doesn't have unreasonable expectations of what the analysis can achieve.

   Consider this scenario: A senior officer approaches an analyst and states that they want a piece of analysis that if enacted will cut dwelling burglaries by 20 percent. This is a completely unrealistic expectation.

   In contrast if the same senior officer approaches the analysts and states "in Borough X we have a problem with overnight burglary of dwellings and I want to tackle the issue; what can you suggest?" Then the analyst as part of the terms of reference is free to discuss their ideas for a product that could assist. This could be a report or Problem Profile that frames the issue and contains within it temporal analysis that highlights peak times for burglaries, this would allow for patrols to take place at optimum times. It may also contain Crime Pattern Analysis looking at the properties targeted, items taken and the modus operandi used to break in. This would allow a pattern to be identified and to discard those offences that don't make up a distinct grouping. Once a clear modus operandi (MO) has been established, research can be conducted on suspects who use this MO and inferences drawn as to who is responsible.
2. Understand the different techniques that will be used and what they offer. Inevitably a product will be dominated by a particular technique, however a good product will consist of a number of techniques.

   Consider this scenario: It has been decided that a proactive investigation targeting the supply of cocaine and the associated violence in Borough Y will be implemented. It is the start of the investigation and the SIO wants an analytical product that frames the problem and gives an understanding of who's involved, in the past they've requested Network Analysis and would like this again. Although Network Analysis would be useful to give an understanding of the situation in order to give a more complete intelligence picture Criminal Business, Market and even Demographical Analysis could be included.
3. Outline the sources of information available. This will be discussed in greater depth under the heading of "Collection Plan". Suffice it to say here this provides an understanding to the customer of what data sources will be utilised in the creation of the product and ensures that the product is of sufficient scope.

The terms of reference will vary greatly in size and content depending on what the requested product is to cover. However as a minimum will usually include the following:

- Details of the requesting customer.
- Your details as the analyst assigned.
- Reason for requested analysis.
- Aims and objectives of the analysis
- Methodologies to be employed
- Scope of the analysis.
- Predicted limitations.
- Deadline for completion.

The terms of reference for the analyst allows for self-critique of the product and will establish if the product itself was successful by meeting the customer's needs. In terms of managing investigations or operations it allows the senior investigating officer or senior intelligence professional to do two key things:

1. Allow the work that has been negotiated with the analyst to form part of a wider investigative or intelligence strategy.
2. Allow the Terms of Reference to provide criteria in part for Results Analysis to assess whether or not the investigation or operation was a success.

As a final aside it is important to note that as an investigation progresses amendments may need to be made to the Terms of Reference. This can be captured as an appendix, however it maybe that the Investigation has progressed to a point where a new product is required, in which case a fresh Terms of Reference maybe required.

Collection Plan

As part of the Terms of Reference, a discussion will have occurred as to what sources of data will be used. A Collection Plan is primarily an analytical tracker and provides an audit trail of the data sources used. This can be as simple or complicated as the analyst needs it to be and a simple Excel© spreadsheet will often suffice. As a basic standard it should provide the following:

- The type of data that is being sought.
- How the data will be obtained.
- Who will obtain the data?
- How the data will be stored.
- Is it an open source, i.e. a source of data that is readily available to the public?
- Is it a closed source, i.e., a source of data that is not available to the public?
- Is it essential to the analysis being undertaken or is it non-essential or even optional?
- Under what legislation will closed sources be obtained and what authorities need to be in place in order to do so?
- The estimated time frame for the data to be made available.

Although this is predominately an analytical tool that assists in collating the data, it can be of use to the SIO managing their investigation or the SIP managing an intelligence package in a number of ways.

1. Provide a greater understanding of the analytical work that they have requested which can form part of the intelligence strategy.

2. Ensure that the correct legislation is being utilised and ensure all aspects of the investigation are carried out lawfully.

3. Assist with costing, particularly in protracted investigations where external closed sources of data are being utilised.

4. Provide an awareness of the time frame that it will take to obtain the data. If the product is required sooner, then an alternative source of data maybe identified that can provide similar answers. An example that is common is where data is required from a particular software application whose servers are based in a different country and not covered by your national legislation.

5. Identify alternative sources of data where applications for a particular data source are refused on the ground that they are not proportionate. A potential scenario is as follows:- Two customers approach you wanting products that will identify individuals involved in criminality. Network 1 is involved in the supply of Class A drugs including cocaine and heroin which they enforce with violence. The SIO wants to understand who's involved and identify a potential hierarchy so as to most effectively deploy Police resources. Network 2 is a group of youths who are involved in anti-social behavior which is starting to escalate. Early intervention has been identified as the best way to prevent their behavior escalating; the SIO is particularly keen to identify the ring leader and any potential facilitators, as dealing with them is likely to 'nip the problem in the bud'.

The most effective product is likely to be a Problem Profile that utilises Network Analysis. In the case of Network 1 communications data is likely to be a key source of data and application for the data that sets out the necessity and proportionality of obtaining it is likely to be approved. The chances of obtaining communications data in relation to Network 2 are infinitesimal. At this point an alternative source of data, such as an open source social media, would allow analysis to be conducted that could provide answers to the questions being posed by the customer.

Collating and Evaluating

Following the production of your Collection Plan and having collected the relevant data it is import to evaluate the reliability of the Intelligence and other data. In the UK across all government organisations there is a common framework for evaluating intelligence known as the 5x5x5 and evaluates intelligence as follows:

Source Evaluation

- A - Always reliable
- B - Mostly reliable

- C - Sometimes reliable
- D - Unreliable
- E - Untested source

Intelligence Evaluation

- 1 - Known to be true without reservation
- 2 - Known personally to source but not to officer
- 3 - Not personally known to source but corroborated
- 4 - Cannot be judged
- 5 - Suspected to be false or malicious (National Intelligence Model, Appendix 3).

Handling Code

To be completed at time of entry into an intelligence system and reviewed on dissemination

- 1 - May be disseminated to other law enforcement and prosecuting agencies, including law enforcement agencies within the European Economic Area (EEA) and the European Union (EU).
- 2- May be disseminated to UK non-prosecuting parties.
- 3- May be disseminated to non-EEA law enforcement agencies.
- 4- May be disseminated within the originating agency only.
- 5- No further dissemination: refer to the originator for handling requirements imposed by the officer who authorised collection.

In 2016, a new grading system was being rolled out which was likely to be completed by late 2017. This has no direct bearing on the principles discussed in this chapter. To allow future readers to align the principles with incoming doctrine I have included a brief explanation at the end of the chapter (see Addendum 1)

There is no need to discuss the handling codes in any depth as they are specific to the UK and each country will have their own variation on these. What is important to note is the evaluation of the source and the intelligence. This provides a standardised way of evaluating the Intelligence that has been collated as part of the Collection Plan. When it comes to creating an Intelligence Product it is important to provide the provenance of the Intelligence when it is mentioned. This will, particularly in the case of inferences, allow the customer who is reading it to have an understanding of the reliability of the source that it is built upon.

A report will want to engage the reader while communicating to them the vital parts of analysis. In my personal experience many of my customers have found multiple footnotes with an Intelligence report reference, an evaluation code and date to be ascetically unpleasing and also jarring whilst reading, consequently I would recommend endnotes. A report should flow well and therefore once the intelligence and data have been collated can be delineated as follows:

1. Recent Intelligence – this should be intelligence that is less than three months old.

2. Historic Intelligence –this should be intelligence that is over three months old.

3. Reliable Intelligence – this should be intelligence that is graded B2 or higher on the previously mentioned scale.

4. Untested Intelligence - this should be intelligence that is graded less than B2.

It could be tempting to talk of unreliable intelligence or corroborating intelligence in the same way, however unreliable intelligence (particularly if one suspects counterintelligence) is an area of great concern that should be specifically highlighted in your work and one would hope is not a general theme of your product[16]. Corroborating intelligence should be discussed as part of the Intelligence picture and a theme that has been identified as part of your analysis. Otherwise the clear delineation of recent/historic and reliable/unreliable with its permutations could become convoluted.

Where your analysis involves using data from a number of open sources it is important to decide how you will evaluate these. In order to assist your customer the most helpful methodology is to consider how it can fit in with the existing evaluation criteria. There is no singular way of approaching this; however let us consider the following scenario:

As part of their data collection plan an analyst has conducted open source research on "Topic X". Theanalyst has come across a blog on "Topic X" written by an author whose identity is not readily identified and a monograph on "Topic X" published by an academic who holds postgraduate degrees in his field. In terms of the blog the author is not identifiable and what he/she has written on the subject has not been identified as verifiable. This doesn't equate to the blog being spurious but rather that it would neatly fit the criteria of untested intelligence. In contrast the academic monograph has been authored by a reputable source with the content containing appropriate footnotes sighting its sources. Consequently this would fit the criteria of credible intelligence.

These approaches will allow for succinctness in writing, allow your product to 'flow', avoiding the verbosity and visual clutter that multiple footnotes on a page can convey.

The Analytical Product
As part of the Terms of Reference the techniques to be used in order to conduct your analysis and the most suitable product for it will have been agreed upon. As a section this is trickier than the previous subjects to comment on. Each individual reading this textbook for guidance will be approaching this with their own problem that they are trying to address and attempting to find a solution to form intelligence analysis, whether this be in support of an investigation, an intelligence operation or other area. As already discussed each problem should be approached as its own unique situation requiring a bespoke response. Consequently how one conducts their analysis will depend on the techniques employed and the approach of the individual analyst. It is beyond the scope of this chapter to discuss the various techniques available to the intelligence analyst in order to the help them analyse data in support of the challenge posed to them. What can be discussed here are some fundamentals that go into making a good product and some considerations for intelligence analysts as they create them.

---

[16] The obvious exceptions would be an analyst working in an intelligence agency or specialist department etc.

A maxim often quoted to intelligence professionals by management is "you're only as good as your last product". To a great degree this is true, unless you work with someone frequently they are unlikely to remember the products that you have delivered in the past. Reputation is a precious thing and ultimately your product will not only reflect on you but your department and depending on the customer who reads it, Intelligence as a whole. Therefore as an intelligence analyst one should strive to create the best product that they can with suitable acknowledgement to the relevant constraints put upon them. A product, for example, created during a fast time 'Crime in Action' needs to be timely, relevant and accurate but the luxury of creating a product that is comprehensive with supporting appendices is unlikely to be available.

With all the aforementioned in mind, the product you create is going to present the greatest opportunity for you to have an influence on your customer whilst making a lasting impact, even more so than the initial dissemination of your product[17]. Your product will still be in the archives long after you've changed roles or moved to a new organisation and, in some cases, will come back to haunt you.

A personal anecdote helps to illustrate this. Whilst working in one of my former departments, the Investigations Intelligence Unit, I produced a product primarily based on Network Analysis in support of an operation looking at tackling the supply of Class A drugs. The operation was developed as best as it could be, unfortunately as is sometimes the case the investigation petered out. Approximately a year later the Officer in charge of the case came to see me and was clutching my product in his hand. With a broad grin on his face he stated "your past has finally caught up with you. We're going to re-visit the investigation and I've just been re-reading your product to look for a starting point".

With all of this in mind let us approach the writing of the product itself. It has already been noted that it is not possible to address all eventualities. We can however look at some key areas that will assist in creating an analytical product that will successfully support an investigation or operation.

1. Writing

The ability to write is a skill set that is essential to being a good intelligence analyst. It is important that you are able to communicate your ideas in a format that is easy to understand and communicates the salient points to your intended audience. After all they have requested Intelligence Analysis in support of their investigation or operation. They will not be able to consider or make an informed choice based upon your work if you can't communicate your concepts. Paraphrasing intelligence professional Barbara Brookover in her chapter on "Effective Crime Analysis Writing" in *Exploring Crime Analysis* there are six key questions to answer for yourself prior to writing your product:

- Why are you writing?
- What level of knowledge and experience does your audience have in the related subject?
- What response do you expect from your audience to your product?
- What do you need to do in order to get the response you want? (Normally implementing your recommendations.)
- Are there responses that you wish to avoid?
- How will you know if your writing has been successful? (Brookover, 2016, p.334)

---

[17] This will be discussed in depth in a later section.

Having considered these questions we are ready to proceed with the following thought in mind. Analytical writing is unique. To a degree it is expository and aims to explain your findings to the reader. In addition the content of the writing, having been analysed, draws conclusions for the readers based upon the available facts, intelligence and inferences that have been created.

2. Product Outline.

Most organisations have requirements for their written work and templates in place. Whilst following the policy and procedures that are in place all templates should be adapted to aid the creation of the product and make it reader friendly. We have already discussed the Five Product Family and the Intelligence Products found in NIM. This as part of your Terms of Reference will dictate the length and scope of your work. As a minimum a good product will include the following:

- An introduction
- Executive Summary detailing the salient points.
- The analysis/intelligence picture[18].
- Intelligence gaps identified.
- Intelligence requirements coming out of the product.
- Intelligence recommendations
- Conclusions
- Supporting appendices such as I2 charts, GIS Maps, call schedules etc.

3. The Intelligence Picture

As an intelligence analyst you are attempting to paint a picture, an intelligence picture. This is the key to assisting your customers in how they will manage operations and progress investigations. It will also form the basis for identifying strategies and solutions for essential problem solving.

The analysis you have undertaken will attempt to answer the 5WH - Who, What, When, Where, Why, and How. This may allow solid answers, or at least highly probably answers to be arrived at in part. Where these are not readily available your analysis should allow you to create inferences based on either deductive or inductive reasoning[19] to plausibly answer them.

4. Intelligence Gaps, Requirements and Recommendations.

Where it is not readily possible to answer one of the 5WHs or a part of it these provide readily identifiable intelligence gaps. This in turn does three things:

- Allows the reader to understand the limitations of the product.
- Identifies the obvious intelligence requirements.
- Informs the SIO's and/or SIP's thinking for the investigative or intelligence strategies for the operation.

Following the identification of the intelligence gaps and requirements, the analyst is free to make recommendations in order to fill them. This is also an opportunity for the analyst to make recommendations in order to corroborate or test the inferences and identify additional analysis that can be

---

[18] This will be discussed more fully at a later stage.

[19] It is beyond the scope of this chapter to fully explore these however there are many good analytical and logical reasoning resources available that can provide a comprehensive overview of this.

undertaken in support of the investigation or operation. When making recommendations these should fall into two areas:

    1. Tactical/Short-term recommendations.
    2. Strategic/Long-term recommendations.

In making recommendations it is important for the analyst to have a good understanding of what their colleagues in Intelligence and other departments can offer. This can allow for an appropriate owner to be allocated in order to progress the recommendation.   In writing up recommendations the following should be included as a minimum:

- Identify whether the recommendations are essential or simply desirable.
- What authorities will need to be obtained or legislation observed in order to progress.
- Estimated time frames for completion and whether they are tactical or strategic.
- Who will complete the recommendation?
- Alternative solutions where one is likely to be unviable.
- Highlight where collaborative working may be required.

There is an old maxim that states "the reward for good work is more work". A good analyst will identify opportunities for more analytical products with ongoing work being self-generating to a large degree. Whilst the SIO or SIP is considering your recommendations you can have the advantage of 'leaning forward.'.

There is a third area for recommendations and these are operational. Depending on the culture of your organisation this can be something that an analyst can be partially engaged in, fully engaged in or, at the opposite, extremely criticised for engaging in. I have found in my experience that this often comes down to two factors:

    1. The relationship that you've managed to cultivate.
    2. The personality and open-mindedness of the SIOs or SIPs

Thankfully in my experience I've worked with those whose attitude has always been "no-one has a monopoly on good ideas" and are more than open to everyone contributing their ideas. A culture where it is frowned upon is understandable if individuals are consulted for their expertise and each person is required to remain within their remit. The problem, however, is cross-pollination; an analyst who has worked in support of specialist departments for a decent length of time is likely to acquire a reasonable working knowledge of operational tactics and their analysis may identify opportunities where these can be deployed to great success. This can ironically be further exacerbated when the teams responsible for implementing such tactics have requested work from the analyst in support of utilising them. The best way forward in making operational recommendations is to do so in consultation with a tactical expert. This is something that I utilise in my products and have a number of individuals that I've built up an excellent working relationship with that I regularly consult when I want to discuss making an operational recommendation. By doing this and making it clear in your product that they have been consulted you have the advantage of adding additional credibility to your recommendation whilst avoiding the potential pitfall of inadvertently 'getting offside' with some who doesn't like Analysts making operational recommendations.

    4.   Conclusions
All good writing finishes with conclusions, particularly analytical writing. At a minimum this will

pull together the salient points of your analysis and this is an opportunity for you to consider what are the key findings and recommendations that you want your customer to take away with them. Your product should, based upon your findings, make predictions regarding the Intelligence picture that you have drawn together. Where the work is of sufficient scope it should also attempt to forecast potential outcomes based on:

1. No changes occurring to the intelligence picture.
2. Changes brought about the subjects under investigation.
3. Changes brought about law enforcement agencies by implementing partial recommendations. This should highlight which recommendations are key to implementing meaningful change and those which are optional.
4. Changes brought about law enforcement agencies by implementing all recommendations.

SIOs and SIPs will be using the product to inform a potentially large part of their decision making process. This will feed into the management process of the investigation or intelligence operations. As an analyst, your conclusions will be an influential factor and, coupled with the overarching investigation and/or intelligence strategy, will allow for the following to be identified:

1. Immediate opportunities for 'quick wins' to be identified and implemented.
2. Strategies for disrupting criminal activity.
3. Long-term solutions to the problem identified in the intelligence picture or crime under investigation.

Ultimately as an intelligence analyst with a product that is timely, relevant and with recommendations that are actionable, you can make a significant contribution to an investigation or operations and ultimately be a major contributing factor in their success.

Dissemination

It is not the purpose of this chapter to discuss in any depth effective mediums for communication and methods for disseminating products. Each individual is different and will have different strategies to assist them in effective communication. The two key points to dissemination are simply this: Ensuring that the right audience receives your product and ensuring that the right audience understands your product.

That being said this chapter has at times touched on dissemination already and will now offer the following suggestions:

a. **Your originating customer is your primary target audience**. It is important that they fully understand what your product is trying to communicate, what your findings are and what your recommendations are. Your report may be disseminated 'far and wide' to other departments, partner agencies and even internationally but your first duty is to the requester of the work. Therefore, it is highly recommended that dissemination to them is done in a context which allows face-to-face interaction with the opportunity for plenty of questions and answers, where needed, so you can provide clarification. Action taken when the analysis undertaken isn't fully understood may have a detrimental effect.

b. **Peer Review.** Prior to the dissemination of your product a peer review of it by another analyst is invaluable, although in a fast time scenario this is not always practical. This can guard against small errors that can creep into any written work. What is of greater benefit however is that they, coming fresh to the problem, may be able to identify additional points that add even greater value to the product.

c. **Review by non-Analysts**. As is often the case products requested of an intelligence analyst are by often customers who don't possess the technical knowledge that forms part of an analyst's tool kit. Whereas a complex piece of analysis in the right hands maybe highly effective the inverse is true when a customer is seeking answers from analysis but the findings are not readily understood. The best work and dissemination of it is when all the salient points are both communicated and understood by the specialists and laypersons alike. In order to try and ensure this I will often ask the other intelligence staff to read my products, see if there is anything that is ambiguous and if so what requires clarification.

d. **Personal Reputation.** Earlier in the chapter the concept of reputation and consistently producing good products was discussed. It is a fact of life that we generally accept information more readily from those that we find credible. An analyst that is credible is one who has a good reputation, produces a good product and has the force of personality to "sell it". The first two are something that can be consistently strived for while the latter is something that can be cultivated and developed. By doing so you are farmore likely to get your findings across and have your recommendations adopted. Even in the case where your product is emailed and read by someone without face-to-face interaction, if they have heard of you in the context of producing reliable, quality products that in itself makes the reader more favourably disposed.

Ultimately the dissemination of your product is your last chance to sell it, so with the opportunities afforded you need to sell it well.

Evaluating the effectiveness of your Analysis

A product that seeks to evaluate the effectiveness of an Operation or Investigation may be requested by the customer and will typically employ Results Analysis as the dominant technique (National Policing Improvement Agency, 2008, pp. 62-63). This will usually be an in-depth piece of work examining the contributions made by all departments involved with operation or Investigation and involve collaborative work with colleagues who are performance analysts. It is not always practical to conduct such lengthy work on all operations and investigations once they have drawn to their conclusions. As an analyst however you can evaluate the effectiveness of your own work. This can be done in a number of ways, the two most common are evaluating your work against the Terms of Reference produced at the start of the operation or investigation and seeking direct feedback from your customer.

1. Evaluating your work against the Terms of Reference. This is by far the simplest way as the criteria for success has already been identified, all that remains is to ask these simple questions:

- Did the product achieve its aims and objectives?
- For any not achieved what were the reasons for this?
- Were there any risks or limitations that were not initially identified?
- For any not identified what were the reasons for this?
- How accurate were the inferences developed?
- If your recommendations were implemented how successful were they in achieving their objectives?

This can be done for each individual product produced and serves as an excellent method for self-assessment. A second and perhaps more effective method, particularly with regards to the subject of the intelligence products supporting the management of operations and investigations, is to review all the work undertaken as a whole. This allows the overall contribution made by intelligence analysis to be reviewed and examined to determine how effective the strategies and solutions recommended were.

2. Feedback from the customer. There are a number of ways this can be utilised but should always be done in conjunction with your Terms of Reference so as to remain in context. Feedback can be captured in any number of ways ranging from feedback forms to a recorded interview. Regardless of the medium employed, there are two principal ways of soliciting feedback from your customer. The first is to ask specific questions so as to gain direct answers on key areas that are of interest to you as the analyst. A second is to have a more open-ended approach where you discuss with your customer in open dialogue the work produced for them. This has the advantage of obtaining their perspective, offer insights into how they think they've utilised your work and an overall perspective of the operation. Where possible it is recommended that both methods are employed to gain well-rounded feedback.

Ideally all of the above will be applied in order to meticulously assess the contribution that intelligence analysis has made and how it has assisted in the overall management of the investigations and operations.

Miscellaneous: The role of Analysis in support of Proactive Investigations and Evidential Analysis
As part of the research undertaken for this chapter I conducted an interview with Detective Inspector Matthew Chapman [20] who over the last three years has been my most frequent customer, particularly during his tenure overseeing the Local Proactive Team. The interview was centered on the following areas:
1 The contribution Intelligence and Analysis makes to investigations.

2. The role Intelligence and Analysis plays in managing the operation.
3. Strategies and solutions from intelligence analysis.

From our discussions the following insights were established:

As an SIO in the world of proactive investigation, the role of analysis along with the wider function of an intelligence unit were viewed in a supportive role which changed depending on the stage at

---

[20] Interview conducted April 2016.

which the investigation was. At the outset of an investigation where an initial investigative strategy is formulated, the key considerations centred on: the victim, suspect(s), motivation for the crime and the question of whether it took place in isolation or if it formed part of a wider series?

The first 24-48 hours are key to preserving evidence. At this juncture he would be looking for what contribution intelligence analysis can make in trying to locate key individuals, an example that was highlighted to me was the analysis of communications data. Alongside this Intelligence work, analytical or otherwise that could assist in identifying and helping to manage any risk posed by individuals, particularly with regards to firearms or violence were viewed as being key.

As an investigation progressed from the initial stages so did the opportunities for the contribution from intelligence analysis. Using the example of a conspiracy the investigative strategy may have initially identified a possible time frame to focus the investigation. Temporal Analysis could support the Investigative hypothesis or suggest a widening of the parameters. In addition intelligence analysis that assisted in establishing the following were cited as being extremely valuable:

1. Identifying an M.O.
2. Attributing a phone to an individual.

As the investigation team builds their case they would then be looking for Intelligence Analysis to build a more in-depth intelligence picture with a view to seeing where it confirmed or negated the ongoing investigative hypothesis. Under UK legislation (Criminal Procedures Investigations Act of 1996), as in most countries, the analyst has a duty to follow all lines of inquiry. From the intelligence picture has the analysis confirmed, cast doubt or even identified new lines of enquiry?

All criminal investigations' ultimate aims are to have the guilty charged and convicted. At this stage the investigtor would be looking for the analyst to take the complicated data sets used in the Investigation, together with the findings from analysis, and distil them down into an easily comprehendible product that can ultimately be understood at Crown Court. (End of Interview)

In support of prosecutions a product from intelligence analysis can be turned into evidential material. Evidential Analysis is different in that there are no inferences or intelligence picture to be presented. Here we are dealing with the facts that have established from intelligence analysis during an investigation or operation. These can range from being extremely complex to comparatively simple. The role of the analyst here is to present their work in a way that is easily understood by a jury and will often make use of the software products such as i2 and Geographical Information Systems (GIS).

Marilyn Peterson notes in her book, *Applications in Criminal Analysis*:

"The use of analysis within the prosecutorial setting is generally an untapped field which may result in the development of new techniques and more beneficial uses" (Peterson, 1994, p. 9).

It would seem that this is the case on an international level and also with a number of intelligence analysts that I have spoken with in both the private and public sector (outside of law enforcement) in the UK. My advice to intelligence analysts involved with agencies that bring either private or public prosecutions is to consider what added value you as an analyst can bring to this field.

As an intelligence analyst working in law enforcement for Surrey Police, my job description always included "where necessary attending court to give evidence". Part of my analytical training included two courses from the City of London Law School's Continuing Professional Development (CPD) programme "Written Evidence for Analysts" and "Witness Familiarisation". Throughout my career these have proved to be invaluable. The vast majority of my contemporaries produce evidential products on a regular basis that are used in support of prosecutions. This can involve a number of different stages:

1. Analysis that assists in convincing the CPS[21] to authorise charges and in some cases hold suspects on remand.
2. Evidential Analysis that has been served on the defence which may assist in procuring early guilty pleas.
3. Attending court to give evidence as a professional witness[22].

Giving evidence at court can be seen as the pinnacle of dissemination during which your evidence is presented, explained by you during "examination-in-chief" and "cross examination". Here the skills of presenting and explaining your work in a way that is easily understood are the forefront.

During this chapter we have discussed and explored at great length the role that intelligence analysis plays in the role of managing police investigations and operations, particularly in the area of decision making. At court your product and evidence can make a significant contribution to the verdict that is returned by the jury, in the case of a guilty verdict this is the ultimate decision that can be made at the end of a successful investigation/operation.

Conclusion

This chapter has demonstrated that intelligence products produced through intelligence analysis support both SIOs and SIPs in the management of police operations. These products allow for more effective working by producing recommendations that highlight opportunities by formulating strategies and solutions through the intelligence analysis of crime problems.

To those who have read this chapter as practitioners I would say that analysis is a science, but intelligence is an art form. In your work is the opportunity to blend both and therefore be creative. Many who you work with can think analytically and therefore will have a great appreciation for the work of an analyst.

For the SIO or other individuals who have the ability to make use of an intelligence analyst this chapter will have demonstrated how intelligence analysis can add value at every level. Whilst acknowledging that the intelligence picture created at the time may not be what an investigation has revealed at its close this should not prevent you from continuing to take full advantage of the services

---

[21] Crown Prosecution Service

[22] A Professional Witness (sometimes called a Witness of Fact) differs from an Expert Witness in that a Professional Witness provides professional evidence from their Analytical Findings. An Expert Witness is an individual who based on experience and qualifications is considered by the Judge to be an expert and may offer an opinion on evidence or facts that is within the remit of their expertise.

offered by an intelligence analyst. As Marilyn Peterson notes in her book *Applications in Criminal Analysis*:

> "A word of advice to managers: do not use the so-called failures of intelligence to hold you back from using intelligence in support of decision making and planning. More mistakes are made by managers who chose to ignore the data provided by their intelligence process than by those who use the intelligence function" (Peterson, 1994, p. 267).

Finally paraphrasing the words of fictional Intelligence Officer George Smiley created by John le Carre' in the *Honorable School Boy* (le Carre, 1977, audio book):

> "If we don't engage in this as professionals then amateurs will do so on our behalf".

This is a reminder to intelligence analysts to always place themselves at the forefront and be proactive in looking to add value to whatever situation they find themselves in. Whether this is daily business, supporting investigations, protracted operations or crime in action there is always something that intelligence analysis can make by way of meaningful and influential contribution.

This chapter has been written from a UK perspective and specifically from that of the author, the applications of it however are myriad. It is up to the reader to apply the concepts discussed in their own cultural context. Ultimately though the objectives of creating an intelligence picture from analysis and influencing those who are in a position to make overall decisions about an investigation or operations will be a constant contribution. It is up to you to take these concepts and apply them in your context personally, professionally and for the good of the organisation.

Addendum One - The 3x5x2 – Intelligence Report[23]

This presents a more simplified system for the evaluation and dissemination of intelligence under three headings:

Evaluation of the source's reliability:

Reliable (1) – This grading is used when the source is believed to be competent and information received is generally reliable.

Untested (2) – This relates to a source that has not previously provided information to the person receiving it or has provided information that has not been substantiated.

Not reliable (3) – This should be used where there are reasonable grounds to doubt the reliability of the source.

Assessment of the information/intelligence received:

Known directly to the source (A).

Known indirectly to the source but corroborated (B) – Refers to information that the source has not personally witnessed, but can be verified by separate intelligence that carries an assessment of **(A)**.

Known indirectly to the source (C) – Applies to information that the source has been told by someone else.

Not known (D) – Applies when there is no means of assessing the information.

Suspected to be false (E) – Regardless of how the source came upon this information, there is a reason to believe the information provided is false.

Dissemination of the Intelligence.

Lawful sharing permitted (P) – May be disseminated for a policing purpose.

Lawful sharing permitted with conditions (C) – May be disseminated but requires the receiving agency to observe any specific handling instructions that accompany it.

---

[23] https://www.app.college.police.uk/app-content/intelligence-management/intelligence-report/ -retrieved 25/03/17 at 18:12hrs

Additional conditions for the use of the Intelligence Unit

A1 covert development – intelligence may be combined or corroborated with other intelligence but direct action cannot be taken.

A2 covert use – covert action may be taken on this intelligence although the source, technique and any wider investigative effectiveness must be protected.

A3 overt use – overt action is permitted on this intelligence.

S1 delegated authority – the originator of the intelligence permits the unsupervised sanitisation of the material in order to allow dissemination to a wider audience.

S2 consult originator – the originator of the intelligence does not permit the sanitisation of the material for wider dissemination without prior consultation.

Chapter 4: Intelligence-Led Policing and Privacy Issues

By Gregory Thomas, Ph.D., Kerri Salata, J.D.[i24] and Linda Randby, J.D.

Introduction

Law enforcement agencies have had long-standing requirements for intelligence as it is an important component in various strategies against criminal activity. In an early example, Godfrey and Harris (1971) examined the significance of intelligence in law enforcement efforts against organized crime. They related that to combat organized crime, law enforcement agencies needed strategies that rested on solid intelligence. Similarly, Dintino and Martens (1983) stressed the importance of the intelligence function to the decision-making process in organized crime control.

This book presents additional examples of the value of intelligence through the strategy of intelligence-led policing in investigating various types of criminal activity, including drug trafficking, white collar and financial crimes, human trafficking, street gangs, and cyber crimes.

Even as early proponents stressed the necessity of intelligence in United States law enforcement efforts, they also were aware of privacy and civil rights issues and the potential for abuse of intelligence. Godfrey and Harris (1971) provided legal aspects to consider in regard to constitutional rights and privacy issues with the intelligence function. In addition, Dintino and Martens (1983) examined criticisms and abuses surrounding U.S. domestic intelligence programs. However, they also recognized the benefits that can be derived from a legitimately-run intelligence function. Martens (2000) described historic abuses and misuses of intelligence in the U.S. during such events as the McCarthy hearings of the 1950s, the FBI counter intelligence program of the 1960s, the Watergate scandal and cover-up of the 1970s, failures and abuses during the drug war of the 1980s and 1990s, and in the investigations of extremist groups and corrupt public officials.

These abuses negatively impacted the domestic intelligence functions of law enforcement agencies. More recent misuses of intelligence include the reporting by some U.S. state and local fusion centers of information that could have "potentially endangered the civil liberties or legal privacy protections of the U.S. persons they mentioned" (Permanent Subcommittee on Investigations, 2012, p. 35.). This chapter discusses issues surrounding the rights to personal privacy in the implementation of intelligence-led policing.

What are privacy and civil liberties?

The U.S. Department of Justice defines the term civil liberties as:

"...fundamental individual rights such as freedom of speech, press, or religion; due process of law; and other limitations on the power of the government to restrain or dictate the actions of individuals. They are the freedoms that are guaranteed by the Bill of Rights – the first ten Amendments – to the Constitution of the United States. Civil liberties offer protection to

---

[24] The views expressed by Kerri Salata are hers and not those of the Bank of Montreal.

individuals from improper government action and arbitrary governmental interference..." (U.S. Department of Justice, 2003, p. 5)

This definition also is found in the U.S. Department of Justice's *Privacy, Civil Rights and Civil Liberties: Policy and Templates for Justice Information Systems.*

Similarly, the term civil rights encompasses obligations that are imposed on the government to promote equality. It is a term that implies that states have a role in ensuring that all citizens have equal protection under the law as well as equal opportunities to exercise the privileges of their citizenship, regardless of race, religion, sex or other such characteristics. (U.S. Department of Justice, 2003, pp. 5-6). Thus the term civil liberties involves restrictions placed on government and the term civil rights relates more to positive/affirmative government action.

The term privacy has also been defined in the U.S. *National Criminal Intelligence Sharing Plan* (2003) to reference individuals' interests in preventing the inappropriate collection, use and release of personally identifiable information. Such interests include privacy of personal behavior, privacy of personal communications, and privacy of personal data. The U.S. Constitution does not explicitly mention a right of privacy (*Carey v. Population Services, Intern.*, 431 U.S. 678, 1977; *Roe v. Wade*, 410 U.S. 113, 1973). However, courts have recognized that a right to personal privacy, such as the right to be free from unwanted governmental intrusion, is implicit in the U.S. Constitution[25] (*Katz v. U.S.*, 389 U.S. 347, 1967; *Runyon v. McCrary*, 427 U.S. 160, 1976; *Griswold v. Connecticut*, 381 U.S. 479, 1965). The right of privacy is basically a protection drawn from several constitutional provisions placing certain aspects of life beyond the reach of government intrusion.

Laws and policies regarding personal privacy

As stated 46 years ago by Godfrey and Harris, "The collection in secret of detailed information concerning the activities, habits, and beliefs of large numbers of citizens–whatever the form of criminal conduct in which it is believed they are engaged–involves substantial constitutional questions" (1971, p. 107). This section looks closer at these issues.

Realizing that privacy protections are an international concern, in 1980, the Organisation for Economic Co-operation and Development (OECD)[26] created a set of internationally agreed upon principles that describe handling practices with regard to the privacy and security of information and personal data. The OECD Privacy Guidelines (revised in 2013) include *Basic Principles of National Application*, described in Figure 4.1 (Organization for Economic Co-operation and Development, 2013). These principles apply to personal data collected by law enforcement agencies as well as other organizations that handle sensitive information about individuals.

---

[25] The general concept of individual liberty and the limitations on the government's powers that are expressly stated in the U.S. Constitution (otherwise known as "enumerated powers") were recognized in the Ninth Amendment, which provides that people retain rights beyond those specifically enumerated in the U.S. Constitution.

[26] The Organisation for Economic Co-operation and Development (OECD) is an intergovernmental organization with 35 member countries, founded in 1961, and committed to democracy and the market economy.

Figure 4. 1

Basic Principles of National Application

Collection Limitation Principle
There should be limits to the collection of personal data and any such data should be obtained by lawful and fair means and, where appropriate, with the knowledge or consent of the data subject.

Data Quality Principle
Personal data should be relevant to the purposes for which they are to be used, and, to the extent necessary for those purposes, should be accurate, complete and kept up-to-date.

Purpose Specification Principle
The purposes for which personal data are collected should be specified not later than at the time of data collection and the subsequent use limited to the fulfilment of those purposes or such others as are not incompatible with those purposes and as are specified on each occasion of change of purpose.

Use Limitation Principle
Personal data should not be disclosed, made available or otherwise used for purposes other than those specified in accordance with the Purpose Specification Principle except:
   a)   with the consent of the data subject; or
   b)   by the authority of law.

Security Safeguards Principle
Personal data should be protected by reasonable security safeguards against such risks as loss or unauthorised access, destruction, use, modification or disclosure of data.

Openness Principle
There should be a general policy of openness about developments, practices and policies with respect to personal data. Means should be readily available of establishing the existence and nature of personal data, and the main purposes of their use, as well as the identity and usual residence of the data controller.

Individual Participation Principle
Individuals should have the right:
   a)   to obtain from a data controller, or otherwise, confirmation of whether or not the data controller has data relating to them;
   b)   to have communicated to them, data relating to them
        i.   within a reasonable time;
        ii.   at a charge, if any, that is not excessive;
        iii. in a reasonable manner; and
        iv.   in a form that is readily intelligible to them;
   c)   to be given reasons if a request made under subparagraphs (a) and (b) is denied, and to be able to challenge such denial; and
   d)   to challenge data relating to them and, if the challenge is successful to have the data erased, rectified, completed or amended.

Accountability Principle
A data controller should be accountable for complying with measures which give effect to the principles stated above.
(Organization for Economic Co-operation and Development, 2013)

Overview of Laws Relating to Policing and Personal Privacy

This section provides an overview of laws in the United States and Canada as they relate to personal privacy. A comparison shows that in some respects, the case law is not as developed and the law enforcement intelligence sharing not as pronounced in Canada as in the United States. This overview also indicates that law enforcement intelligence privacy issues are continually evolving.

- United States

As stated previously, in the U.S. the right of privacy is a protection drawn from several constitutional provisions placing certain aspects of life beyond the reach of government intrusion. The courts have found specific sources of privacy in the U.S. Constitution, such as the First, Fourth, Fifth and Ninth Amendments as well as the first section of the Fourteenth Amendment. While all of these sources of privacy are important, for purposes of understanding the principles of privacy, civil liberties and civil rights in the intelligence setting, only a few will be highlighted.

The Fourth Amendment

The Fourth Amendment states:

> The right of the people to be secure in their persons, houses, papers and effects against unreasonable searches and seizures, shall not be violated, and no Warrants shall issue, but upon probable cause, supported by Oath or affirmation, and particularly describing the place to be searched, and the persons or things to be seized.

Generally, the Fourth Amendment requires that all searches must be reasonable and that any search based upon a search warrant be based upon sworn facts that demonstrate the existence of probable cause to search a particular place or to seize a person or thing. To establish probable cause, a law enforcement officer must show that the place to be searched will turn up evidence of a crime or that the person arrested committed a crime. Generally, a search conducted without a warrant, is considered unreasonable.

To determine whether a search falls under the scope of the Fourth Amendment, a "reasonable expectation of privacy test" should be conducted. Under this test: (1) a person must exhibit an "actual (subjective) expectation of privacy" and (2) "the expectation [must] be one that society is prepared to recognize as reasonable" (Katz, 1967). If it is determined that a reasonable expectation of privacy exists, then it is considered a search under the Fourth Amendment. Because this determination is rendered on a case-by-case basis in conjunction with a review of the totality of the circumstances, this doctrine has resulted in numerous court cases interpreting whether particular circumstances give rise to a reasonable expectation of privacy.

For example, in *Riley v. California* (2014), the U.S. Supreme Court held that a warrant is required to search the digital information on a cell phone that is seized during the course of arresting an individual. The Supreme Court determined that cell phones are different from other physical "papers and effects" which may be found on an arrestee's person. Accordingly, unless there is an exception to the Fourth Amendment warrant requirement, such as exigent circumstances, law enforcement must obtain one prior to searching cell phones in these instances.

In another case, *United States v. Jones*, (2012), the U.S. Supreme Court strayed from the "reasonable expectation of privacy test" and held that the installation of a GPS device on a car without a warrant was a search under the Fourth Amendment. For something to be deemed a valid search under the Fourth Amendment, a warrant must be obtained or one of the exceptions to the warrant requirement must apply. The Court reached this determination because it determined that the installation of the device constituted a trespass on a person's property. Some of the justices concurred with the determination that this was a search but followed the "reasonable expectation of privacy test." In determining that this was a search under the reasonable expectation of privacy standard, the justices felt that the use of extensive long-term surveillance violated that expectation thereby making these circumstances a search.

Many courts have held that dissemination of information from one agency to another does not implicate the Fourth Amendment because the dissemination itself is not a "search" or a "seizure" (*Jabara v. Webster,* 1983). However, if erroneous information is disseminated about an individual and law enforcement authorities act based on this information, that individual's Fourth Amendment rights may be implicated, particularly if the individual was "seized" and/or his or her property was searched.

Additionally, individuals who retain a reasonable expectation of privacy may lose Fourth Amendment protections when they relinquish that control to third parties. For example, an individual may transmit information to third parties electronically, such as sending data across the Internet or retaining information on a shared computer network. At this point, the individual who transmitted or shared the information may have lost his or her reasonable expectation of privacy. Regardless of whether this individual retained his or her reasonable expectation of privacy, the third party who received the transmitted information or has access to the shared information may disclose it to law enforcement so long as the third party has common authority over the information (*United States v. Young,* 2003). The general rule is that an individual's Fourth Amendment rights dissipate as the individual's right to control the third party's possession diminishes (*United States v. Allen,* 1997).

The Fourth Amendment "is wholly inapplicable to a search or seizure, even an unreasonable one, effected by a private individual not acting as an agent of the Government or with the participation or knowledge of any governmental official" (*United States v. Jacobsen,* 1984). So, when a private individual who is acting on his or her own accord conducts a search and then makes the results available to law enforcement, no violation of the Fourth Amendment occurs. It is important that the law enforcement officials who receive the results limit their investigation to the scope of the private search when they are searching without a warrant. An example of the application of this doctrine would involve an individual who takes his or her computer in for repairs and the repair technician finds evidence of criminal activity which is turned over to law enforcement. The repair technician's search is not violative of the Fourth Amendment.

There are also numerous exceptions to the warrant requirements of the Fourth Amendment. Some key exceptions include consent, exigent circumstances, plain view and searches incident to arrest. If one or more of these exceptions apply, a warrant is not required, although probable cause must still exist.

The First Amendment

One of the more difficult challenges facing law enforcement engaged in intelligence gathering activities is handling information involving First Amendment protected activity. The First Amendment to the U.S. Constitution provides that "Congress shall make no law respecting an establishment of religion, or prohibiting the free exercise thereof; or abridging the freedom of speech, or of the press; or the right of the people peaceably to assemble, and to petition the Government for a redress of grievances" (Bill of Rights, 1791). Law enforcement agencies should never collect or disseminate information based solely on First Amendment protected activities nor should they conduct investigations on this basis.

There are five core freedoms in the First Amendment. The first is religion. The government is prohibited from establishing a religion. It is each person's right to practice (or not to practice) any faith without government interference. Speech is also protected. Individuals have the right to speak freely, without interference from the government. The freedom of press gives individuals the right to publish news, information and opinions without government interference. This freedom does not just apply to media outlets, it includes other public areas such as the Internet or self-published newsletters. The First Amendment also provides that individuals or groups have the right to gather in public to march, protest, demonstrate, carry signs and otherwise express their views. Individuals can also join and associate with each other in groups and organizations without government interference. Finally, the freedom to petition the government provides individuals the right to appeal to the government in favor or against policies that affect them or about which they feel strongly. The types of activities protected under this freedom include gathering signatures in support of a cause, lobbying legislative bodies or filing lawsuits.

Of all of these freedoms enunciated in the First Amendment, the most difficult area of intelligence gathering for law enforcement agencies are situations involving "expressive activity". It is important to understand that expressive activity that incites violence or constitutes a threat is likely not protected by the First Amendment. On the other hand, a group of individuals who hold signs advocating their position in front of a government building may be protected from prosecution. However, if that same group is in front of the government building waving guns and knives while advocating their position, the outcome may be different.

Some individuals and groups express what others consider extreme views such as those related to animal rights, protection of the environment, anti-government stances, white supremacy, or anarchy. Although these expressions may not be criminal, they may be viewed as a threat. This places law enforcement in the position of determining whether the behavior is simply an individual or group making a firm statement of their beliefs or a threat–a difficult position that is somewhat subjective. It is important that law enforcement officials ensure the safety of the general public while protecting the privacy, civil liberties, and civil rights of individuals or groups who are exercising their First Amendment rights.

Groups and individuals also have protection under the First Amendment when associating with other groups or individuals. "[I]mplicit in the right to engage in activities protected by the First Amendment" is "a corresponding right to associate with others in pursuit of a wide variety of political, social, economic, educational, religious and cultural ends" (*Roberts v. United States Jaycees,* 2000). The Supreme Court "has recognized the vital relationship between freedom to associate and privacy in one's associations" (*NAACP v. Alabama,* 1958). "Inviolability of privacy in group association may ... be indispensible to preservation of freedom of association, particularly where a group espouses dissident beliefs." *Id.* "Government actions that may unconstitutionally burden this freedom may take many forms, one of which is 'intrusion into the internal structure or affairs of an association'…" (*Boy Scouts* at 648).

Importantly, the right of expressive activity and association is not absolute. The freedom can be overridden if the need to gather intelligence serves a compelling government interest. (*Roberts* at 623.) Additionally, large gatherings of people may present public safety concerns, especially if the gathering relates to a passionately held belief or position. These gatherings may be subject to time, place and manner restrictions without running afoul of the First Amendment. (*Clark v. Community for Creative Non-violence*, 1984).

In determining whether a particular intelligence gathering program unconstitutionally infringes on a group member's rights of expressive activity or association, the analysis set forth by the U.S. Supreme Court in the *Boy Scouts* case is instructive. First, it must be determined "whether the group engages in expressive association" (*Boy Scouts* at 648.). Second, it must be determined whether the intelligence gathering "significantly affected" or "significantly burden[ed] the group's ability to engage in expressive association" (*Id.* at 650, 653). Finally, these two factors should be weighed against whether the government's interest in gathering the intelligence is "compelling" (*Id.* at 657).

Remedies

To the extent law enforcement activities violate an individual's or group's privacy, civil liberties or civil rights, a remedy is available. Title 42 U.S.C. § 1983 allows for civil lawsuits for deprivation of constitutional and federal statutory rights by persons acting under the color of law. Section 1983 lawsuits against law enforcement agencies most frequently involve issues under the First, Fourth and Fourteenth Amendments. Generally, to be successful, plaintiffs must show that the law enforcement agency failed to provide due diligence in protecting individuals' civil rights. This can be accomplished by showing that the government agency showed "deliberate indifference" toward such protections. Some of the evidence that a plaintiff would put forth includes showing that a particular agency lacks clear policy and procedures on intelligence gathering or that an agency does not have a clear, articulate policy in place that addresses intelligence gathering activities and their relationship to citizens' privacy, civil rights and civil liberties. There are immunities available to government officials depending upon the role and place of employment of the government employee. However, these immunities are not typically granted without judicial involvement.

A plaintiff who is successful under § 1983, may recover compensatory and punitive damages as well as injunctive relief. Compensatory damages have been awarded for costs such as medical care, lost wages, physical and emotional pain and suffering. Even in the absence of compensatory damages, a jury can return a nominal award which may allow for the imposition of punitive damages and attorneys' fees. Additionally, losing a § 1983 civil rights case, while costly and embarrassing, can also result in the imposition of significant new restrictions on a law enforcement agency's intelligence gathering functions (U.S. Department of Justice, 2009, pp. 156 – 158).

28 CFR 23

In 1979, the U.S. Department of Justice (DOJ) developed guidelines for the management of criminal intelligence records that state and local law enforcement agencies maintained. These guidelines were codified in 28 *C.F.R.* Part 23 – Criminal Intelligence Systems Operating Policies. These regulations are published under the authority of the Justice System Improvement Act of 1979 (42 *U.S.C.* § 3789g c).[27]

Title 28 *C.F.R.* Part 23 (hereinafter Part 23) governs inter-jurisdictional and multi-jurisdictional criminal intelligence systems which are operated by or on behalf of state and local law enforcement agencies and which are funded by federal funds (U.S. Department of Justice, 2009, p. 34). It provides guidelines on the collection, retention, review, dissemination and purging of criminal intelligence records. Part 23 requires that any records maintained in state or local law enforcement agencies' criminal intelligence systems contain sufficient evidence to establish a reasonable suspicion that an individual or organization in involved in criminal behavior. While it is not mandatory for state and local law enforcement agencies to follow Part 23, to the extent such agencies receive federal funds for the purpose of maintaining a described above database, they must agree to follow its requirements. (U.S. Department of Justice, 2009, p. 149)

Regardless of the receipt of federal funds, many agencies have adopted Part 23 as the *de facto* standard for managing intelligence information. After the *National Criminal Intelligence Sharing Plan* recommended that agencies adopt Part 23, its adoption became more widespread and it has become a recognized national standard for state and local law enforcement agencies to follow when managing intelligence information.

In 2008, in an effort to aid law enforcement agencies with developing policies and procedures related to implementing Part 23, the Law Enforcement Intelligence Unit (LEIU) re-issued the *Criminal Intelligence File Guidelines.* The purpose of these guidelines is "to bring about an equitable balance between the civil rights and liberties of citizens and the needs of law enforcement to collect and disseminate criminal intelligence on the conduct of persons and groups who may be engaged in systemic criminal activity" (Law Enforcement Intelligence Units, 2008, p. 2).

Part 23 sets forth operating principles concerning the collection and maintenance of criminal intelligence information. One specific principle relates that participating agencies, "shall not collect or maintain criminal intelligence information about the political, religious or social views, associations, or activities of any individual or any group, association, corporation, business, partnership, or other organization unless such information directly relates to criminal conduct or activity and there is reasonable suspicion that the subject of the information is or may be involved in criminal conduct or activity" (28 *CFR* 23). While these regulations are required of all federally funded intelligence projects, they can be applied to all law enforcement agencies performing an intelligence function and should be followed as general guidelines.

---

[27] …**(c) Criminal intelligence systems and information; prohibition against violation of privacy and constitutional rights of individuals**

All criminal intelligence systems operating through support under this chapter shall collect, maintain, and disseminate criminal intelligence information in conformance with policy standards which are prescribed by the Office of Justice Programs and which are written to assure that the funding and operation of these systems furthers the purpose of this chapter and to assure that such systems are not utilized in violation of the privacy and constitutional rights of individuals….

National Criminal Intelligence Sharing Plan

In 2002, the Criminal Intelligence Sharing Summit (Summit) was convened by the International Association of Chiefs of Police. The attendees of the Summit included law enforcement executives and intelligence experts from across the United States. As a result of the summit, the Global Intelligence Working Group (GIWG) was created. GIWG was tasked with developing a national criminal intelligence sharing plan, which was one of the recommendations adopted at the Summit.

The *National Criminal Intelligence Sharing Plan* (NCISP) was formally released in May 2004. The *NCISP* provides state, local, tribal and federal law enforcement agencies with the tools and resources that they need to develop, gather, access, receive and share intelligence information. It established a series of national standards that have been formally recognized by the professional law enforcement community as the role and processes for law enforcement intelligence today (U.S. Department of Justice, 2009, pp. 44-45). The NCISP contains over 25 recommendations and action items which address numerous issues and concerns related to law enforcement intelligence operations.

Some of the recommendations and action items relate specifically to privacy and constitutional rights. Recommendation 6 states:

"All parties involved with implementing and promoting the *National Criminal Intelligence Sharing Plan* should take steps to ensure that the law enforcement community protects individuals' privacy and constitutional rights within the intelligence process" (*National Criminal Intelligence Sharing Plan*, 2004, p. v-vi).

The *NCISP* also states the following in Recommendation 9:

"In order to ensure that the collection/submission, access, storage and dissemination of criminal intelligence information conforms to the privacy and constitutional rights of individuals, groups and organizations, law enforcement agencies shall adopt, at a minimum, the standards required by the Criminal Intelligence Systems Operating Policies Federal Regulation (28 *CFR* Part 23) regardless of whether or not an intelligence system is federally funded" (*NCISP*, 2004, p. v).

Recommendations 13 – 16 all relate to specific action items related to implementing an intelligence program that appropriately addresses the public concerns related to overzealous intelligence gathering while overlooking privacy interests and the constitutional rights of individuals. The recommendations encourage training on these issues, the implementation of a policy of openness to the public regarding an organization's criminal intelligence functions and the development of a privacy policy (*National Criminal Intelligence Sharing Plan*, 2004).

The need to ensure that individuals' constitutional rights, civil liberties, civil rights, and privacy interests are protected throughout the intelligence process is explained in *NCISP*. The development of a privacy policy is encouraged to attempt to "eliminate the unnecessary discretion in the decision-making process, guide the necessary discretion and continually audit the process to ensure conformance with policy goals" (*NCISP*, 2004, p. 6). The specific elements of the privacy policy are also addressed including the need to involve all interested parties in the development and implementation of the privacy policy.

NCISP also recommends training "all levels of law enforcement... on constitutional rights, privacy issues and safeguards as they relate to the criminal intelligence function" (*NCISP*, 2004, p. 15). Openness and transparency with the general public regarding the operating principles of the intelligence process is encouraged (pp. 15 – 16). *NCISP* also recommends that law enforcement agencies set up a system of accountability. "Accountability is essential to the effective implementation of a policy designed to protect individuals' privacy and constitutional rights" (*NCISP*, 2004, p.16).

Two of the prevalent recommendations from *NCISP* relating to privacy, civil liberties and civil rights involved 28 *C.F.R.* Part 23 and the implementation of a privacy policy for law enforcement engaged in intelligence operations.

The *NCISP*, revised in 2013, adopted recommendations specifically relating to privacy, civil rights, and civil liberties. In fact, it recommends that all law enforcement agencies adopt the standards set forth in 28 *C.F.R.* 23 regardless of whether or not an intelligence system is federally funded.

Guides and templates for policy development and training are available. For example, the U.S. Department of Justice, Bureau of Justice Assistance published *Privacy, Civil Rights, and Civil Liberties Policy Development Guide for State, Local, and Tribal Justice Entities (2012)*, which provides agencies information regarding the planning and implementation of privacy protections, and includes templates to aid in policy development.

Canada

The United Nation's *Universal Declaration of Human Rights* to which Canada is a party, defines privacy as an inalienable human right. "No one shall be subjected to arbitrary interference with his privacy, family, home or correspondence, nor to attacks upon his honour and reputation. Everyone has the right to the protection of the law against such interference or attacks" (United Nations,1948). Canadians do not have explicit constitutional rights to privacy, but over time, these rights have been interpreted in sections 7 and 8 of the Charter of Rights and Freedoms and are connected with concepts like the right to liberty, dignity, and autonomy which are considered fundamental to our democratic society (Khullar, 2010). Canadian Courts interpret the constitutional right to privacy generously, broadly, and liberally to balance the individual's expectation of privacy with the goals of law enforcement (Hunter et al. v. Southam Inc. 1984; R. v. Dyment, 1988): "grounded in man's physical and moral autonomy, privacy is essential for the well-being of the individual. For this reason alone, it is worthy of constitutional protection, but it also has profound significance for the public order. The restraints imposed on government to pry into the lives of the citizen go into the essence of a democratic state" (R. v. Dyment, 1988, para. 17). Privacy legislation and other supporting legislation like the *Criminal Code of Canada* provide exceptions allowing the collection, use, and disclosure of personal information for the purpose of law enforcement. When conducting intelligence-based investigations, it is important that law enforcement has an understanding of the impact of the *Charter* and other legislation relation to consent on investigations, searches, and seizures especially with recent and rapid advancements in technological and digital realms.

The Charter

The right to privacy is a fundamental right protected by both sections 7 and 8 of the *Charter* "[e]veryone has the right to life, liberty and the security of the person, and the rght not to be deprived thereof except in accordance with the principles of fundamental justice" (Section 7); "[e]veryone has the right to be secure against unreasonable search or seizure" (*Canadian Charter of Rights and Freedoms*, 1982). For the purpose of discussing intelligence-led policing, the focus of this section will be an individual's informational privacy rights protected by section 8 of the *Charter*.

In the 17th century, Sir Edward Coke declared, "[t]hat the house of every one is to him and his Castle and Fortress" (77 Eng. Rep 195, 1604) but the Supreme Court in Canada held that the right to privacy is a personal right protecting the individual, not simply their home. There are three high-level categories of privacy rights: 1) spatial or territorial protections; 2) those of the physical person; and 3) information related to the individual (R. v. Dyment,1988, para 19). If an individual believes their *Charter* rights have been infringed, they can seek a legal remedy "that is appropriate and just in the circumstances" (Section 24, Canadian Charter of Rights and Freedoms) and they can also ask that the Court not use evidence obtained by law enforcement against them in a trial (Human Rights Program). Hunter et al. v. Southam (1984) is the first post-*Charter* case to clarify that the right to privacy afforded in section 8 of the *Charter* protects all individuals against unreasonable search and seizure. In circumstances where an individual alleges unjustified state intrusion, consideration must be given as to whether the defendant has a reasonable expectation of privacy and the extent of that expectation. The accused has an onus of proof to establish that they had a reasonable expectation of privacy in the circumstances (*Canadian Encyclopedic Digest*, Constitutional law) which is based on the 'totality of the circumstances' and may include: presence at the time of the search, whether the accused is in possession or control of the property or place searched, the historical use of the property or item, and the accused's ability to regulate access (R. v. Edwards, 1996). Searches are reasonable when authorized by statute but a search carried out without a warrant is "presumptively unreasonable" (*Canadian Encyclopedic Digest*, Criminal Law). The Crown is then required to establish reasonableness on a balance of probabilities: 1) that the search was authorized by law; 2) that the authorizing law was reasonable; and 3) that the authority to conduct the search was exercised in a reasonable manner (*Canadian Encyclopedic Digest*, Criminal Law, R. v. Cole, 2012). An assessment must be made by the Court about the reasonableness of a warrantless search and whether an intrusion on an accused's privacy rights advances law enforcement goals and is in the public's best interest.

Law enforcement should obtain the consent of the individual, a subpoena, warrant, or order when conducting intelligence-led investigations and be cautious in situations of warrantless searches since the Court may have to consider whether the search was conducted in a reasonable manner (R. v. Edwards, 1996, para. 33). Even items seized in plain view during the execution of a search warrant may require another warrant to analyze that item (R. v. Little, 2009). Electronic devices owned by individuals, including cellular phones, computers and storage devices, are considered personal because the potential for discovering highly personal information exists. Recent cases are essential for law enforcement's understanding of what is and is not considered private in an increasingly digital era.

Cellular Devices

Like the rest of society, criminals are increasingly conducting their affairs through electronic messaging, and intelligence-led policing requires clear guidance on appropriate ways to gather this evidence. The search of a cellular phone without a warrant is not justified by common law, whether or not the phone is password-protected. An unlocked cellular phone does not mean an individual waives their privacy interest, just like an unlocked door to a home. Like the home, cellular devices remain intensely personal, even when not password-protected (R. v. Fearon, 2014, para. 160) because they contain private and personal communications through text and SMS messages, emails, and application-based communications, mobile apps which may or may not have passwords, and personal information like banking or finances. There are certain instances when is it reasonably necessary to infringe on an accused's privacy rights such as when the accused calls someone for "backup", the police or the public are threatened, or when there is reasonable suspicion that the search is necessary to prevent bodily harm or death: "[t]herefore, a warrantless search of a cell phone on arrest will be justified when (1) there is a reasonable basis to suspect a search may prevent an imminent threat to safety or (2) there are reasonable grounds to believe that the imminent loss or destruction of evidence may be prevented by a warrantless search" (R. v. Fearon, 2014, paras. 178-179). The use of software-assisted searches on an accused's cellular device can be considered an unreasonable search and seizure (R. v. Vye, 2014). In R. v. Marakah, the Court found that the sender of a text message has a reasonable expectation of privacy in the contents before it reached its destination, but once the message reaches the recipient, it is no longer in the control of the sender and there is no longer a reasonable expectation of privacy. The Supreme Court of Canada, which heard this case in 2017, wrote there was a reasonable expectation against unreasonable search and seizure in both sent and received text messages in some cases (R. v. Marakah. 2017 SCC 59).

Computers

Computers must be treated cautiously by law enforcement when intelligence gathering because they contain highly confidential and personal information about an individual. Computers, "…contain our most intimate correspondence. They contain the details of our financial, medical, and personal situations. They even reveal our specific interests, likes, and propensities, recording in the browsing history and cache files the information we seek out and read, watch, or listen to on the Internet" (R. v. Morelli, 2010). Since computers contain highly confidential and sensitive personal information, there is a heightened expectation of privacy. In the course of a warranted search, computers in plain view can be seized, but a further warrant is required before the computer is searched in the course of intelligence-led investigations (R. v. Vu, 2011, para. 24).[28] Law enforcement should restrict their searches to the crime being investigated pursuant to the warrant and not "rummage through the entire computer contents in search of evidence of another crime" (R. v. Jones, 2011, para. 42). Individuals also have a reasonable expectation to privacy in the informational content of their work computers, although this is a somewhat diminished expectation.

In R. v. Cole (2012), law enforcement obtained photos, files and a laptop from the accused's employer, a school, when the technician discovered child pornography and a partially nude photo of an underage student. Law enforcement did not obtain a search warrant before analyzing the computer. The Supreme Court of Canada held that the police should not have seized and searched the computer. Instead, the school should have informed law enforcement of the discovery of the materials which would have allowed law enforcement to obtain a search warrant before accessing personal information on the computer (R. v. Cole, 2012). Though the Supreme Court of Canada did not exclude the evidence in this case because it decided its admission would not bring the administration of justice into disrepute,

---

[28] Section 489 of the Criminal Code allows law enforcement to seize items not listed in a search warrant in plain view.

individuals have a heightened expectation of privacy relating to information on their computers, even work-issued computers.

USBs (also known as "thumb drives") or other mass storage devices are treated similarly to computers because of the storage capacity and type of information that can be stored on these devices. In R. v. Tuduce (2014), the accused was pulled over for a speeding offence when a USB device was discovered in the backseat of his car. Law enforcement used an intelligence expert in forensic examination of electromagnetic, optical, and storage devices, to search the USB key and discovered information leading to charges for unauthorized use of credit card data. The court applied the same considerations that apply to searches of personal computers for the following reasons: 1) A USB key can store significant data; 2) Data can be on a USB device without a user's knowledge and includes information about the user (dates, times, who modified the information); and 3) Data can be salvaged from a USB key even when the user deleted it (R. v. Tuduce, 2014, at paras. 71-73).

An individual's name and address connected to an Internet Service Provider (ISP) is also considered personal information and cannot be shared by a third-party corporation without a warrant, court order or consent of the individual. R. v. Ward (2012) and R. v. Spencer (2014) are two leading cases where through cyber-intelligence, law enforcement discovered inappropriate activity related to an ISP address and obtained personal information about the individual from the communications provider without a warrant or consent of the individual. In Ward, law enforcement obtained information from a third-party Internet provider, Bell Sympatico. The personal information obtained led police to obtain a search warrant which then led to charges against Ward for possession of and accessing child pornography. The Ontario Court of Appeal found that while the accused had an expectation that his ISP address would remain private, Bell Sympatico, had the right to prevent its services from being used to access child pornography. In Spencer, the accused was charged with possession of child pornography and making available child pornography. Again, in this case law enforcement discovered an ISP address used to store child pornography on an Internet file-sharing program. Law enforcement obtained information from a third-party Internet provider, Shaw, by relying on a provision of the Personal Information Protection and Electronic Documents Act (PIPEDA) which allowed disclosure of information to a law enforcement agency. Shaw provided the information to law enforcement based on the terms of a written contract with its clients which mirrored the language in PIPEDA and allowed them to disclose customer personal information, "necessary to…satisfy any legal, regulatory or other governmental request" (Spencer, 2014, para. 55-61). The matter was heard by the Supreme Court of Canada where Justice Cromwell determined that Spencer was entitled to anonymity in Internet searches but that the use of the information obtained by law enforcement would not bring the administration of justice into disrepute.

In response to several cases involving warrantless searches by law enforcement, the *Digital Privacy Act* received Royal Assent in June 2015[29] resulting in some substantial changes to PIPEDA for the private-sector. The *Digital Privacy Act* is important for law enforcement because it changed the ability of private-sector entities to disclose personal information of an individual to law enforcement without the consent of the individual or a subpoena, warrant or order. The *Digital Privacy Act* allows non-consensual disclosure of information to another organization when reasonable for the purposes of investigating a breach of an agreement or contravention of a law that has been, is being or is about to be committed (Digital Privacy Act, 2015 at section 7(3)(d.1)). The *Digital Privacy Act* also allows non-

---

[29] "Royal Assent" is the final stage of the legislative process where a bill passes through Parliament to become law.

consensual disclosure of information to another organization in circumstances of fraud prevention when detecting or suppressing fraud or preventing fraud that is likely to be committed (Digital Privacy Act, 2015 at section 7(3)(d.2)). In both cases, there must be a reasonable expectation that disclosure would compromise the activity and non-consensual disclosure can only be made to another organization, not law enforcement; "[t]hey are not broad exceptions that permit disclosure without consent to other parties such as law enforcement…" (Office of the Privacy Commissioner, 2017). PIPEDA still allows the private-sector to disclose personal information without consent when there is an emergency that threatens the life, health, and security of an individual, in matters of national security, defence of Canada, the conduct of international affairs, or for anti-money laundering purposes or terrorist financing purposes (Office of the Privacy Commissioner, 2017). However, unless the disclosed personal information clearly falls under a legislative exemption, valid consent for search and seizure is still required.

Open-Sources Searches

Most law enforcement intelligence agencies in Canada use open-source Internet searches in investigations and information gathering. Open-source searches include Boolean searches using search engines, open social media profiles, and even the creation of false accounts with the intention of befriending a suspect, their relatives or close associates online. All information available online is not necessarily public information. Open-source searches are relatively untested in Canadian courts and not well-defined in legislation. In a special report to Parliament, the Office of the Privacy Commissioner of Canada's position was, "that the public availability of public information on the Internet does not render personal information non-personal" (2014, p. 11). In the same report, the Privacy Commissioner of Canada discussed the need to reform existing privacy legislation to reduce unnecessary collection and regulate access to open-source information and investigations available from public sources (Office of the Privacy Commissioner of Canada, 2014). Without legislation, common law is assisting to define an accused's privacy rights online. In a 2016 case, based on an intelligence-led investigation, a series of Tweets were accepted into evidence. The Court compared Twitter event hashtags with public meetings, billboards, or announcements on the street corner and considered them information that anyone could see or read (R. v. Elliott, 2016, p. 43.). When law enforcement use chatrooms to speak with suspected child pornographers, the Courts have found that, "catching the perpetrators and abusers after they have violated children and spread their pictures all over the Internet is not enough. Ways must be found to deter would-be pornographers. One way of doing so is by deterring those who are interested in acquiring the pornography (R. v. Kwok, 2007, para. 52.)." Despite that this case touches on using the Internet as a preventative measure against child abusers, there is little caselaw in support of law enforcement using a false online profile or false online identity in other more private or closed social networking and chatroom forums, like Facebook or Instagram. It is possible that the Courts may come to see this form of online use by law enforcement intelligence agents as a fishing expedition or a form of entrapment and law enforcement should be cautious when using these investigative techniques.

Use of Technology in Investigations

Privacy is described as a "broad and evanescent concept" (Dagg v. Canada, 1997) which has become even more ambiguous with new technology and innovative investigation techniques like electronic, cellular, and aerial surveillance and data collection. Laws like the Canada Evidence Act, the Criminal Code, and Police Services Act provide guidance to law enforcement on search and seizure powers, rules of evidence, and disclosure requirements when intelligence gathering,[30] but Canadian Courts are increasingly developing common law approaches to address gaps in legislation. To determine if intelligence-led investigative techniques related to technology offend section 8 of the Charter, the court established that an evaluation of the current capacity of technology is required and that assessment should not be based on the technology's capacity in the future (R. v. Tessling, 2004, para. 55). While section 8 protects persons who have a reasonable expectation of privacy in their home, the court determined that individuals are also entitled to anonymity in public places:

> The mere fact that someone leaves the privacy of their home and enters a public space does not mean that the person abandons all of his or her privacy rights, despite the fact that as a practical matter, such a person may not be able to control who observes him or her in public. Thus, in order to uphold the protection of privacy rights in some contexts, we must recognize anonymity as one conception of privacy… (R. v. Spencer, 2014, para. 44).

Technology advancements like drones illustrate that privacy concepts, like anonymity in public spaces, still require interpretation by the Courts and legislatures. Drones are cost-effective law enforcement aids (Office of the Privacy Commissioner of Canada, 2013) used in agencies in the United States, United Kingdom, and Canada for scene photographs and aerial surveillance (RCMP – Lower Sackville, 2015), but drones can be used for other intelligence gathering initiatives. Law enforcement should approach drone surveillance in gathering intelligence on individuals by using the "reasonableness approach" and consider intelligence records gathered from drones, "subject to the same privacy law requirements as with any other data collection practice" (RCMP – Lower Sackville, 2015, p. 15). However, it is notable that drone technology use by law enforcement is relatively untested in Canadian Courts. Similarly, in 2015, records released by the American Civil Liberties Union (ACLU) about law enforcement's use of "StingRay" technology in Florida caused representatives in the House of Commons of Canada to question whether law enforcement were using StingRays in intelligence gathering (American Civil Liberties Association, 2015). StingRays can perform active surveillance of digital cellular telephones which can be mounted in vehicles, drones or carried by individuals (Pell and Soghoian, 2014). In April 2016, an information access request was filed with the Office of the Privacy Commissioner of Canada, launching an investigation into the use of StingRays by the Royal Canadian Mounted Police (RCMP) (CBC News, 2016). The Office of the Privacy Commissioner of Canada reports partial disclosure of the information requested, however, the use of Stingrays in policing remains a current issue with significant privacy considerations.

For a permissible warrantless search, an individual has to waive their section 8 Charter rights and law enforcement must establish valid consent to search (R. v. Wills, 1992). It is becoming increasingly important with new technological advances and innovative investigative techniques that law enforcement be open and transparent with the public about intelligence techniques and establish processes to demonstrate that the intelligence activity is permissible by legislation or common law. With continued technological advancements, law enforcement should ensure that new and innovative intelligence techniques follow current and permissible data collection practices in policy development to maintain public confidence.

---

[30] "Law enforcement" include public-sector government agencies that enforce laws including, but not limited to, the Royal Canadian Mounted Police, Ontario Provincial Police, and provincial, and municipal police services.

Production of Personal Information

Fundamental privacy principles exist in laws at all levels of the Canadian legislature: federal, provincial or territorial, and municipal. These principles include consent, limited collection, accuracy, openness, limited use, disclosure, and retention of information. Canada has two federal privacy laws that govern the protection of personal information in both public and private-sectors:[31] the Privacy Act which applies to federal government institutions and PIPEDA which applies to private-sector organizations and federally-regulated organizations. The Privacy Act applies to federal government institutions like the Department of National Defence (including the Canadian Forces), Canada Border Services Agency, Canadian Security Intelligence Service, the RCMP and the Communications Security Establishment (Privacy Act, 1985). The 10 provinces and three territories in Canada also have public-sector legislation.[32] In addition, many municipalities have freedom of information laws entitling individuals to protection of records and information kept about them by municipal governments and organizations. It is important that law enforcement operate with the understanding that individuals have the right to access and correct personal information collected during intelligence gathering unless the information was collected or used for the purpose of detecting, preventing or suppressing a crime, enforcing a law, or it involves a threat to Canadian security, may impact a lawful investigation, or reveal a confidential source of information like a confidential informant (Privacy Act, 1985).

National Intelligence Collaboration

Similar to the U.S., Canadian law enforcement have a national forum to exchange information and intelligence on organized criminal activity. Though sharing between law enforcement is not as well-defined at municipal levels, federal intelligence agencies seem to have networks to share information related to national importance. Police agencies, agencies with specific law enforcement roles, and agencies complimentary to law enforcement can become member agencies of the Criminal Intelligence Service Canada which allows them to exchange intelligence information through a national Criminal Intelligence Network (Criminal Intelligence Service Canada, 2014). [33] There is also a partnership between various intelligence agencies of law enforcement in Canada engaged in a strategy called the Canadian Law Enforcement Strategy to Combat Organized Crime committed to contributing information to a national intelligence database for investigative and threat assessment purposes. This committee is

---

[31] The "Public-Sector" is a governmental-run organization; the "Private-Sector" includes for profit and non-profit corporations and partnerships.

[32] PIPEDA applies to all private-sectors except in provinces with "substantially similar" legislation. Provinces with "substantially similar" legislation to PIPEDA include Quebec, British Columbia and Alberta.

[33] Category I – Police Agency: The agency has full police officer authority provided under a Canadian federal or provincial police act. The primary role of the agency is law enforcement and the agency contributes to the criminal intelligence process.

Category II – Agency with Specific Law Enforcement Role: The agency has specific but limited law enforcement responsibilities. Its authority is provided under specific federal or provincial legislation (e.g. Customs Act, Immigration Act, Provincial Wildlife Act). Category II Membership may be granted to a foreign law enforcement or intelligence agency if, as determined by the respective Provincial Executive Committee, it is deemed to be in the best interest of the broader criminal intelligence community.

Category III – Agency with Role Complementary to Law Enforcement: The agency has no direct law enforcement authority but provides assistance to law enforcement agencies.

governed by a National Executive Committee and Provincial Executive Committees (Criminal Intelligence Service Canada, 2014).

Application to Intelligence-Led policing

While it is imperative for police, as public agents, to be as transparent and accessible with information as possible, the nature of the criminal investigative process sometimes requires police to collect and analyze information that is not available publicly or that contains sensitive, personal details. Criminals attempt to conceal or disguise their activities from public view so law enforcement agencies must use certain unobtrusive and covert methods, such as electronic surveillance and undercover operations, to obtain private information without alerting suspects. Also, on occasion, as part of a criminal investigation, law enforcement officers obtain information pertaining to the practices, habits, possessions, and associations of suspects of criminal activity. While law enforcement agencies have a requirement for this information, they also have a responsibility to maintain the security of this sensitive information and use it in a manner that protects individual rights and civil liberties.

As described in this book, intelligence-led policing is a model for proactively and strategically addressing law enforcement issues. If properly managed, intelligence identifies social problems before they become criminal problems. These are the objectives of intelligence-led policing. Intelligence, in this sense, is a process that derives knowledge from information about one's opponents in order to guide decision-makers. According to Martens, "intelligence is certainly a key component in any viable crime control program, particularly when addressing crime that is systematic, systemic, and organized" (2000, p. 37). These are the targeted elements of intelligence-led policing.

Intelligence itself does not necessarily equate to clandestine and covert activity. In fact, a large amount of information used by police for investigative purposes is available publicly. Property records, corporate documents, criminal and civil court filings, county records, and telephone directories that contain personal information have long been available for public inspection. Add to this, information available from social media and is it possible to obtain a wealth of personal information about an individual.

However, the fact that such information is readily available to law enforcement officials does not mean that they can freely collect and maintain this information on individuals. Gordnier (2011), explains that information collected for intelligence use must be for a legitimate law enforcement purpose. In order to perform this function, officers must establish a reasonable suspicion that an individual is involved in criminal activity or that there is an identified criminal predicate. U.S. policy explains that, "Reasonable Suspicion or Criminal Predicate is established when information exists which establishes sufficient facts to give a trained law enforcement or criminal investigative agency officer, investigator, or employee a basis to believe that there is a reasonable possibility that an individual or organization is involved in a definable criminal activity or enterprise" (28 *CFR* 23). Gordnier (2011) relates that the concepts of "legitimate law enforcement purpose" and "reasonable suspicion" are lesser invasions of privacy and constitutional rights than such standards as proof beyond a reasonable doubt or probable cause to believe someone committed a crime. The concept of reasonable suspicion also requires less certainty, another reason why law enforcement authorities must prevent the public disclosure of criminal intelligence. Without meeting these thresholds of a legitimate law enforcement purpose and reasonable suspicion of criminal activity, law enforcement agencies do not have a valid justification to collect or maintain sensitive information on subjects.

Conclusion

Intelligence is an integral component in criminal investigations involving ongoing, conspiratorial activities, such as organized crime, fraud, corruption, racketeering, and the trafficking of illicit goods and services. Intelligence-led policing plays an important role in focusing and prioritizing these types of investigations. As has been demonstrated, intelligence involves sensitive, personally identifying information, and if misused, can have serious repercussions on the subjects of investigation as well as the agencies conducting the investigation. For these reasons, it is important to understand privacy issues as they pertain to the collection, storage, use, and dissemination of intelligence and their application in intelligence-led policing.

Section II. Applications

Chapter 5: Strategically Combating Organized Crime: An Intelligence-Led Policing Approach

By Andrew Wright and Lt. (N) Lee Heard

Introduction

Organized crime is inevitable. The number of people who rely on illicit goods and services may vary from community to community, or culture to culture, but their presence in society is unavoidable. There will always be those who supply, support, and/or operate illicit enterprises, making organized crime a constant aspect of any community, but it must be mitigated and targeted so it is not allowed to grow, gain power, or rule through violence.

Organized crime elements remain poised to circumvent society's rules and gain profit wherever possible. The state's laws, and by extension its authority, although necessary for legitimacy, is subsequently threatened by its own legality. When a state must abide by law, while fighting those who do not respect or accept those same laws, the state becomes mired in its own fight. The state must then find other methods and techniques that adhere to the law yet still allow for the upper hand.

Organized crime "complicates law enforcement attempts to develop proactive strategies to detect, disrupt, prevent, and investigate" (Coyne & Bell, 2015, p.13. Despite the many challenges, leveraging data can be a necessary law enforcement response. Law enforcement may use a variety of analytical methods to strategically target high-value aspects of criminal organizations in order to disrupt or deny them. The use of intelligence leads to the development of stragies that best target organizations' major weaknesses, which disrupts them. Enhanced strategies through data analysis build a better understanding of the threat, since simply *reacting* to detected street-level activity is not sufficient when fighting organized crime. Strategic targeting needs to mitigate the widespread socio-economic consequences that arise from organized crime activities, curbing groups so criminal elements do not become more powerful or entrenched. But what are these analytical methods?

There are three significant analytical tools that can be leveraged in this fight against organized crime. This chapter focuses on Social Network Analysis (SNA), Communications Analysis and Center of Gravity Analysis (COG). SNA is one solution that may be leveraged against organized crime, as will be explained in the following pages. Communications Analysis has been the backbone of organized crime analysis for a half-century. Additionally, COG may be used alone or in conjunction with SNA to fight organized crime by focusing on critical elements for an organizations' survival. SNA, Communications Analysis and COG can be used to identify the most vulnerable aspect of a criminal organization so that law enforcement can target them to fundamentally disrupt its activities and keep communities safe.

Targeting Organized Crime

The very nature of organized crime is dynamic and pervasive, which makes enforcement challenging. As a result, targeting organized crime requires a clear understanding of what constitutes a threat. By definition, *organized crime* is crime that is linked together in some way over space and time for profit. Offenders work in concert, sometimes unbeknownst to active members, committing crimes that endure over time to generate profit. As such, bonds and relationships are formed over time and various power centres can be spread across larger social, criminal, communication, and/or financial networks. Associations and power centres form through co-offending, sometimes regardless of any defined group identity or gang affiliation.

Organized crime has historically been described as any aspect of society reliant on "violence, a code of secrecy among the conspirators, access to black markets to sell [any] stolen wares, and connections to the political elite to protect and even sanction their predatory activities" (Schneider, 2009, p.8). The United Nations Office of Drugs and Crime (UNODC) defines organized crime as something structured, meaning at least three or more persons linked in some way, as per the United Nations Convention Against Transnational Organized Crime[34] (Calvani, 2010). Furthermore, according to Abadinsky (2010), organized crime can be hierarchical atop having exclusive membership. Some law enforcement is now starting to define organized crime as networks of co-offenders. In total, organized crime is therefore a series of linked and structured sub-cultures, dependent on close bonds among members, with varying degrees of networked interaction.

Structured sub-cultures can form various patterns of association. The UNODC identifies several typologies of organized crime around the world. *Standard hierarchies* are groups with clear leadership and defined structure; *regional hierarchies* exist where leadership is largely decentralized but shares power amongst leaders of local groups or cells within a larger criminal entity; *clustered hierarchies* are defined by having structure within a number of criminal groups, gangs, or organizations that are independently operated but have a central overseeing body; a *core group* is a criminal network with a core central authority, surrounded by loose cells or other sub-networks. Finally, there is simply the *criminal network*, which is defined by the activities of the individual, working in concert with others, but with routinely shifting alliances or allegiances (UNODC, 2002). Regardless of the structure, all consist of various actors, all linked together in some way, with some individuals or clusters of individuals holding more power than others.

In order to further understand the threat posed by organized crime, law enforcement must understand how to detect and fight these various structures. As stated by Abadinsky, "in order to understand how the varied and large-scale tasks of criminal organizations can be accomplished, we need to examine the structures that contemporary organized crime manifest (2010, p. 2)." Identifying the hierarchy and understanding the structure of organized crime allows law enforcement to target the network, rather than the individual crimes being committed in a given jurisdiction. Understanding the UNODC typologies aids law enforcement in this effort (Le, 2012).

---

[34] *Article 2 ... For the purposes of this Convention: (a) "Organized criminal group" shall mean a structured group of three or more persons, existing for a period of time and acting in concert with the aim of committing one or more serious crimes or offences established in accordance with this Convention, in order to obtain, directly or indirectly, a financial or other material benefit.*

Despite the growing understanding of the true nature of organized crime, law enforcement continues to attempt to categorize and frame stand-alone groups rather than identify the interplay between various power brokers or individuals, all within larger networks (CISC, 2007). By delineating groups in this manner, law enforcement is able to adhere to the commonly accepted RICO statute[35] or Canadian criminal code definitions[36], but fail to address the real issues. By sticking to a strict legal definition, law enforcement is unable to identify true network dynamics or key facilitators. The traditional legal approach has major drawbacks since statute definitions do not always reflect the reality of the criminal phenomena, or capture ongoing and constant changes. By looking at the interplay among the co-offending networks however, law enforcement may be able to build better strategies for combating the issue in a more holistic way (Hashimi, Bouchard, Morselli, & Ouellet, 2016).

For law enforcement, building better strategies is the ultimate goal, but one not easily achieved. Law enforcement is often limited in its ability to carry out routine strategic targeting, and often opts for a more tangible tactical response. Disruption of a criminal network's operations should become the objective, not simply going after every detected street-level crime. When the latter occurs, this may only result in the promotion of low- or mid-level players, not true disruption. If operations are not conducted strategically, law enforcement actions may in fact fuel organized crime elements: eliminating competition, increasing illicit market value by restricting supply, or facilitating new criminal partnerships through incarceration. Tackling overt street-level activities may not disrupt or even have an effect on the larger networks responsible for production, source, smuggling, and/or supply of some illicit commodity. Therefore, by not considering larger criminal networks at play, in favor of more routine street-level crime enforcement, police agencies may actually have positive effects (in favour of the criminal element) on the overall organized crime picture, and may even have adverse or unintended effects on public safety.

Studies have shown that rarely the entire known or named criminal gang or organization is the true entity committing crimes. Instead, it is often co-conspirators from an array of named groups, sometimes acting with those not affiliated with any gang or known named group, committing crimes. Co-offending networks can operate independent of any defined groups (Bouchard & Konarski, 2014). What's more, the "identification of the 'core' members of a gang may, or may not, be an exercise worth undertaking" (Bouchard & Konarski, 2014, p. 90).

Law enforcement needs to know what the bigger picture looks like, and interdict appropriately and pre-emptively, with the resources available. Strategic work needs to be done so law enforcement can contextualize, forecast probable outcomes, and be ahead of any foreseeable consequences at any moment. Only when law enforcement understands the total makeup of an organization can they be effective in disrupting a group or dismantling it. Analytical tools thus become necessary in order to go beyond what

---

[35] *RICO law refers to the prosecution and defense of individuals who engage in organized crime. In 1970, the U.S. Congress passed the Racketeer Influenced and Corrupt Organizations (RICO) Act in an effort to combat Mafia groups.*
[36] *467.1 (1) The following definitions apply in this Act. criminal organization means a group, however organized, that (a) is composed of three or more persons in or outside Canada; and (b) has as one of its main purposes or main activities the facilitation or commission of one or more serious offences that, if committed, would likely result in the direct or indirect receipt of a material benefit, including a financial benefit, by the group or by any of the persons who constitute the group. It does not include a group of persons that forms randomly for the immediate commission of a single offence.*

has been identified. Law enforcement can then start targeting the critical, yet less-obvious, components of a criminal network through the use of SNA, Communications Analysis, or COG, and target those elements that have remained in the shadows.

Strategic Criminal Intelligence and SNA

Criminal intelligence is all about using analysis and about going beyond what is detected, leveraging all the information known at a given moment, and estimating what is probable. It goes beyond the facts in order to pre-empt a threat or issue by informing decision-makers. Intelligence-led policing (ILP) is a process that uses incomplete police data, employs inferences, all to inform and ultimately level the playing field between any law enforcement agency and any given criminal organization. "Network analysis has proven to be a useful tool for extracting intelligence information…it allows for the detection of key players or clusters of persons significant to a criminal organization or conspiracy" (Hashimi & Bouchard, 2016, p. 3).

SNA is an analytical technique that can be used in ILP to make sense of real-world organized crime activity and various multifaceted societal issues that underpin it. SNA is a process of examining dynamic social structures and characterizing them in terms of entities or nodes (individual actors, people, or things within a given network) and the ties or edges that bind them (any relationships or interactions between two or more entities or nodes). It was in 1973 that research showed the significance and analytical capability inherent in network analysis. Research showed that the ties that bind us together, whether weak or strong, hold statistically relevant meaning (Granovetter, 1973) and it was estimated by Sparrow (1991) that it could be used to identify various vulnerabilities in different types of criminal organizations using centrality scores (the measure of importance of a given person or node in the context of a larger criminal network).

SNA may be used then to counter organized criminal enterprise as it addresses the various structures and organizations present in a given network. SNA can be used to quantify and then assess the different structures often present within an array of network-types (structures), and makes sense of the various relationships and entities that exist within. When using SNA, the analyst has the ability to draw out greater meaning from detected and seemingly random relationships (previously or historically detected), regardless of and sometimes in spite of any previously assumed structure. Analysts are then able to draw inferences and make strong recommendations, as to how to move forward to combat any criminal element strategically.

Despite the different typologies of organized crime (UNODC, 2002), with their defined titles, roles, and responsibilities, the identification of true power brokers still proves difficult. Defined roles may not reflect actual importance or power. Plus, many organized crime groups or cells operate anonymously to avoid detection and may not show obvious signs of membership, as they often belong to larger criminal networks and link across geography and morph over time. What's more, in any given hierarchical group, those with higher positions may not be those that pose the greatest threat; taking the head-off-the-snake, so to speak, may not have a true effect on a given organization's functioning or capability (their overall threat), and it may still continue to operate. One study shows that taking out a leader may weaken a criminal organization temporarily, but will cause fragmentation, which fosters new groups; new groups form to address market demands; and this process promotes violence in the longer-term (Philips, 2015).

An analysis of various police data shows that overall, SNA is a viable analytical tool when looking at criminal networks and criminal behavior; "SNA is a promising tool in law enforcement and intelligence investigations" (Hurst, 2009, p. 118). SNA helps law enforcement identify and choose the best and most-valuable targets. It arms them with a stronger and unbiased understanding of the total organized crime issues in a given jurisdiction. SNA can be used to strategically combat organized crime at any moment, and may be one of the only tools that give law enforcement the upper hand against those who are skilled at remaining undetected and always one step ahead. In fact, SNA makes any assessment strategic first, and then allows law enforcement to measure, assess, investigate, and ultimately disrupt those organized crime elements that pose the greatest threat.

SNA becomes a vital aspect of the ILP process as a whole and so requires considerations at every stage of the intelligence cycle: planning/direction, collection, collation, analysis, and reporting. SNA first must be planned for; it lays at the intersection of collation and analysis; and a strong SNA may only occur after data has been collected and properly collated or organized; it can then be used at multiple stages of analysis, from beginning to end. SNA is a tool that needs to be interpreted, and the results are then available as a starting point for subsequent intelligence planning, further collection, and more refined analysis.

In order to conduct an intelligence analysis using SNA, an analyst must gain access to the necessary volume of data that reveals relationships amongst offenders. Initial collection is done through routine police work; front-line police, detectives, and other police staff are in the business of recording associations between criminals on an ongoing basis. Random police information culminates in analysts being able to map out large and complex criminal networks, even those that have attempted to remain undetected. Using SNA, analysts can understand and unlock more meaning from this inter-related data than ever before.

Collating association data is important, so that specific pieces of information can be utilized at a given moment. Collation should account for all necessary elements of a criminal network such as people, relationships, structure, criminality, and geography: there will always be people, and people interact in only a finite number of ways, organizational structure or lack thereof, when serious crime is being committed, all in a given jurisdiction. This list is not inclusive however; it relies on the planning phase of ILP to define what association types will be needed to be collected and then collated, sometimes case-by-case. Often times, police records systems account for these necessary elements, but it is perhaps necessary to build-in other relationship-types in a more refined data system, to store more refined and pertinent data.

Once the information is assembled and organized, analysis can begin. SNA is the natural extension of association analysis, a routine criminal-intelligence analysis tool used to uncover criminal conspiracy involving numerous players all linked together. After an association analysis is applied, analysts have to start looking beyond what the individual links are, view them as a whole, and in a larger context, to unlock even more understanding. "Each organized crime group is a network in itself, and operated in a wider network" (Strang, 2014, p. 6). SNA builds upon association analysis and is the one advanced analytical technique that can be used to effectively understand a range of relationships all at once. "Network analysis can help identify which approaches will be most effective and efficient when the analysis incorporates descriptions, and assessments of network functioning as well as of the network structure" (Strang, 2014, p. 22).

While conducting SNA, it is critical that the correct logic is applied. Conclusions derived from SNA results must be taken further via *inference*, not deduction. Interpretations of SNA will be based on a series of inferences based on existing relationships and will enable an analyst to arrive at some theory about what is going on beyond those relationships detected. Once analytical conclusions are drawn, further analysis and proper intelligence reporting must take place to inform decision-makers, who will then plan subsequent collection activities, ultimately driving the intelligence cycle forward. All inferences and conclusions must be tested through further intelligence collection.

While the results of SNA appear absolute and definitive, scientific almost, SNA results in the ILP realm should serve only as an intelligence-lead, because they are built upon inference and not corroborated fact. SNA helps the analyst conclude who may be the most critical targets, but it is only the start. Subsequently, qualitative analysis must continue to make sense of any given result, adding context and substance where required. SNA therefore is not evidentiary.

Ultimately, once data is collected and properly collated, analysts can identify those who have high *centrality* scores, correlate past and present associations of targets, and may reveal who could be at the center of a given conspiracy. These new targets may be those who have not been the subject of past investigations, and may not have been obvious to police prior to analysis. In fact, these targets' roles or significance may not even be obvious amongst the co-offenders actually operating in the criminal network itself. As a result, the detection of these targets may only result from association analysis and SNA, not via any other means, not even confidential source information or wiretaps.

SNA Theory

The purpose of SNA is to measure the extent of relationships between people, organizations, or other entities, in order to understand how a network functions or operates. Not only does SNA provide a visual depiction, but also an analytical and measured one. Centrality measurements can suggest who may be the best or most likely probe/intelligence target; it can be used to identify source opportunity; or it may be used to find new investigative leads. Applied SNA methodology leverages theoretic graph and network concepts to understand criminal associations by deriving meaning from discrete mathematics and statistics. It is based upon concepts such as graph theory, used to analyze structures through scientific methods, and network theory, used to empirically demonstrate associations (Hanneman & Riddle, 2005). The mathematical base of this theory has been found to have practical applications in ILP and strategic criminal intelligence (Sparrow, 1991). Overall, SNA is a sociological method that can directly measure major elements of organized crime as they play out in the real world, leveraging detected relationships, but its application in ILP is more complex.

The main concepts to consider for the application of SNA are: *entities or nodes, links or edges,* the various *centrality results* (terminologies such as degree, closeness, betweenness, and eigenvector), the *k-core,* and of course the overall nature/dynamic of the network, via *cohesion* or *density* calculations. These terminologies are reflective of SNA's statistical origin, but they can be easily understood in real terms, and are necessary for the application of the theory to criminal intelligence analysis. SNA terminologies define any given network's dynamic parts, which describe the various significant persons, links, and/or relationships relating to any entities and/or nodes.

A strong understanding of the concepts of SNA is imperative. *Entities or nodes* can be people or some other real thing or object. In the applied analysis to organized crime, they may be various physical things representative of elements of a crime: a place, criminal organization, business, weapon, bank account, and/or vehicle. *Links or edges* are how the entities or nodes relate with one another; they are the associations that define the network. Centrality scores are the importance of an entity or node, given their relationship to other entities or nodes.

For SNA to work, each network being assessed must be homogenous, with only one distinct entity type per network. Although there is the ability to assess what is called 'two-mode' data, the relationship of some entity to some other type of entity, for practical applications in SNA, networks should only be comprised of one entity type and the various relationships that can bind only those entities. For example, if assessing a network of persons and how they relate, the entity type can be comprised of only people, not related vehicles or phones. Another example may be assessing a network of bank accounts; the entity-type can only be the bank account, not the account holder or banking institution.

The first centrality result is *degree*, which is a measure of the total number of links any individual entity has (Hanneman & Riddle, 2005). This measure is often conducted at the most basic level in association analysis. A given entity's score (total links) is compared with all other entities within the network. Having multiple links can suggest different status in the network, depending on the shape, size, and structure of a given network, but generally the more links any one entity has, the higher the degree. A high degree can translate to expression of power. Those persons with more associations, for instance, may have more opportunities to make social connections and to facilitate or generate (criminal) opportunities.

Another aspect of the degree score is the concept of *network capital*. A detailed analysis can take into account the relative strength and importance of a given actor in the network, in relation to the types of links that bind various parts together or given attributes of the entity itself (Schwartz & Rouselle, 2009). Some links between persons may not be equal; therefore a weighted factor may be applied to individual links. This may result in a factor being applied to a link, since some roles carry more weight in network capital. For instance, co-offending versus family links may have different relevancy in different analyses. Also, given some factor attribute to an entity in the network, perhaps an armed, dangerous, or violence flag or alter for a given offender, could be applied also.

Next, *closeness* is another centrality measure. It is similar to high degree but it measures the number of connections relative to the *position* that given entity has in relation to others (Hanneman & Riddle, 2005). How close one entity is to another, forms their ability to interact directly with other actors in a network. This may translate into even greater power status; being at the center of a network may be more significant than being on the fringe, dependent on the criminal typology. Closeness will depend on the shape, size, and structure of the network, and becomes more significant as linear relationships are formed across larger networks. Yet, as was stated, any result must be interpreted. Closeness for instance could result in not identifying a leader, who may appear on the peripheral of a network given limited connections to associates for security reasons. Also, closeness could simply identify a number of mid-level actors, who may be redundant in the network structure, thus not making viable targets for strategic enforcement.

The next centrality result is *betweenness*, which quantifies the total number of times an entity acts as a bridge along the shortest path between any two clusters (Hanneman & Riddle, 2005). If two people in a network are not directly linked but need to interact, they would need to engage the person with a high degree of betweenness. These are the entities that are most likely to know something about the overall workings of the network, and may also be known as 'gatekeepers'. Their relative position as a bridge makes them key facilitators in some way for information or actions that need to flow or be transferred from one entity to another. This centrality result can often mean a strong source development opportunity, but could be frustrated if this person is also involved in criminality directly, so again, the results must be properly interpreted.

The first two centrality results identify entities that may hold the most power, the third identifies an entity with the most working knowledge, but the fourth, the *eigenvector* score, is the entity with potentially the most *influence* (Hanneman & Riddle, 2005; Sparrow 1991). Influence may be defined as having the most access to power brokers, but not holding power itself. An eigenvector score is subsequently a measure of the total number of times an entity links to other entities that scored high with regard to the above noted centrality results.

Although the eigenvector value is absolute, the real-world translation requires extensive analysis. Influence often gets misinterpreted as power itself; this is where the intelligence analysis process must translate the result. This influence score can reveal an entity at either the lowest- or highest-level of authority in a network. In relation to a drug trafficking network for instance, 'influence' may be found in street-level users who associate with numerous dealers or high-level traffickers who manage those same number of dealers (Personal Communication, 2016). The street-level user however should not be dismissed if given this score. The eigenvector result still reveals meaning around a given entity's access to power. A focus on the street-user may reveal activities of other dealers who were not previously known or detected.

One more result of SNA is the *K-core*. A K-core is a value assigned to clusters of entities, based on total mutual links therein (Hanneman & Riddle, 2005). This is the number of unique links binding several entities together, not necessarily multiple links between the same two entities. The more interconnected entities are, the more cohesive a cluster is assumed to be. K-core identifies the most interrelated clusters of a network, the various 'cores', but does not measure how cohesive the entire network is overall.

Cohesion, in the intelligence analysis of organized crime is also an important metric; it can reveal the strength or resilience of a criminal organization. Cohesion may be an interpretation of the density of the network; the denser the network is, the harder it may be to disrupt. In SNA, cohesion goes beyond just the cohesion of a k-core, and an entire network's cohesion is also measurable. In the most basic form, a network's density is simply the proportion of all possible ties that are actually present (Hanneman & Riddle, 2005). And cohesion is an important aspect of assessing organized crime overall because it can reveal the strength of a group, its susceptibility for infiltration, or its overall threat (CISC, 2007). One study found that "variations in gang cohesion are related to the conditions under which the gang is founded or developed, the characteristics of the members, their collective choices, and the level of loyalty expected" (Dunbar, 2012, p. 1).

What makes these measures so powerful is the predictability of human behaviour; we are bound by our routines. Even when people operating within clandestine or 'shadowy' environments attempt to break routine and act unpredictably, the single act of breaking the routine is a pattern unto itself. When any individual is not operating per their normal routine, the absence of a pattern appears when properly assessed, using appropriate results can reveal these behaviours. Relationships detected over time provide insight into how a network operates presently, even if or after a given actor has become more sophisticated and is now able to go undetected.

Historical links may reveal a current network, despite individuals being cautious in order to avoid detection. Yesterday's delinquents are today's mid-level players, so detected relationships over time have significant analytical value. Historical centrality results can offer some knowledge about the present. Offenders learn over time how to be cautious, yet there are likely historical records that show noteworthy associations early on in their career. It is not uncommon for investigations to be mired in the present, but the past detection of a relationship can be assumed to be valid until it is proven otherwise.

The reason for assuming a relationship has endured, versus dissolved, is a matter of practicality. Arguably, those who share major co-offending experiences also share an emotional bond, as compared to average interactions. Those engaged in shared criminal occurrences are therefore more likely to continue to associate, given their shared involvement in a criminal sub-culture. Also for more routine police checks, social links are indicative of an entrenched friendship. Police observations may record an encounter between two criminals who are meeting for the first time, which carries potential significance since that encounter could have been arranged to facilitate future criminal enterprise. In the same way, just as two CEOs may meet for a formal dinner to facilitate subsequent business.

Another element of relationships between entities, either historical or present, is the *direction* of the link. Direction can represent authority or information flow. Within the context of using SNA within the ILP process, direction is largely ignored as it is not known at the outset. In fact, direction among clandestine relationships is precisely the element an analyst is attempting to understand when he/she uses SNA. Therefore, it is assumed that a relationship has mutual direction and that all actors are of equal importance until proven otherwise.

Assessing links between entities requires critical thought and hypothesis-testing. Where some relationships can be assumed based on other factors, the *null-hypothesis* is equally valid in SNA, where the absence of information or links among a network is observed. The absence of any observable or detectable associations may be interpreted as network sophistication. Despite considering unique circumstances, it is generally accepted that any individual suspected to be involved in criminality, but is absent from the network, is trying to avoid detection.

One weakness of SNA is incomplete data, due to the clandestine nature of organized crime networks. The alternative method is a qualitative analysis of the data, but this can be subjective to the analyst's experience and bias. Interestingly though, SNA will reveal preliminary outcomes regardless of incomplete data sets. These preliminary leads are substantial enough to drive the intelligence cycle through various iterations until viable targets are revealed. Any incomplete set of links, or any incomplete understanding of a total network, will reveal gaps, suggesting new avenues to investigate. SNA also has the power to assess murky data. It inherently provides immediate opportunity for data refinement or collection. Employing SNA within ILP allows law enforcement to build strategies for disruption or dismantling. It is the perfect ILP tool.

The true power of SNA is that it reveals aspects of a network that go beyond the knowledge held by those operating within it by using centrality or other measures to show who or what is truly at play. It reveals insights into networks that may not be known to anyone previously. Often, it may be a tactic of organized crime players to keep elements of their operations secret from each constituent part of the organization/network. Yet, when known aspects of clandestine networks are mapped out, based on various pieces of intelligence (both historical and contemporary), new observations and various assumptions can be tested against a social or criminal network map, and a successive SNA can reveal the extent or scope of an operation within a given organization in spite of deception methods.

SNA Applications

The practical application of SNA is derived from the perspective it provides on organized crime as a phenomenon of a whole, and allows an analyst to go beyond any of its constituent parts. This is important as "criminal networks transcend the current notions that organized crime should be solely viewed from either an organization, patron-client or enterprise lens…human relationships form the least common denominator of organized crime" (Mcillwain, 1999, p. 319). Once one starts using SNA, it becomes the only lenses one can see organized crime through (Bouchard & Amirault, 2013). Yet, applying this theory is less straightforward.

The following is an example of a deployment of SNA, both in terms of the tactical-level (to start) or a strategic-level (the intent). At a tactical-level, an analysis of any given organized crime element may begin with the detection of some activity, apart from any strategic understanding of any overarching network at play. Information in these cases may come from a variety of sources, such as: confidential informant debrief, surveillance deployed for some other reason, or extraneous information gleaned from some preliminary investigation. Once something has been detected, preliminary research should occur to learn any associations related to those targets detected.

Police data and/or open source information will likely be available to map out a network that surrounds any new target, placing them in at least a smaller group or cell. Although major aspects of a new or emerging network at some early stage may be historic, based on unrelated police records, some existing data will likely be able to inform a baseline network. A rough network will therefore be available at any given time, if the targets have been living or operating in a given jurisdiction for some given time. A base-line network may then be used as a triage tool to decide which actors of the smaller group or cell would be more viable as a potential additional target for interviews, surveillance, or further investigative efforts (based on centrality results). If no network or association data is available, this at the very least has identified an intelligence gap, or may indicate a level of sophistication, and/or suggest that perhaps they may have operated previously in another jurisdiction (suggesting an analyst should look elsewhere for additional information).

So in total, to begin using SNA, the tactical-level steps subsequently are: 1) learn of a target; 2) data mine known sources of data for any and all associated entities to target(s), 3) collate this data based on entity descriptions and their subsequent relationship types (potentially co-offenders if listed in a criminal case file, or socially if listed in a routine information-type file), 4) then map out these known entities and relationships, 5) then apply SNA centrality calculations (using some available software)[37], 6) interpret the results, make assumptions/inferences, draw conclusions, and develop recommendations, and 7) inform management and units responsible for additional intelligence collection.

Once further information is collected on an initially detected cell, or if substantial information was available from the first search, a full strategic SNA can then take place. For the strategic-level (the objective), a substantial data-set is necessary. This could have been available from previously collected information or will come over time. A strategic collection effort should be ongoing, based on some key criteria (or intelligence priority), so that certain aspects, or knowable aspects, of any given network can be drawn on to make a strategic determination about a target's importance or significance in a larger network, at any moment. Often, this information is collected and collated as part of routine police action (as was noted) and will be captured in the more common police records management systems or RMS. The issue with relying on routine police records however is the volume of data, and the potential for significant noise (non-pertinent information), which can cloud or skew the final results. A dedicated intelligence database will ensure quality and relevancy of the data. Prior planned and directed collection can thus make any result strategic at the same instance a tactical answer is available. So if data is collected routinely, then targets may be identified beyond the tactical-level.

The strategic-level steps subsequently are: 1) plan the data collection criteria (for drug trafficking for example, likely develop collection priorities around certain drug types or *modus operandi*), 2a) detect some target through tactical-level processes, or 2b) routinely collect and collate data and then routinely run an SNA analysis in order to determine new avenues for data collection outside the scope of any passive detected activities or investigation, and 3) inform management and units responsible for additional intelligence collection.

So how might this look in real terms? A target becomes known to an intelligence unit through some means. Notionally, a Crime Stopper's tip could suggests that some individual or target, an Aaron ACTON (AA), is selling drugs in some area of the city. As outlined in the crime stoppers tip, AA has one associate named Brent BUTTON (BB). From here, these individuals are run in the local RMS and these checks reveal further historic information on both entities. AA is previously listed in two records or occurrences from some years past. In a case file, AA is found to be an associate of a Greg GHOST (GG); they were previously co-accused in some drug possession file. Also found in a street check, AA is an associate of a Fred FROST (FF). Further searches reveal that BB only has one past occurrence and he is listed in another Street Check along with an associate Chris CURTON (CC); the two were seen together outside some bar downtown. So far this network consists of five persons, linked via 4 edges and looks like the following network:

---

[37] *There are a number of ways of calculating centrality results or analyzing a total network. There is UCINET, a software designed by Steve Borgotti (University of Kentucky); there is IBM's I2 Analyst Notebook software which includes basic SNA capability; then there can be simply Excel, which can be used if the formulas or calculations are known and understood by the analysts.* See Apendix 2 for varied analytic software.

Figure 5.1

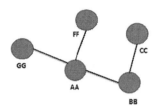

Initially, without an SNA, AA may have become the most obvious target, based on his detected involvement in criminality (drug trafficking via the Crime Stopper's tip) and him being visually the most apparent center of the network. What is the consequence of being so narrowly focused on AA as a target? Without any larger network context or understanding where this cell fits in a larger drug supply picture or criminal landscape, this targeting may be misguided. What happens when the next person is more violent, or what happens when that original target is incarcerated and becomes more sophisticated, and is then releases back on the street? Has this initial targeting actually led to an increase in other crime-types, or has it fueled the fire of organized crime as discussed previously? Might BB have been a better target? More analysis is required.

An analyst's search continues for any additional associates, and another Street Check is found that now associates CC with FF, and CC is also listed in a past Case File along with two additional associates, Darren DEEDS (DD) and Eric EATON (EE). FF is also listed in one additional Street Check and is found to associate with a Harry HUGHES (HH). These searches find that many more associates, now associates of associates, form a larger network. Another case file reveals that GG is an associate of two others, Jack JUKES (JJ) and Igor IVANOV (II). The network is for now complete, with one last record found, one more Street Check, which associates HH to II. There are no more returns on any of the associates identified when searched in all available data sources. The intermediate result is a more substantial network composed of now 10 entities and 13 links resulting from one Crime Stopper's tip, five street checks, and three case files (see addendum 1 for full data set). Shown another way, these links form the following network, the *A to J cell*. Given associates have common links to various other entities within this network, where HH is found to be a common associate of II and FF, the inference that this is a cohesive network is strengthened. Who now is the next most viable intelligence target?

Figure 5.2

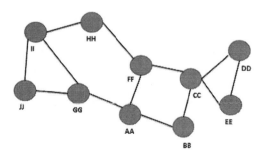

If an SNA is now done on what is known, using some calculation tool, centrality results answer this question. In this simple network so far, the entity with the highest degree of centrality is CC (not AA), as he is found to have four known links, represented by street checks and case files; CC is found to be a more prolific offender. The number of links CC has may suggest some sort of power in this network, and may reveal him as a more high-value target, for yet unknown reasons. CC also has the highest score in both the betweenness and the eigenvector centrality results, further suggesting his significance. In addition, the entity with the highest closeness centrality score is FF; as he has three known links, and is more central. In this smaller network then, CC and FF may be recommended intelligence targets. Both CC and FF may have no criminality detected as of late, but given their significance in the network combined with AA's current drug trafficking activities, it may be inferred CC and FF are still active and are more significant power brokers.

Based on this analysis, any enforcement unit may now have some greater deployment/ collection/ investigative options, which go above the original source information, and which triage ten possible targets down to two, yet provide more options beyond the originally detected criminality. The crime stoppers tip revealed something immediate, the selling of some drug commodity by some person named AA. An immediate strategic question was if enforcement action is taken upon AA, will the network that supplies AA just replace him?+ This links back to the initial strategic considerations; by extension, another question becomes will there be violence related to any competition for this turf if AA is arrested or removed? The analysis suggests that CC or FF may be higher-value targets, given a new understanding of the total network. There may be a change for source development, or surveillance task opportunity, either of which may reveal more aspects of the network, before enforcement launches a drug investigation into AA. Ultimately, more understanding of the network and a choice of a different target could disallow a replacement of AA, as well it could cut off his drug supply. Targeting another beyond AA might now have an effect on the organized crime enterprise operating, fracturing and disrupting the total network at play.

In this notional scenario thus far, some new and significant targets have been revealed. If collection action was dispatched as a result, either a directed patrol or perhaps some surveillance effort, what is then learned? If a surveillance team locates and tracks CC for an amount of time, based on the previous findings, he is observed with a Paul PARKER (PP) and a Kevin KONSKY (KK). These new links and associations would not have otherwise been detected without an SNA being done, and may not have been revealed during a targeted investigation on AA only.

Although this analysis was noted to be tactical initially, it is now becoming strategic, and the process continues, data collection and collation continues, and more compressive enforcement strategies may unfold. Our network now looks like the following, and we now have an A-K+P crew.

There are now two more associates to run checks on, and these checks reveal subsequent network connectivity beyond KK and PP, linking the known network to an even larger network. Collection tasks plus more searches reveal now two networks that were not previously known to be linked. These links only were found because of the SNA and subsequent analysis and recommendations.

Figure 5.3

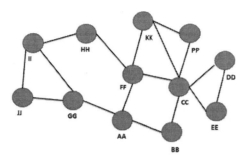

The entity KK was consequently found to be listed in two other Street Checks, linking him to an Oscar OLDS (OO) and a Mike MASTERS (MM) respectively. OO was listed in a Street Check with PP and a Tyler TURKOT (TT). PP was further listed in another Street Check with a Steven SAUNDERS (SS), and a Case File along with Ugo UBON (UU) and a Victor VISEK (VV). We have now linked up two cells (that of AA and PP), based on some information gleaned from a recommendation made based on SNA. We now have an ever growing network that now looks like the following network.

Figure 5.4

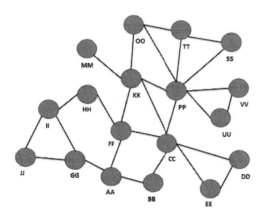

Again, searches continue and uncover more of the network. Additional searches reveal links between MM and TT, who are listed as co-accused in a Case File along with Noel NEVIT (NN); MM and NN are also listed along with Len LOWES (LL) in yet another Street Check. New SNA calculations are run and find that now PP comes out with the same degree score as CC. Surveillance then continues to monitor PP, who is later seen with a Quincy QUIAD (QQ). The surveillance report states that after the two met (PP and QQ) QQ went on to have a meeting with NN, SS, and a Robert REESE (RR).

Meanwhile, a previously unrelated source is reporting on a Xavier XANDUS (XX) and a William WIDER (WW), who are reported to be down-lines to VV. XX is further noted to be in a Street Check with a Yaffa YAKOV (YY) and WW was reported in another Crime Stopper's tip to be an associate of Zander ZULOS (ZZ), both suspected to be criminally active; they were noted also to be selling drugs. The collection, collation, and analysis are starting to reveal a larger criminal network, and by extension, a potential criminal drug conspiracy, where an analyst can start to infer, source, supply, and various other roles and responsibilities of the organization. The intelligence cycle has been implemented with SNA as the primary analytical tool and driver which has brought about a better understanding of a criminal organization, which may now inform decision makers.

Figure 5.5

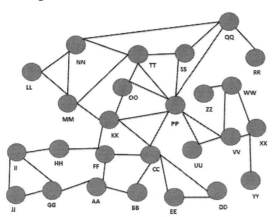

The full extent of the information is now available, and reveals a drug trafficking network composed of 26 distinct entities (+ one source or CI) and 45 distinct links (Tasked Surveillance, Street Checks, Case Files, Crime Stoppers Tips, and Source Reporting) called the Alphabet Crew or A-Z Crew (see addendum B for a full data-set of this new network).

From this data, a strategic analysis may reveal various aspects about the total network, and an analyst may now infer various power relationships and higher-value targets. Based on what is now known, the top two targets with the highest degree of centrality, so the most likely power brokers in this network are PP and NN; the highest closeness score is again PP, but this time followed by KK; the highest betweenness centrality score is PP followed by CC (who has access to the drug trafficking cell around AA via FF and BB); and finally the highest eigenvector score (those with the most influence) are now NN along with PP as number two. The K-core results show, KK, MM, SS, QQ, NN, OO, RR, TT, and PP, as the most cohesive elements in the network, or the core of it.

From this analysis we can infer that NN may hold control over this network, but PP is the highest value target, potentially holding both power and authority in the network. The core of the A-Z crew currently has 3 known drug trafficking cells and the targeting of PP could disrupt the drug supply to these cells. SNA has revealed several possible avenues of enforcement around this network, but further analysis continues. In the context of ILP, we are now able to inform decision-makers of other courses of action beyond AA, but the analysis is not yet complete. Even further collection is required and the intelligence cycle must continue. Other intelligence questions emerge and must be answered before recommendations should be made to an enforcement unit. If this is a potential drug conspiracy, is the supply the most effective target, is the leadership, or is it best to go after the money laundering aspects, which are not revealed through the analysis so far?

An SNA can be applied to multiple network-types, such as person networks (social or co-offending networks), and it can be applied to communications networks, or financial transaction networks. Once an SNA is run on various networks sharing common players within a financial network, and a communications network, or any other type, there will be different power brokers found per network. Now which ones does an intelligence unit target? When is it better to go after those visible and active in the community and on the street (a social network), or when is it better to go after the financial network (money flow), or when is it better to go after those that communicate the most frequently (facilitators)? Figuring out which network to target becomes the next analytical challenge or perhaps targeting select central actors across multiple network-types is critical for true disruption.

Communications Analysis [38]

Communications analysis can be divided into two forms: metadata analysis and content analysis. Under 'metadata analysis,' falls the most commonly used form of analysis in the 1980s: telephone record analysis. Organized crime and narcotics cases both depended upon knowing who was communicating with whom, when, and how. At that time, records were received (via subpoena) from a telephone company. The data included were numbers called, dates and times of calls, length of times of the calls and if the calls were "collect" or "direct." In some instances, the city and state were included; in others, area code information allowed the analyst to determine the city and state that was called. In rare cases, calls were considered 'third party' calls because they connected two numbers that did not include the number that had been subpoenaed (and were billed to a third telephone number).

These calls were originally analyzed by placing the data on 3" X 5" cards, with the subpoenaed number at the top and the data on calls listed below. These were reviewed by an analyst and the "primary numbers" were determined (those called most frequently). "Unusual calls" were also determined by time of day or day of week. Calls were considered "unusual" if they were outside the normal geographic spans by the caller, or were at an unusual time of day (for example, the middle of the night), or were significantly longer than the average calls. The underpinning of the analyses was pattern analysis – frequency, dates, times, days of the week, etc. But the number of records analyzed was usually limited to a few hundred, due to the complexity of the analysis and the limitation of human capability.

An additional step that was needed was the submission of the "primary numbers" or "unusually called numbers" to the telephone company so that the identity of the owners of the numbers called could be determined. But even at that point, only surveillance of a subject might prove that a certain individual was on the phone at the time of a particular call rather than another member of the household.

---

[38] This section was provided by Marilyn B. Peterson.

Nonetheless, even in this form, the analysis could warn of an impending crime and/or indicate the geographic range of the criminal activity. Communications are key in the planning stage of a crime and increased communication could indicate that a crime was imminent. Pre-knowledge of a potential crime could allow for prevention or mitigation.

One example of a helpful telephone record analysis completed was the review of the records of an individual whose calls showed significant activity both prior to and immediately after a major sporting event. This supported other indicators that he was involved in an illegal sports betting operation.

Thus the use of communication analysis in intelligence-led policing is to be expected. If communication is a warning of crime, then that crime might be forestalled or interdicted by those with that knowledge.

Today, phone record metadata are still analyzed, but they've been joined by all the other metadata related to modalities of communication available to people in the 21st century: email, texts, tweets, Instagram, Facebook, and all the other forms of social media. There remains the underlying metadata which reflect communication occurring and thus the ways they can be analyzed continues.

Telephone record analysis is defined as "the compilation, review and analysis of telephone communications that shows patterns of communications among individuals or companies. The underlying methodology of telephone record analysis uses the tools of association analysis, frequency distribution and link charting" (Peterson, 1990, p. 85).

Telephone record analysis was described in an article for the IALEIA newsletter in the mid-1980s. This was followed by a book chapter on the topic in 1990. That chapter gave a step-by-step process for doing telephone record analysis manually, which was the only way available to analyze them at the time (Peterson). By 1990, computer applications and databases were developed that allowed for thousands of records to be analyzed, rather than a few hundred. That has since expanded to hundreds of thousands of records being able to be analyzed. Software has also enhanced our ability to do more complex analysis and charting of communication records.

One of the value added aspects of analyzing phone records in the 1980s was that identifying the most connected numbers in the records reduced the number of subscribers that had to be identified which, in those days, was an additional investigative step that needed to be taken.

The advent of pagers, cell phones and VOIP (Voice Over Internet Protocol) calls has widened the availability of data to investigators and analysts looking to uncover networks. And while the phone bills of 30 years ago only showed long-distance calls, some of the telephone records of today show not only the local calls, but also the calls in as well as out. Cell phone calls of today can also allow geographic tracking through mapping the cell towers used in the communication or the GPS (global positioning system) function of the phone used.

Steps in Telephone Record Analysis
Telephone record analysis is a multi-step process that reviews and analyzes the records to provide the investigation with helpful data. The process is as follows:

1. Obtain the records to be analyzed
2. Define the scope of the calls (beginning and ending dates)
3. Determine the frequency of calls by date and day of the week
4. Determine the frequency of calls to specific numbers
5. Determine the length of time spent on the calls
6. Develop a primary listing of numbers called by frequency in steps 4 and 5
7. Analyze frequently called numbers for patterns (day, time, etc.)
8. Analyze calls by time of day of the call
9. Review all records for geographic distribution
10. Prepare matrices and charts if applicable
11. Ask critical questions of the data
12. Identify information gaps (what additional information do we need to know)
13. Combine all of the above into a comprehensive written report (modified from Peterson, 1990, p.86)

In addition to getting records from telephone companies in earlier decades, law enforcement also used a "trap and trace" device, also called a Dialed Number Recorder (DNR). This was a mechanical device that could be attached to a telephone line and would collect the date and time of the call by recording when the phone was taken "off hook" and when it was put "on hook."

While the above steps were initially developed to apply to telephone company records, they are easily applied to cell phone records and Internet traffic. One important step not noted in 1990 was comparing the calls among multiple subscribers. When looking at networks of conspirators, the numbers contacted by multiple individuals provide insights into others involved in the activity that might not have previously been identified. In some agencies, hundreds of thousands of calls have been reviewed to ascertain the breadth of the criminal network. This can also allow us to view the hierarchy of calling. In a simple link analysis, we look at who is connected to whom. Communications transactions allow us to view this in terms of not only links, but the temporal realm and the direction of the communication. We may reflect who may be giving orders and who may be taking them.

This caused a significant difference in the matrices used from the "typical" triangular matrix used in link analysis. The telephone record matrices were square to allow for the "to" and "from" issues of the communication to be seen. An example of a telephone record matrix is shown in Figure 5.6.

The telephone record matrix shows a total of 31 calls among nine telephone numbers. There were telephone calls from six numbers and calls to an additional three numbers. The dates of the calls were put inside the cells of the matrix; times could also have been added if more space had been available. The numbers in the final cells represent the total number of calls made to or from that particular number to other numbers in the group of potential conspirators.

Figure 5.6 Telephone Record Analysis Matrix

FROM

TO	555-222-1234	555-222-2345	555-222-3456	555-222-4567	555-222-5678	555-222-6789	
555-222-1234	X	1/2, 5/6	2/27, 1/5		3/23		5
555-222-2345	2/1,3/14	X			3/21,4/21		4
555-222-3456			X	2/5,4/1		4/15	3
555-222-4567	3/11,3/18		2/2,3/31	X	4/1,4/2		6
555-222-5678			1/1		X	4/22	2
555-222-6789	4/4			2/22		X	2
555-435-2876		1/3,2/14			4/12		3
555-562-7611			2/7,4/5				2
555-877-3857	1/15,2/15			2/21,3/8			4
TOTALS	7	4	7	5	6	2	31

(Source: Peterson, 2017)

Communications analysis also gives us a gateway to other activity, besides the most simple form of calls among individuals or businesses. People now use their telephones and computers to do banking, connect to varied forms of social media, make appointments, purchase items, book a table for dinner, pay for a parking spot, apply for loans and so on. One of the indicators of an impending terrorist attack, identified after 9/11, was transferring leftover funds back to their source immediately before the attack. If this were done by phone or Internet, this would be key to uncover.

Communication analysis charts vary from the "typical" link chart in several ways. First, the frequency of the communication is indicated using a small circle along the line denoting the communication. Second, arrows are used to show the direction of the communication. An example of a communication chart is shown in Figure 5.7.

In this chart, 11 IP addresses are referenced, with emails going to or from each address. The small circles along the line show the number of emails done. It can be seen that some of the addresses are emailed by three addresses, while others are only contacted by two.

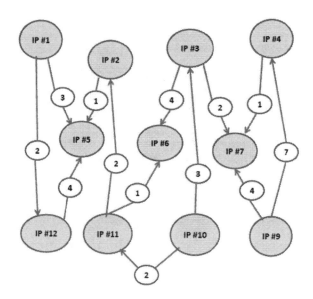

Figure 5.7 Communication Record Chart (Source: Peterson, 2017)

One use of telephone record analysis has been to provide probable cause to be allowed to do a wire intercept. While the telephone record analysis gives the 'metadata' of the call, its actual content can only be received through monitoring the conversations on the phone. There are very specific laws regarding the interception of conversations in this manner and law enforcement must take care to "minimize" its listening to conversations not relevant to criminal activity.

Social media and online games have given criminals additional ways to evade detection of their activity and conversations. While telephone calls may have driven them to use code words and phrases, being able to "meet" virtually inside a site or game on the Internet, using "avatars" or other means enables them to distance themselves from the conversations being held and the plans being made.

Another aspect of communications analysis is content analysis. Content analysis is "a research technique for making replicable and valid inferences from data to their context" (Krippendorff, 1989, p. 403). Content analysis is applied to both written and spoken words. It has been used on media reporting, films, court testimony, political speeches and a variety of other communications. Sometimes simple analysis of communications can show results. For example, when the *Washington Post* and *New York Times* published the manifesto of Theodore Kaczynski, his brother, David, recognized his writing style and notified the FBI, allowing them to capture a 'lone wolf' bomber who had eluded them for 17 years (Simon, 2013).

According to Shuy, this form of analysis, began to be used in the 1980s in Germany and has been used in wider contexts ever since, particularly in criminal and civil litigation (2015, p. 823).

Krippendorff wrote that there are six steps to doing content analysis:
1. Design (defining the context of the analysis),
2. Unitizing (identifying the units of analysis),
3. Sampling (determining the parameters of the data to be analyzed),
4. Coding (interpreting the semantically complex text),
5. Drawing inferences and
6. Validation (looking for corroborating evidence to validate inferences) (1989, pp. 406-7)

Within law enforcement, content analysis has been used on conversations that have been captured through electronic surveillance (wire intercept). In the previous century, much of this was laborious and painstaking as it required the analyst to spend hours transcribing the audio tapes before they could analyze them.

In 1990, Shuy wrote about the process as it related to analyzing the statements of organized criminals. He made an important point when he noted that actual tape recordings were the evidence, not the transcripts that were made from the tapes as the latter were "filtered" by the transcript maker and could be an incorrect interpretation (Shuy, 1990, pp.120-121). At that time, transcripts were being used as "primary" evidence although they did not reflect tone of voice or level of voice. For example, a simple sentence in a transcript might say, "You don't really believe that, do you?" which might be interpreted as a simple question or as a sarcastic remark.

Shuy noted there are some common misperceptions about language, including:

1. Meaning is primarily in individual words.

2. Listening to a tape once will be enough to determine its content.

3. Reading a transcript of a tape is as good as hearing the tape itself. Transcripts are accurate and they convey everything that is on the tape,

4. All people in conversation understand the same things by their words, and

5. People say what they mean and intend" (Shuy, 2004, n.p.).

Content analysis may also be called discourse analysis or forensic linguistics. The term "discourse analysis" has been used when referring to the analysis of statements given in an investigative setting; that is, witness statements or defendant statements. When it is termed "forensic linguistics" it may refer to its analysis of legal testimony and other witness statements.

Transcripts are used in accord with varied laws and regulations. In *Steve M. Solomon, Jr., Inc. v. Edgar*, the court stated: A proper foundation for [the use of a mechanical transcription device] must be laid as follows: (1) It must be shown that the mechanical transcription device was capable of taking testimony, (2) It must be shown that the operator of the device was competent to operate the device, (3) The authenticity and correctness of the recording must be established. (4) It must be shown that changes, additions, or deletions have not been made, (5) The manner of preservation of the record must be shown, (6) Speakers must be identified. and (7) It must be shown that the testimony elicited was freely and voluntarily made, without any kind of duress (88 S.E.2d 167 (Ga. Ct. App. 1955)).

Some contend that if the electronic surveillance recording is in English (or the native language if other than English) and devoid of background distracters, letting a judge and jury listen to the tape is preferable to using a transcript as the latter has been "interpreted" by a person who may, or may not, be accurate (Fishman, 2006).

It should also be noted that listening to a tape or reading a transcript can be misleading if one does not understand the terms being used. According to Lewin & Lewin, in the *Random House Thesaurus of Slang* (1989) there were 223 terms for marijuana at that time. Likewise, terms such as "ice" could refer to diamonds, methamphetamine, to kill someone, or to the U.S. government agency of that name.

In today's environment, there are numerous software programs that assist content analysis. Computerized coding is the automated tabulation of words, phrases, etc. that have been compiled for the analysis. Researchers may create their own dictionaries of key words, etc., or use pre-determined ones. Some of the computerized programs used to assist in content analysis can be seen in Appendix 2, under "Content Analysis".

The potential for using communication analysis as a methodology to assist intelligence-led-policing is significant. Lawfully obtained conversations can provide warning of impending criminal or terroristic acts that could then be prevented. What may be necessary is the further exploration of this form of analysis and its techniques included into the methodologies that are taught to both law enforcement and national security analysts.

Centres of Gravity Analysis

The concept of centres of gravity is not new. It was first introduced by Carl Von Clausewitz in the eighteenth century in his seminal work '*On War*, which states:

> "*Out of these characteristics a certain centre of gravity develops, the hub of all power and movement, on which everything depends. That is the point against which all our energies should be directed*" (Fowler, 2002, p. 1).

The concept of centres of gravity continues to be highly praised by various militaries throughout the globe in their counter-insurgency operations:

> "*The center of gravity concept is useful as an analytical tool while designing campaigns and operations to assist commanders and staffs in analyzing friendly and enemy sources of strength as well as weakness*

and vulnerabilities...In theory, destruction or neutralization of enemy centers of gravity is the most direct path to victory" (Bennett, 2002, p. 6).

While the usefulness, form and history of the theory of the centres of gravity concept and related analysis has been a subject of debate within military intelligence and operations circles since the days of Von Clausewitz, its introduction and use within law enforcement intelligence and operations circles is still in its infancy and has yet to be integrated within the Intelligence-Led Policing model which we will strive to accomplish throughout this chapter.

Definitions
1. Centres of Gravity (COG): primary sources of moral or physical strength, power and resistance.
2. Critical Capabilities (CC): primary abilities which merit a centre of gravity to be identified as such in the context of a given situation.
3. Critical Requirements (CR): essential conditions, resources and means for a critical capability to be fully operative.
4. Critical Vulnerabilities (CV): critical requirements or components thereof which are either deficient or vulnerable to neutralization, interdiction or attack in a manner achieving decisive results (Eikmeier, 2013, p.2).

The main, modern usage of the centres of gravity concept in the military has always been best suited to counter-insurgency and operations against networked opponents. The same can be said of its applicability in law enforcement intelligence where the utility of the theory and related analysis is best suited to target criminal networks with enforcement operations designed to achieve the disruption and/or degradation of organizational and networked structures. Like insurgencies, criminal networks form a complex, shifting mosaic that can contain multiple centres of gravity as they conduct operations at local, regional and national and international levels. This means that in one area a criminal network can be weak and subsequently be conducting small-scale operations and in another area the same criminal network may be strong and conducting larger scale operations. From a strategic perspective, these variations form a mosaic not of small coloured tiles but of areas of varying criminal efforts. This mosaic is made all the more complex when larger or transnational criminal networks are examined as they are often made up of alliances or working relationships between multiple criminal networks. This increased complexity can often be a critical weakness however because it is the alliances between groups that become one of the main centres of gravity for the criminal network, that when targeted, may lead to the disintegration of the network and a disruption in the functioning and operations of multiple organized crime groups (Klug, 2012, p. 2)

As seen in the opening quotes of this section, in the military context centres of gravity apply to both friendly and enemy forces as once the enemy centres of gravity are determined the friendly forces are supposed to concentrate all or the majority of their forces (friendly centres of gravity) to defeat the enemy centres of gravity. While the same is true in law enforcement we will cover basic centres of gravity in a policing context and then concentrate on determining criminal centres of gravity through analysis. Much like military and criminal centres of gravity, police centres of gravity may have many commonalities and may differ from geographic location as well as the size, nature and purpose of the police service being examined. For our purposes then we will use a police centre of gravity identified in a UK study that determined that the centre of gravity for police was that they are the "sole legitimate and statutory basis for protection of life and property, the detection and prosecution of offenders and upholding and enforcing the law"(Chapman, 2014, p. 10). At once it is evident how the criminal centres of gravity negatively impact upon the police centre of gravity as any success that criminal networks profit from withou police detection or successful enforcement operations detracts from the legitimacy of the police service. It suggests that they are incompetent or incapable at the very least at carrying out the core functions within their centre of gravity, namely protection of life and property, the detection and prosecution of offenders and upholding and enforcing the law. Similarly, one can see that if the police service centre of gravity is operating at peak performance and efficiency and is directed at the centres of gravity of criminal networks, the opposite is true, the legitimacy of the police is restored as they successfully protect life and property and detect and prosecute the offenders involved thereby degrading and/or disrupting the operations of the criminal networks involved.

Underlying Theory of Centers of Gravity Analysis

Centres of gravity can be divided into moral and physical types. Moral centres of gravity could include leaders and popular support, while physical centres of gravity could include the members of the criminal network, the economic power the group or network wields in illicit and grey markets and the support of the local criminal populace in any given geographical area (Klug, 2012, p 5). While there is no single structure under which criminal networks operate, there are similar functions or capabilities required. The same functions required for running a business can be applied to the analysis of a criminal network, and while they do not convey a hierarchical structure, it is also possible to have networks in which hierarchical organizations are key participants (Williams, 2001, p. 65). To be successful, a criminal network must conduct some common functions. Conducting centres of gravity analysis using these required capabilities is a useful way to determine appropriate approaches to effectively target criminal networks.

Of these key features there are some that figure more prominently than others when trying to determine a centre of gravity, especially strategic leadership in the form of a charismatic leader that is able to expound a powerful ideology, which may be the centre of gravity of these targets in many cases. The analysis of the necessary roles and functions that must be filled in criminal networks is also essential to determining the critical capabilities, requirements and vulnerabilities of these groups in order to finally determine and analyze their centres of gravity. Criminal networks, much like businesses are constantly looking for growth opportunities, new markets, and ways to realign their structures and strategies to maximize profits (Cole, 2012, p. 50).

Critical capabilities can be defined as the primary abilities that allow the criminal network to continue to operate such as staying alive, informed, influential and able to communicate. Critical requirements are the conditions, resources or means required to make a critical capability fully effective, such as the support of the criminal populace and charismatic leaders as mentioned earlier. Finally, critical vulnerabilities are the vulnerable components of critical capabilities and requirements which one can target in order to exploit centres of gravity (Klug, 2012, p. 5).

Examples of centres of gravity from a law enforcement standpoint include:

- Personnel, such as key facilitators, technical experts etc;
- Logistics, such as key nodes in a distribution system, major transportation assets, etc.;
- Equipment, such as customized vehicles for smuggling operations etc;
- Lines of Communication, such as encrypted phones, servers, etc.; and,
- Finance such as locations where narcotics and firearms are bought and sold and money laundering facilities.

An important point to note is the fact that criminal networks are parasitic, they have little ability to produce the resources needed for their organizations on their own. While exceptions to this rule can be seen in the functioning of methamphetamine labs, marihuana grow ops and other home grown drug production facilities by criminal networks, most of the required products are produced or imported after being manufactured or obtained by allied criminal networks in source countries and passed through middle men or criminal transportation networks or hubs. In order to disrupt their centres of gravity any territorial sanctuaries they enjoy need to be removed whether it is a certain neighborhood or a networked criminal drug subculture in a geographical area, as this removal will deprive them of financial income and support from the local criminal populace and assist in the prevention of regeneration (https://netwar.wordpress.com/2007/08/30/counterinsurgency).

It is for this reason criminal networks will rarely present a physical operational centre of gravity by concentrating their manpower in any one place as they prefer to disperse their personnel to complete drug trafficking, debt collection and other criminal activities to continue the functioning of the criminal network and to avoid unwanted law enforcement attention and possible interdiction (Klug, 2012, p. 6).

Steps to Complete Centres of Gravity Analysis
1. Identify the organization's desired ends.
2. Identify ways or actions that can achieve the desired ends. Select the ways the organization is most likely to use. Those selections are the critical capabilities.
3. List the organization's means or resources available needed to execute the critical capabilities.
4. Select the entity from the list of means that inherently possess the critical capability. This is the centre of gravity.
5. From the remaining means select those that are critical for execution of the critical capability. These are the critical requirements.
6. Identify those critical requirements that are vulnerable to adversary actions. (Elkmeier, 2014).

We will now examine each of these steps in detail while covering any sub steps that may also need to be completed in order to successfully determine the centres of gravity of a given criminal network.

1. Identify the organization's desired ends.

For the purposes of this example we will be examining an imaginary Outlaw Motorcycle Gang (OMG) criminal network called the MOTHRA Motorcycle Club (MC) which is a 1% OMG[39] operating in

---

[39] "1 % motorcycle clubs" are those whose members employ violence and criminal activities as part of their lives, while the other 99% of the motorcycle clubs' members are law-abiding citizens.

Ontario, Canada, with multiple chapters across the Province controlling prostitution and engaging in drug trafficking specializing in methamphetamine and cocaine. The organization's desired ends in this case are to continue to control prostitution and to sell as high of volumes of methamphetamine and cocaine as possible.

2.   Identify ways or actions that can achieve the desired ends. Select the ways the organization is most likely to use. Those selections are the critical capabilities.

In terms of prostitution, there are many things that the MOTHRA MC network will have to do to maintain control. First they will have to continue to recruit victims for prostitution and control and/or secure suitable venues and advertise services. In addition since controlling prostitution in the Province of Ontario is their end goal in this case they would also need to tax or dissuade competing groups to maintain control of the market. With regards to methamphetamine trafficking, the most likely actions would be to set up and operate methamphetamine labs to produce the product and then transport it and sell it to customers while attempting to expand their markets and customer base. In terms of cocaine trafficking, the MOTHRA MC network will need to secure their supply in a source country, facilitate importation and transportation and subsequent sales to customers and the expansion of their markets and customer base.

3.   List the organization's means or resources available needed to execute the critical capabilities.
For this step if you are dealing with multiple critical capabilities for complex criminal networks, it is better to create a table to track all of the required means or resources available or needed to execute the critical capabilities as seen in the diagram below.

Figure 5.8: Critical Capability Tracker-MOTHRA MC

Prostitution	Methamphetamine Trafficking	Cocaine Trafficking
Recruiters	Production Specialist	Source Country Contact
Handlers (Pimps)	Transporters	Importation Specialist
Venues	Traffickers	Transporters
Advertising (Internet)	Dealers	Traffickers
Customers (Johns)	Customers	Dealers
Enforcers/Protection	Debt Collectors	Customers
		Debt Collectors

(Source: Andrew Wright, 2017)

The values in the table above are the critical requirements needed in order for the MOTHRA MC criminal network to accomplish its ends. It is important to note that in this example, cocaine trafficking by the MOTHRA MC criminal network is a more complex activity compared to prostitution and methamphetamine trafficking as it involves the extra steps of having a source country contact as well as an importation specialist. Direct importation is only usually undertaken by criminal networks who are high volume multi-kilo traffickers while smaller networks would rely on already imported supplies that will usually be of lower quality due to the cutting process that is likely to occur at each stage once the narcotics have departed from the source.

4.   *Select the entity from the list of means that inherently possess the critical capability. This is the centre of gravity.*

As we have used three different criminal activities that the MOTHRA MC criminal network is involved in, there are likely to be different centres of gravity for each unless the activities are closely linked for example the methamphetamine and cocaine trafficking activities would share the same critical capabilities of transporters, traffickers, dealers and debt collectors. However, the centre of gravity for methamphetamine would be the production specialist and the operation of the methamphetamine lab as without it there would be no product for the network to transport, traffic and deal. Similarly, for cocaine trafficking, the centre of gravity would be the source country contact and the importation specialist for the same reasons as described in the methamphetamine example as without product, the network is unable to complete the rest of the critical requirements.

In the prostitution example however, things are somewhat more complicated and there are actually two centres of gravity, first would be the recruiters because similar to the narcotics trafficking examples the victims are the commodity that are being trafficked and are key to the operation of the network. In this example however, recruitment of victims is not enough because the recruitment activities do not make any money for the network. This is where the secondary centre of gravity comes into play, that of advertising as it is only through the customers reading and acting upon the ads do we finally see the establishment of a profit stream for the network through the successful completion of dates and sexual services provided.

5. *From the remaining means select those that are critical for the execution of the critical capability. These are critical requirements.*

The critical requirements for the MOTHRA MC criminal network also vary by criminal activity being completed. Stayingwith the prostitution example the critical requirement would be the venues where prostitution occurs because it is that activity which generates a profit for the MOTHRA MC. Similarly with the two narcotics trafficking activities (methamphetamine, cocaine) the critical requirements would be the transportation, trafficking and dealing hubs because without the means to get the products distributed out to the customers the execution of the profit streams cannot take place.

6. *Identify those critical requirements that are vulnerable to adversary actions.*

The centres of gravity already identified should take the priority for targeting as they will most successfully disrupt or degrade the network. The critical requirements that are vulnerable to adversary actions for each criminal activity stream are as follows. First for the prostitution activity stream, the previously identified critical vulnerability of venues, is also vulnerable to adversary actions. Through the deprivation of venues for prostitution we deny the profit stream from taking place as we block the employment of the victims in the completion of sexual services.

The best ways to deprive the prostitution activity stream of the network from the required venues is for law enforcement to analyze those hotel and motel chains and neighborhood streets where these activities occur in the highest volumes and then move to enforcement operations on customers and pimps alike as well as rescues of opportunity for prostitutes and human trafficking victims forced to provide these services. The problem with these actions and the reasons why the aim is disruption and degradation of the network as opposed to outright destruction is the fact that in terms of venues these activities can be moved into private venues such as condominiums and houses or screened by the operation of adult entertainment facilities, all of which are harder to enforce. In addition, action against the prostitution venues may also just lead to the displacement of activities to another neighboring or close-by jurisdiction that has not completed centres of gravity analysis of the criminal network so that the MOTHRA MC can start anew until their activities are disrupted or degraded again, if at all.

In order to target the critical requirements of the narcotics trafficking criminal activity networks, it would be useful to first complete a commodity flow diagram in order to determine the transportation and trafficking routes that the narcotics take from the source after importation or production. Once the primary and secondary routes of commodity flow have been determined, interdiction operations can take place that will disrupt or degrade the network by reducing the supply of the commodity, in this case methamphetamine or cocaine from getting to market. The challenges in targeting this critical requirement however are the constant changes in transportation and trafficking concealment techniques utilized by the MC in order to stay one step ahead of law enforcement interdiction operations. In this case then it is better to target those who have the expertise in transportation trafficking and concealment fields, such as those businesses or individuals that build traps or concealed compartments to transport narcotics, as these are more highly specialized skills than the drivers or other vehicle or vessel operators possess themselves and would be much harder for the MOTHRA MC criminal network to replace, thereby prolonging the disruption or degradation of these narcotics trafficking networks. Following this method will allow an analyst to determine logical centres of gravity, complete with critical vulnerabilities available for targeting. As critical vulnerabilities are identified, they have the possibility to become decisive points or operational objectives to be achieved to reach a desired state. By targeting the centres of gravity, either through direct means or indirectly through critical vulnerabilities, the strength of the criminal network is challenged.

Challenging the strength of the criminal network through network degradation and disruption and subsequent negative impacts on multiple profit streams positively changes the operational environment toward the desired state (Cole, 2012, pp. 51-2). It is important to note at this point that when using this technique to target larger criminal networks such as the MOTHRA MC that may have the previously covered varying levels of criminal effort and activity from the tactical to the strategic, in different or multiple geographic locations and require the application of the friendly centre of gravity. In this case joint forces operations composed of multiple police services and law enforcement agencies against the centres of gravity of the criminal network may be required with the end result being the defeat of the criminal network by an opposing law enforcement network.

How Centres of Gravity Analysis Supports Intelligence-Led Policing

The theory of intelligence-led policing is supported by centres of gravity analysis as it allows an analyst to better inform and influence the decision-maker when operating in a highly networked criminal environment as it specifically aims to disrupt and degrade criminal networks through the identification and targeting of centres of gravity.

1. *Interpret the Criminal Environment:* (Wright, 2011, pp. 212-7). It is in the first stage of the intelligence-led policing model that the analyst would conduct centres of gravity analysis to assist in interpreting the criminal environment and any criminal networks in operation through the identification of Critical Capabilities, Requirements, Vulnerabilities and Centres of Gravity. This would also be where the police service would want to determine its own centres of gravity so that it knows what it can bring to bear upon the criminal centres of gravity once determined in order to cause the largest amount of disruption or degradation to the network. This would typically be where a service, depending on the size of the network being targeted might enter into a Joint Forces Operation (JFO) or other multi-agency project model to ensure economy and efficiency of effort and force is used on the criminal centres of gravity.

2. *Influence Decision-makers:* This stage of the model requires the analyst to inform the decision-maker of both friendly and criminal centres of gravity in existence in the operational environment and then influence them to target the criminal centres of gravity and any associated vulnerabilities identified. The important thing here is actually convincing the decision makers to act upon the analysis provided. Despite many agencies public pronunciations of following an Intelligence-Led Policing model, many only pay lip service to the model. Acting on intelligence takes courage as it is predictive and not 100% verified by facts and evidence like in investigative models. In this context, dismissing the analysis is always the safest, most cost effective and low risk course of action. An old saying in the intelligence trade states that if you are 100% sure, it is already too late, this means analysts using these techniques need to make sure the decision makers are significantly influenced to act before it's too late.

3. *Impact the Criminal Environment:* This final stage requires the decision-makers to target the criminal centres of gravity and any associated vulnerabilities in an effort to disrupt or degrade the criminal networks in operation. This final stage is where the actual impact in terms of network degradation and disruption should occur if we have performed the centres of gravity analysis according to the steps. By this stage we should have determined the criminal network's desired ends and have informed and influenced the decision-makers sufficiently that they are spurred on to implementing the most effective actions against the criminal network's centre of gravity. Important to note here is that you will not always be correct or you may find that the criminal networks may be able to regenerate more quickly from targeting efforts than we had assessed and may become even more resilient as these networks and the cells that compose them are often learning organizations made up of career criminals. Do not be disheartened, because even if there are setbacks in using this method the cumulative degradation and disruption to the networks and the removal of key facilitators in key criminal markets should impact the overall quality of network composition and participants. Over time, this will result in the criminal network increasingly vulnerable to higher order degradation and disruption operations.

Centres of Gravity Analysis of the A-Z CREW

When describing the theory of Centres of Gravity Analysis, I touched upon the fact that many times analysts will be faced with multiple organized crime groups operating in large criminal networks. Lucky for us, this is the case of the A-Z CREW, as they are allied with and operating in the same network as MOTHRA MC which is often the case when speaking in terms of support clubs for OMGs or associated, supporting street gangs.

For the first step, we can assume that the larger network's desired ends remain the same: to control prostitution and sell high volumes of methamphetamine and cocaine, but in this case, the network's ends have expanded to selling high volumes of narcotics as they specialize in the sale of heroin and crack cocaine, which they produce from powdered cocaine supplied by MOTHRA MC.

For the second step we can determine that in terms of heroin trafficking, the A-Z CREW network component will need to secure their supply in a source country, facilitate importation and transportation and subsequent sales to customers and the expansion of their markets and customer base. With regards to crack cocaine production and trafficking, they need to be supplied by the MOTHRA MC, process the powdered cocaine into crack rocks and facilitate transportation and subsequent sales to customers and the expansion of their markets and customer base. In both cases they will need an effective system of debt collection and enforcement to ensure the continued viability of their profit streams.

For the third step we can then organize the required functions to achieve the desired end state into another chart:

Figure 5.9   Critical Capability Comparison-A-Z CREW

Crack Cocaine Trafficking	Heroin Trafficking
Supply From MOTHRA MC	Source Country Contact
Production Specialist	Importation Specialist
Transporters	Transporters
Traffickers	Traffickers
Dealers	Dealers
Customers	Customers
Debt Collectors	Debt Collectors

(Source: Andrew Wright, 2017)

With the crack cocaine illicit networked business model we can already see one potential centre of gravity, previously mentioned, the alliance and supply relationship for cocaine to be turned into crack cocaine by the A-Z CREW. By targeting this centre of gravity we can negatively impact the profit streams of both organizations that make up the network; MOTHRA MC in terms of their powdered cocaine profit stream and the A-Z CREW in terms of their crack cocaine profit stream. In addition, as is the case with many alliances between criminal groups involved in networked operations, they may only have one point of contact between the two groups, in this case, Noel NEVIT (NN) where targeting may cause the alliance to disintegrate and limit the A-Z CREW to a single, heroin based profit stream.

In this case however, we see yet another reason to target NN as he not only plays a controlling function in the A-Z CREW, but he also provides charismatic leadership to the group. We see how multiple centres of gravity can reside in one person, cell or part of the network if it possesses multiple critical capabilities and requirements needed to achieve the desired end state. Also derived from the associated social network analysis on the A-Z CREW the two sub-cell leaders, Paul PARKER (PP) and Chris CRUTTON (CC) are also identified as the key facilitators for trafficking crack cocaine and heroin respectively. As we determined that targeting NN would cut off the supply of crack cocaine, fracture the alliance between groups and deprive the A-Z CREW of charismatic leadership we can further identify secondary centres of gravity. The most vulnerable secondary centre of gravity in this case is CC, in order to disrupt or degrade the heroin trafficking cell. We could also select micro centres of gravity by further examining the cell to determine which of CCs dealers are the most efficient in terms of drug sales to further disrupt the profit stream but in this case we will keep things at the macro level. Going back to the macro level, the best way to cause widespread disruption to the network is not only to target NN for the reasons already mentioned but to have our JFO partners target the methamphetamine and prostitution centres of gravity simultaneously thereby causing many different areas of network degradation and disruption at the same time, weakening its structure as a whole.

Conclusion

It is clear that whether looking at criminal networks at the micro level or the macro level the use of SNA, Communications Analysis and COG analysis can greatly increase the effectiveness and efficiency of strategic, all the way down to operational and tactical targeting. In the information age, coupled with globalization, businesses both licit and illicit, will only become increasingly complex and networked in order to reap the benefits of network proliferation. Unless police services and the analysts embrace these techniques to disrupt and degrade these highly complex networks and their composite parts, law enforcement runs the risk of being outmatched and outmaneuvered by criminal capabilities possessed by 21st century criminal networks. To paraphrase retired General Stan McChrystal, it takes a network to defeat a network and until law enforcement fully embraces this approach and determines its own centres of gravity and those of the criminal networks it opposes, using all of the combined resources available, policing will remain somewhat reactive as opposed to the truly holistic intelligence-led approach it so richly deserves.

Addendum 1: A – J Crew

Entity A (Node)	Link or Edge	Entity B (Node)
Aaron ACTON (AA)	Case File 1	Greg GHOST (GG)
Aaron ACTON (AA)	Street Check 1	Fred FROST (FF)
Brent BUTTON (BB)	Crime Stoppers Tip	Aaron ACTON (AA)
Chris CRUTTON (CC)	Street Check 3	Fred FROST (FF)
Chris CRUTTON (CC)	Case File 2	Darren DEEDS (DD)
Chris CRUTTON (CC)	Street Check 2	Brent BUTTON (BB)
Darren DEEDS (DD)	Case File 2	Eric EATON (EE)
Eric EATON (EE)	Case File 2	Chris CRUTTON (CC)
Greg GHOST (GG)	Case File 3	Igor IVANOV (II)
Harry HUGHES (HH)	Street Check 5	Igor IVANOV (II)
Harry HUGHES (HH)	Street Check 4	Fred FROST (FF)
Igor IVANOV (II)	Case File 3	Jack JUKES (JJ)
Jack JUKES (JJ)	Case File 3	Greg GHOST (GG)

Addendum 2: Full Alphabet Crew

Entity A (Node)	Link or Edge	Entity B (Node)
Paul PARKER (PP)	Tasked Surveillance 2	Quincy QUAID (QQ)
Noel NEVIT (NN)	Tasked Surveillance 2	Steven SAUNDERS (SS)
Robert REESE (RR)	Tasked Surveillance 2	Noel NEVIT (NN)
Noel NEVIT (NN)	Tasked Surveillance 2	Quincy QUAID (QQ)
Quincy QUAID (QQ)	Tasked Surveillance 2	Robert REESE (RR)
Robert REESE (RR)	Tasked Surveillance 2	Steven SAUNDERS (SS)
Steven SAUNDERS (SS)	Tasked Surveillance 2	Quincy QUAID (QQ)
Fred FROST (FF)	Tasked Surveillance 2	Kevin KONSKY (KK)
Chris CRUTTON (CC)	Tasked Surveillance 1	Kevin KONSKY (KK)
Paul PARKER (PP)	Tasked Surveillance 1	Kevin KONSKY (KK)
Paul PARKER (PP)	Tasked Surveillance 1	Chris CRUTTON (CC)
Len LOWES (LL)	Street Check 9	Noel NEVIT (NN)
Noel NEVIT (NN)	Street Check 9	Mike MASTERS (MM)
Len LOWES (LL)	Street Check 9	Mike MASTERS (MM)
Paul PARKER (PP)	Street Check 9	Steven SAUNDERS (SS)
Kevin KONSKY (KK)	Street Check 8	Mike MASTERS (MM)
Kevin KONSKY (KK)	Street Check 7	Oscar OLDS (OO)
Paul PARKER (PP)	Street Check 6	Tyler TURKOT (TT)
Oscar OLDS (OO)	Street Check 6	Tyler TURKOT (TT)
Paul PARKER (PP)	Street Check 6	Oscar OLDS (OO)
Harry HUGHES (HH)	Street Check 5	Igor IVANOV (II)
Harry HUGHES (HH)	Street Check 4	Fred FROST (FF)
Chris CRUTTON (CC)	Street Check 3	Fred FROST (FF)
Chris CRUTTON (CC)	Street Check 2	Brent BUTTON (BB)
Xavier XANDUS (XX)	Street Check 10	Yaffa YAKOV (YY)
Aaron ACTON (AA)	Street Check 1	Fred FROST (FF)
Source 1 (Drug User)	Source Report	William WISER (WW)
Source 1 (Drug User)	Source Report	Xavier XANDUS (XX)
Steven SAUNDERS (SS)	Down line 2	Xavier XANDUS (XX)
Victor VISKEK (VV)	Down line 1	William WISER (WW)
William WISER (WW)	Crime Stoppers 2	Zander ZULOS (ZZ)
Brent BUTTON (BB)	Crime Stoppers 1	Aaron ACTON (AA)
Noel NEVIT (NN)	Case File 5	Mike MASTERS (MM)
Tyler TURKOT (TT)	Case File 5	Mike MASTERS (MM)
Noel NEVIT (NN)	Case File 5	Tyler TURKOT (TT)
Paul PARKER (PP)	Case File 4	Ugo UBON (UU)
Paul PARKER (PP)	Case File 4	Victor VISKEK (VV)
Ugo UBON (UU)	Case File 4	Victor VISKEK (VV)
Igor IVANOV (II)	Case File 3	Jack JUKES (JJ)

Jack JUKES (JJ)	Case File 3	Greg GHOST (GG)
Greg GHOST (GG)	Case File 3	Igor IVANOV (II)
Eric EATON (EE)	Case File 2	Chris CRUTTON (CC)
Chris CRUTTON (CC)	Case File 2	Darren DEEDS (DD)
Darren DEEDS (DD)	Case File 2	Eric EATON (EE)
Aaron ACTON (AA)	Case File 1	Greg GHOST (GG)

Chapter 6: Proactive Approaches to White Collar Crime

By Marilyn B. Peterson

White Collar Crime has been defined as "an illegal act or series of illegal acts committed by non-physical means and by concealment or guile, to obtain money or property, to avoid the loss of money or property, or to obtain business or personal advantage." (National District Attorneys' Association, as quoted in Edelhertz and Rogovin, 1980, p. 4). The term was coined by Edwin H Sutherland in 1939 (Geis, Meier and Salinger, 1995, p. 2) to describe the politicians, professionals and businessmen who engaged in this activity.

The words "The pen is mightier than the sword" were first written by novelist and playwright Edward Bulwer-Lytton in 1839, but he could well have been referring to them as a modern reflection of theft by deception. According to the *2014 Report to the Nations on Occupational Fraud and Abuse* by the Association of Certified Fraud Examiners, global losses due to fraud were nearly $3.7 trillion (www.acfe.com). Some definitions of white collar crime focus on economic crimes such as fraud, embezzlement, stock manipulation and insurance fraud, while others believe that white collar crime is committed by individuals who hold powerful positions in society and can victimize others through these positions (Moore, in Edelhertz and Rogovin, 1980, p, 21). Bribery and corruption have also been placed inside the bounds of white collar crime as has the newer-minted cyber crime.

Because white collar crime is often a crime of opportunity, it is challenging to prevent. Nonetheless, more has been done, by both government and commercial industries, to prevent it than possibly any other type of crime. Analysis and intelligence play a key role in preventative efforts, as are discussed in this chapter.

Introduction

In 1996, the federally-funded National White Collar Crime Center (www.nw3c.org) determined that "white collar crimes are illegal or unethical acts that violate fiduciary responsibility of public trust committed by an individual or organization, usually during the course of legitimate occupational activity, by persons of high or respectable social status for personal or organizational gain" (Association of Certified Fraud Examiners, 2002, p. 863). "Fiduciary responsibility" could include a range of actions, from that of a home health care worker who pockets a few extra dollars for herself each time she runs an errand for her elderly patient to those of investment bankers who swindle clients of millions of dollars a week. The commonality between these two scenarios is that the client assumes a level of honesty that isn't there.

Is there a distinction between white collar crime and fraud? Fraud is a sub-set of white-collar crime. The legal definition of fraud, as found in Black's *Law Dictionary*, is "some deceitful practice or willful device, resorted to with intent to deprive another of his right, or in some manner to do him an injury. As distinguished from negligence, it is always positive, intentional" (Black's Law Dictionary Free Online 2nd edition).

There is a very broad range of white collar crimes. They include securities fraud, counterfeiting, tax fraud, mortgage fraud, food stamp fraud, insurance and Medicaid/Medicare fraud, bankruptcy fraud, bribery, misfeasance, malfeasance and nonfeasance in office, corporate crimes, credit card fraud, contract fraud and a multitude of variations.

How it can be combated by Intelligence-Led Policing
How can white collar crime be combated or prevented by intelligence-led policing? One keystone to prevention of any crime is knowing indicators that might reveal criminal activity is taking place. For example, if one wanted to bribe a public official to influence a vote, here are some of the initial steps they will need to take to facilitate their crime:

1. Identify public officials who will be voting on the item.
2. Of those, identify officials who might be vulnerable to an offer of money (those with high expenses, large loans, an extravagant lifestyle, etc.). Non-monetary items of value are also used as bribes such as gifts of an expensive family vacation, clothing, jewelry, or other property.
3. Alternately, identify some misbehavior by the individual in the past which might be used to influence him in return for the misbehavior not becoming public (more extortion than bribe). What is the likelihood of your bribe being accepted by that person: do they appear open to influence?
4. Arrange for a private meeting with the individual to be bribed.
5. Remove a large amount of money from the bank to use as payment. In the case of other items of value being exchanged, the manner of transfer may vary. In some cases, money might not be given directly, but transferred to an offshore bank in the recipient's (or a close relative's) name.

If any of these steps are uncovered by an investigator or analyst, (through the knowledge of potential indicators and their identification), then the bribery may possibly be prevented.

According to Barry Zalma in *Red Flags of Insurance Fraud* (2012) several indicators of fire insurance fraud include:

1. "Were there multiple separate fires?
2. Was the premise over-insured?
3. Did the fire spread unnaturally?
4. Was there damage to the structure before the fire?
5. Were pets absent from the home at the time of the fire?
6. Is the insured under economic duress or will he benefit from the fire? " (Zalma, 2012)

If noticed in advance of the crime, some of these indicators could help prevent arson and fire insurance fraud. For example, if the removal of items from a premise were seen, along with suspicious activity around the premise prior to the fire, close surveillance of the property might enable the fire to be anticipated and thwarted. After the fact, these indicators can help the investigator or analyst determine if a criminal investigation is worth pursuing. Timeline, financial and commodity flow analysis (to be discussed later in this chapter) are very helpful analytic methodologies to employ in these kinds of cases.

Other tenets of intelligence-led policing are equally effective in preventing insurance fraud or bringing it to a quick resolution, including information sharing. Numerous organizations have been formed to collect and share information on fraudulent actors and their modus operandi in hopes of ending their activities. One example is the NICB, the National Insurance Crime Bureau, which focused in the past on vehicle insurance fraud, but now also has a healthcare fraud segment. This 100-year old organization fights vehicle-related insurance fraud and crimes, with over 1,100 members around the United States. (www.nicb.org) It provides numerous prevention tips on frauds ranging from staged accidents to identity theft to insurance fraud.

Information is a key ingredient in fraud prevention. The 2016 *Report to the Nation on Occupational Fraud and Abuse* revealed that tips accounted for 39.1% of the initial detection of fraudulent activity. The adage, "if you see something, say something" is as true in fraud prevention as it is in terrorism prevention. In comparison, surveillance/monitoring accounted for less than 2 % of initial detection (Certified Fraud Examiners, 2016, p, 25).

Coderre (2004) suggests there are five conditions necessary to detect fraud:

- studying the organization's environment to identify risk categories and exposures
- understanding the symptoms of fraud
- being alert to the occurrence of these symptoms
- assessing the risks and exposure
- examining the risks and exposures from a fraudster's point of view to understand how he/she would make it possible (pp. 36-7)

In the corporate environment, fraud prevention is critical. Analysts or investigators within the environment can achieve significant fraud prevention activities.

One way that information on white collar crime has become more available is due to non-law enforcement actions such as the adoption of auditing standard 54 which requires financial professionals to notice and report possible criminal activity to the appropriate authorities (AICPA, 2007, p. 1771).

White Collar Crime Analysis Techniques

There are a variety of analytic techniques that are used to prevent or combat white collar crime including financial analysis, pattern analysis, timelines, event flow analysis, indicator development, commodity flow analysis, and network analysis.

Financial analysis comes in many forms and formats. Depending upon the crime being investigated and the records available, a financial database is created that can be manipulated as needed for the analysis. Numerous software companies have developed programs that assist in this effort. The most basic way to analyze financial records is to use a spreadsheet or relational database (such as Microsoft Excel© or Access ©). Both these programs allow analysts and investigators to create simple queries and aggregations to better understand large record sets. The results of this kind of analysis can then be summarized in easy to understand tables, charts and graphs.

In one example of a bankruptcy fraud investigation, a furniture store in a small city had declared bankruptcy, leaving hundreds of customers without ordered furniture after providing the store with sizeable deposits against the cost of the furniture. The married couple who owned the store declared that their poor business acumen had led to the bankruptcy and it was not deliberate or fraudulent.

The investigating agency (a county prosecutor's office) provided varied business documents to a financial analyst. Several years' worth of store orders, receipts, and deposits were placed into a spreadsheet and reviewed. Through the analysis of these corporate and personal financial documents, it was established that the couple was taking additional funds out of the business systematically over the course of several years; this was the drain on income that led to the bankruptcy. In fact, the monies were transferred to an account held by the couple in another state that was their intended retirement location. Further, numerous deposits were transferred to this account and not paid to the furniture manufacturers identified in the orders. Thus, hundreds of thousands of dollars had been siphoned from the business over more than a five year period.

The spreadsheet developed by the analyst for this data included fields such as date of deposit, amount of deposit, person received from, account deposited to, vendor involved, date when ordered furniture was received, and date when the deposit was returned (if any).

The analysis of this data uncovered a pattern of deliberate misdeeds that allowed the prosecutor's office to successfully prosecute the bankrupt couple with charges of fraud. Some funds were returned to customers who otherwise would not have seen any recompense. This analysis is also a good example of how indicators can be used to identify ongoing criminal activity. Positive outcomes such as this can also be helpful for 'best practices' guidance in future cases; thereby discovering and intervening before a bankruptcy occurs (Peterson, 1985).

Pattern Analysis

Patterns of crime are seen in a variety of ways. Within white collar crime, victims may occur in patterns (e.g., the elderly, the poor, hurricane victims, etc.); criminal occurrences may occur in time intervals (e.g., payday scams, pre-holiday shortfalls, etc.), or in geographic patterns (e. g., neighborhoods, zip codes, etc.).

Pattern Analysis is enabled by the human desire for sameness. We all can be creatures of habit. We often do things because we see people like us (or who we want to be) on television buying that certain car, or visiting that particular vacation spot.

Breaks in patterns may be considered anomalies – something so out of the ordinary it calls attention to itself. These may include that phone call in the middle of the night, or the sudden drive to a nearby state to purchase something we could not purchase closer to home.

In one example of pattern analysis in a fraud case, "Medicaid mills" were seen to exhibit similar characteristics which enabled investigators to uncover them easily including that they are:

• found in areas with high concentrations of Medicaid recipients;

- inhabit small, storefront spaces,
- lack basic equipment and supplies necessary for practices;
- change location frequently;
- hide their ownership by using "nominees" and incorporation services;
- may bill through the provider number of a physician who is also an employee;
- use a shell company as a billing entity;
- have a mail-drop corporate address;
- may own more than one clinic (Krayniak and Peterson, 2000, p. 9-10).

Pattern analysis requires that several crimes or crime indicators of a similar nature have already occurred. While this does not prevent the initial crimes, it does prevent their recurrence and thus this can be viewed as part of intelligence-led policing.

Timeline Analysis

Timelines place events into a chronology along a line that is horizontal, vertical, or diagonal, with the events being read either left to right or top to bottom.

Timelines have been used to depict events for centuries. The Bayeux Tapestries, for example, reflected the Battle of Hastings in 1066 from a Norman point of view. The tapestries are 230 feet long, including 50 scenes and were created by numerous seamstresses (http://www.historylearningsite.co.uk/medieval-england/the-bayeux-tapestry/). Charles Joseph Minard's famous timeline, created in 1869, showed Napoleon's march on Russia in 1812-13 (as published by Tufte, 1983). Not only did it reflect the dates of the marches to and from Moscow, but also showed the temperatures, mapped the rivers, and reflected the numbers of troops moving on the particular dates (beginning with 422,000 men and ending in Poland with10,000 men). Timelines are essential to explain the intricacies of many white collar crime investigations.

Timelines tell the story of what happened over time and can be used to easily explain events to management, strategic partners, or even in court. They can be used in a strategic assessment to provide an historical overview; or can show patterns. The steps to doing a timeline are:

1. Gather and review data
2. Extract key dates and occurrences
3. Determine format of timeline (direction of line, length, symbols and markings, etc.)
4. Establish timeline with key dates
5. Summarize occurrences including significant facts
6. Use top and bottom of line as necessary
7. Organize summaries along line in chronological order
8. Review facts for necessary but unknown occurrences (what's missing?)
9. Analyze the information in the timeline

The two sides of the line have varied uses. If there are a lot of occurrences and the developer wants to use as little space as possible, occurrences may be arrayed on either side of the line. If there are two sets of data--for example, what is known and what is suspected, or what has been portrayed versus what has happened--then the sides of the line may differentiate between them. Alternately, if events caused results over time, the two sides of the line could be used to show both the events and the results.

Figure 6.1 Timeline Example

Saga of the missing millions

February 1995	Sept. 13, 1999	Sept. 24, 1999
■ Martin A. Armstrong begins selling his "Princeton Note" securities using accounts at Republic New York Securities Corp., now HSBC Holdings, in New York.	■ Armstrong is arrested on charges he masterminded a global fraud by selling Princeton Notes to Japanese companies while concealing huge trading losses of more than $500 million.	■ Investigators seek to block Armstrong from liquidating his company, Princeton Economics International, offshore in the Turks and Caicos islands.

Armstrong owned this $1.4 million beachfront house in Loveladies. (AP photo)

Oct. 7, 1999	Oct. 14, 1999	Oct. 29, 1999	Dec. 31, 1999	Jan. 14, 2000
■ Armstrong pleads not guilty to 14-count indictment alleging he diverted funds for his own use while deceiving investors. They said he lost $367.8 million in unsuccessful trades from 1997 to 1999.	■ Court-appointed receivers' probe finds Armstrong spent $4.4 million of his investors' money on rare coins.	■ Japanese authorities shut down Armstrong company Cresvale International, of Tokyo, which was implicated in the alleged note scandal.	■ Armstrong refuses to turn over $16 million in gold bars, rare coins and antiquities he is alleged to have, saying doing so would violate his Fifth Amendment rights against self-incrimination.	■ U.S. Magistrate Richard Owen jails Armstrong for failure to turn over the full $16 million, and for allegedly destroying corporate records. Prosecutors say he turned over only about $1 million in assets.

Jan. 22, 2000	Jan. 30, 2001	Feb. 2, 2001	March 6, 2001
■ Armstrong's defense lawyers drop his case after Judge Owen rules they must relinquish $1.2 million in retainers Armstrong paid them.	■ Court-appointed receivers shut down Princeton Economics Institute, an Armstrong company at Carnegie Center in West Windsor.	■ Court-appointed receivers allege that Armstrong diverted $169 million of clients' money for himself and his companies. They said $98 million is still unaccounted for.	■ Armstrong attempts to convince a panel of federal appellate judges that he should be released from jail.

An antiquity in Armstrong's collection

Times graphic by Laura Sommerville

(Source: *Trenton Times* 2002)

The timeline example in Figure 6.1 shows the components of a timeline – dates, direction, and synopses of what occurred on the varied dates. This timeline spans six years and shows how an individual securities salesman made millions, but yet the justice system was unable to track a significant amount of the funds to recover them. The use of photographs in the timeline provides a glimpse of the millions realized from the fraudster's activity.

Another example of a timeline is shown below (Figure 6.2), in the Analyst's Notebook © format. It shows the efficacy of using multiple timelines to reflect the actions of a three individuals, telephone lines and bank accounts, in which interactions occurred on particular dates. It is also able to capture information on meetings held among the three suspects, as well as specific amounts of money being transmitted into the bank accounts.

Figure 6.2 Analysts' Notebook© Timeline

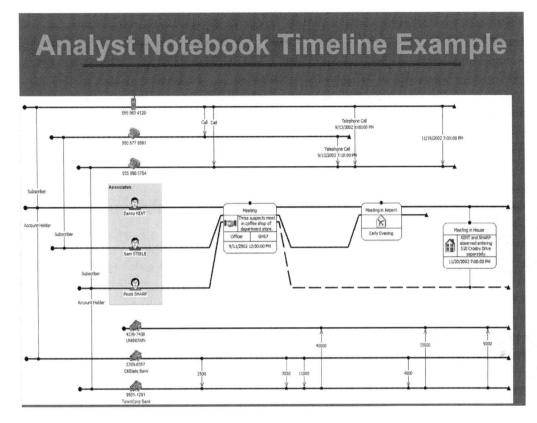

(Source: i2 website)

Event Flow Analysis

Event flow analysis is "the review of raw data to determine the sequence of events or interactions that may reflect criminal activity" (IALEIA, 2004, p.33).   Key to completing an event flow analysis is the development of an event flow chart. However, the chart is not the final product of the analysis but should rather be used to compile the data into a format that is more easily analyzed.

Event flow charts answer the questions when, who, where and how. It's events are most often summarized inside a box or symbol and are placed in chronologic order, connected by lines with arrowheads showing the direction of the flow. Both known and suspected events can be included, with notations being made relative to the suspected events. Suspected or presumed events or flows are often depicted by dashed lines versus solid lines for known activities and flows. If necessary, forecasted future events could also be shown.

Steps in Event Flow Analysis

1. Gather and review data
2. Extract key dates and occurrences
3. Develop flow chart:
    a. determine symbols to be used for occurrences
    b. summarize occurrences including significant facts and dates inside the symbols
    c. organize the symbols in chronological order
    d. review facts for necessary but potentially unknown occurrences
4. Summarize the information in the event flow chart
5. Review the information for inconsistencies, anomalies, patterns, or potential causation
6. Ask critical questions of the data
7. Identify additional data that might be found that would make knowledge more complete.
8. Draw hypotheses about the information

When creating the flow analysis chart, several pitfalls may be seen. The two most common are over-lengthy summarization of the event or not knowing what to include or exclude as an event. The latter can be explained first. Deciding what to include or exclude from the event flow chart is partly a function of the purpose of the chart. If the chart is supposed to show events leading up to an incident, then all events that may be precursors to the incident would be included. If the activities center upon a particular individual and location, then activities extraneous to that person or location could be omitted. Another pitfall that is seen is concluding that certain events cause later events due to their timing. This is not necessarily true.

Summarizing events can be made easier in several ways. First, full sentences are not required; articles and other non-essential words can be left out. A second way to summarize is to break events into smaller parts and place each part into a different symbol. Each symbol should be dated, but specific times can be used as well, and that may allow an event to be broken into smaller pieces. The level of detail provided on the incident should include only what is necessary to explain the incident's relationship to the overall activity.

Similar to the Analysts' Notebook © timeline above, an event flow charts can depict several lines of activities compared, one to another. An example of that is seen in Figure 6.3.

Figure 6.3

MULTIPLE LINE EVENT FLOW CHART

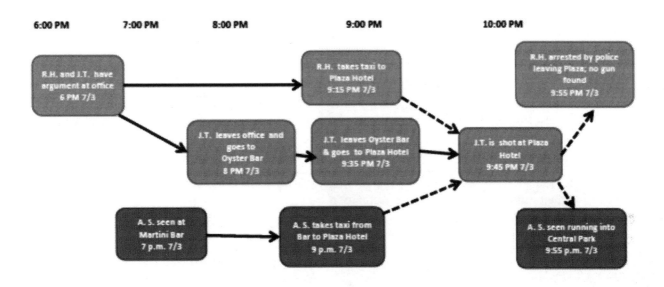

(Source: Peterson, 2017)

In Figure 6.3, three individuals' are shown on different lines of action. How their paths cross is shown by the flow arrows on the chart.

Asking critical questions of the data compiled can point to gaps in the information and/or to potential courses of later action. For example, in the multiple line event flow above:

1. What was the "normal" relationship between RH and JT?
2. What was their argument about?
3. What was the relationship between AS and JT?
4. Was there anyone else seen meeting with them at the Plaza?
5. What did the witnesses report about the shooting?
6. Was AS pursued by officials when he ran into Central Park?
7. Why was RH arrested and not AS? (and so on)

Commodity Flow Analysis

Commodity Flow Analysis has been defined as "A graphic depiction and analysis of the flow of goods or services among persons, entities, or locations. The analysis may give insight into distribution patterns, hierarchy, the nature or extent of a conspiracy, or the processes of an illicit organization" (Peterson 1998, p.38).

Commodity flow charts include movement of something among or between individuals, entities/organization, locations, etc. This chart looks similar to a link chart in that the boxes or other symbols include the names of individual, organizations, groups, etc. However, in commodity flow charts, what is moving and the dates/times of those moves are depicted along the lines between the boxes. The key to not confusing link and flow charts is to remember that only these entities from or to which/whom something has moved can be in a commodity flow chart. Relationships are the basis of link charts, while movement is the basis of a commodity flow chart.

The key to completing a commodity flow chart is to discern where the product, good or services began and then follow its path to its final destination.

Steps in Commodity Flow Analysis
    1. Gather materials

    2. Eliminate extraneous information and translate significant data into a database; include reference numbers

    3. Develop the commodity flow chart:
        a. Choose symbols and place people/entities/locations within symbols.
        b. Indicate what is moving and when, along flow line when possible
        c. Use arrows to show direction of flow

    4. Prepare summary of chart

    5. Review material for patterns, anomalies, and trends

    6. Ask critical questions of the data

    7. Compute net positions where necessary

    8. Draw hypotheses and possible courses of action

Several of these mirror the early steps of event flow analysis. The difference comes in where the entities between whom/which the commodities flow are placed within the boxes or symbols. These names can include identifiers, such as addresses, government identification numbers, bank account numbers, and bank names, etc. depending upon what information you have.

Figure 6.4

Commodity Flow Matrix

		From								
Col Column2	Column3	Column4	Column5	Column6	Column7	Column8	Column9	Column10	Column11
	A	B	C	D	E	F	G	H	Gain
To A					$25,000	$90,000			$115,000
B	$50,000								$50,000
C		$50,000		$100,000					$150,000
D								$150,000	$150,000
E				$75,000					$75,000
F	$40,000								$40,000
G						$100,000			$100,000
H	$75,000					$50,000			$125,000
Loss	($185,000)	($50,000)	0	($175,000)	($75,000)	($240,000)	0	0	
Gain	$115,000	$50,000	$150,000	$150,000	$115,000	$40,000	$100,000	$125,000	
Remainder	($70,000)	$0	$150,000	($25,000)	$40,000	($200,000)	$100,000	$125,000	

(Source: Peterson, 2017)

One difficulty people have with commodity flow charts is that one rule of charting – that no one entity can be shown in two or more places on the same chart – must be followed. In other types of flow charts, persons may be placed throughout the chart. Another rule of charting - not crossing lines - should also be followed here but that may be difficult with complex information.

It could be helpful to note that information can be combined on one line in some instances. For example, multiple payments between two entities can be aggregated by direction (to or from) and placed with a date span along one line.

Because commodities can often flow in circular patterns and may confuse viewers, it might be helpful to also construct a commodity flow matrix showing the 'to' and 'from' flows with net positions for each entity. The next figure reflects the previous matrix in a commodity flow chart.

Figure 6.5

Commodity Flow Chart from Matrix

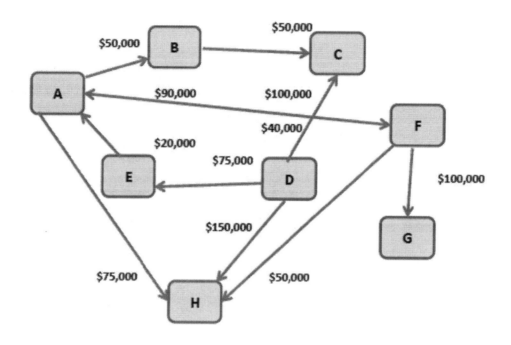

(Source: Peterson, 2017)

In it, you can see that three of the entities (C, E, G and H) appear to keep the profits of this criminal endeavor while A, D and F each appear to possibly be 'pass-through' entities that have less money than they began with. This may be deceptive, however, as the transactions we are tracking may not be all the transactions in which they are involved. It is more likely that, if they are 'pass-throughs', their balances end up like B ($0).

Another thing to remember is that often flow may be presumed in both directions on a flow chart. If contraband is being distributed, it is likely that there is money or some other form of value being passed in return for the goods. For example (Figure 6.6), $1.2 billion in counterfeit goods were seized during 2014 that originated in China (including Hong Kong) (US Department of Homeland Security, 2015).

Figure 6.6

Goods Flowing From China to United States, 2014

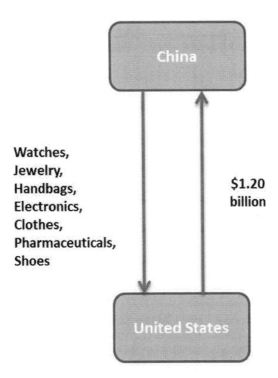

Watches,
Jewelry,
Handbags,
Electronics,
Clothes,
Pharmaceuticals,
Shoes

$1.20
billion

Source: U.S. Dept. Homeland Security 2015

Critical questions

With every analytic product it is necessary to ask critical questions. As an example, let's look at the commodity flow chart shown in Figure 6.6 above.

1. What were the actual dollar amounts for each type of counterfeit goods flowing from China to the U.S.?
2. Are the amounts quoted 'street value' of the goods, or cost to distributors of the goods?
3. What percentage of the total amount of counterfeit goods flowing to the U.S. does the amount from China comprise?
4. What are the smuggling routes used to move these goods into the U.S.?
5. What smuggling methods are used?

6. Are there organized crime groups involved in these efforts? If so, which and who are their leaders?

In some instances, analytic work results in the need for additional information gathering. The above case is an example of that, where obtaining additional records is necessary to pursuing the activity.

Indicator Development

Indicator analysis is "a review of past criminal activity to determine if certain actions or postures taken can reflect future criminal activity. It can result in the development of 'flagging' systems in computerized environments or behavioral profiles" (IALEIA, 2004, p. 33).

The Nebraska Department of Insurance has created indicators for several types of insurance fraud, including what to look for with fraudulent claimants, including:

May often pay premiums in cash…
May show losses relative to times when they are experiencing financial hardship…
May be very well versed on the claims process and/or terminology
May seem over willing to accept a small settlement on a claim…
May be hesitant to submit to an examination under oath… (Nebraska DOI, nd, p. 8)

While this type of knowledge cannot prevent someone from attempting to commit insurance fraud, it can result in the insurer's more detailed investigation into the claim before it occurs.

Network Analysis

Some white collar crimes can be done by single individuals (such as embezzlement, check fraud/kiting, or some forms of elder fraud), but many are done by organizations or networks. Network, or Association, Analysis, is the "collection and analysis of information that shows relationships among varied individuals suspected of being involved in criminal activity that may provide insight into the criminal operation and which investigative strategies might work best" (IALEIA, 2004, p. 31).

Network analysis, applied in white collar crime settings, can lead investigators and analysts beyond the minor players in a scheme and to its final beneficiary. For example, the person who creates false billing statements in a physician's office is not the individual who primarily benefits from the insurance (or other payments) that result. The billing person is following orders from a supervisor, who reports to a manager, who reports to an officer in the company if not to the physician him/herself. This establishes a chain of involvement across the office. The billing person may benefit from the crime by keeping his/her job or receiving an annual bonus. The larger profits, presumably, go to the medical corporation or physician.

There is a more detailed description of how network analysis is done in Chapter 5 and 10.

Predictive Analytics

Predictive Analytics are also now being used to combat fraud. They use historical data to predict future outcomes using models based on a particular business process. It creates a process to show red flags that can be modified when variables alter (Spann, 2014, p. 24).

This form of analytics is particularly helpful when faced with what is now called "big data". These are "any voluminous amount of structured, semi-structured and unstructured data that has the potential to be mined for information" or "extremely large data sets that may be analyzed computationally to reveal patterns, trends, and associations, especially relating to human behavior and interactions" (Tech Target, 2016). Using predictive analytics, one can apply past practices to data and identify key pieces of it to analyze and use to suggest what might occur in the future.

Spann also suggests the use of varied analytic software in support of predictive analytics including:

- VisuaLinks (Raetheon)
- Analyst's Notebook (IBM)
- Analytics 10 (ACL)
- Visual Network Analytics (Centrifuge)
- SAS Analytics
- Comprehensive Financial Investigative Software (Actionable Intelligence Technologies) (Spann, 2014, pp. 6-8).

You may find more information on these, and other, software packages, in Appendix 2.

According to Spann, the gist of fraud analytics is that "organizations must analyze all relevant transactions against all parameters, across all systems and all applications" (2014, p. 17), while predictive analytics "takes a forward-looking approach to determine if the outcome has or will result in a fraud" (Spann, 2014, p. 58). A simple example of this is found in Coderre where he compared employee addresses with vendor addresses and found that a few were similar. Thus, he uncovered fictitious vendor payments being received by employees (2004, pp. 168-9).

Summary/Conclusion

The trillion-dollar industry that is white collar crime has many opportunities to use analysis and intelligence-led policing to end the strangle-hold fraudsters have on both personal and corporate profits. A rich variety of analytic methods can be used to detect and prevent white collar crime. As their use expands in both public sector and private corporate settings, a significant reduction in the number and profits of while collar crime may be seen.

Chapter 7: Cyber-Crime Applications

By Navid Sobbi and Melissa M. Vives, PhD

Introduction

In May 2017, "large scale cyber attacks took down NHS (National Health Service) servers across the UK, as well as disrupting an estimated 200,000 individuals and businesses across 150 countries…(in response many) firms are taking steps to improve cyber security and protect their companies from future attacks" which include two-factor authentication and the use of cloud technology, which mitigates the risk of a ransomware attack (Cunliffe, 2017, p. 1). This was just one example of the far-reaching impact that a cyber attack can have.

Cyber-crime does not have a straightforward, singular definition as it has evolved beyond the singularity of such a term. To determine the reality of what cyber-crimes have evolved into, we must first know where it started, how it progressed and its current state. This chapter reviews a brief history of cyber-crimes and examines the current capabilities of cyber-criminals, the role of law enforcement in combating such crimes and the applicability of intelligence-led policing.

One helpful U.S. document, Presidential Directive 41, defines a cyber incident as "An event occurring on or conducted through a computer network that actually or imminently jeopardizes the integrity, confidentiality, or availability of computers, information or communications systems or networks, physical or virtual infrastructure controlled by computers or information systems, or information resident thereon. For purposes of this directive, a cyber incident may include a vulnerability in an information system, system security procedures, internal controls, or implementation that could be exploited by a threat source" (The White House, 2016, p. 1).

History of Cyber-Crimes

The creation of the Internet has provided global connectivity and instantaneous communication. A new generation has evolved into a technological world that provides immediate responses to any inquiry and tremendous business opportunities. But these advances in technology come with new, sophisticated and lucrative prospects for criminal activity and the increased potential for organized criminal enterprises to prosper. This section reviews the history of cyber-crimes to provide a better understanding of how these enterprises have evolved.

Cyber-attacks are not new and literature suggests that they began as early as the late 1980s with the first self-replicating computer virus known as a "worm" (Andress & Winterfeld, 2014). A worm simply is a malware program that can infect a computer, spread to other computers and slow network speed and computer performance (Weidman, 2014). In 1976, Donn Parker wrote that computer systems represent a gateway to crime. As the technology of computers and the Internet evolved, skilled computer "hackers" infiltrated computer systems with viruses that took years to discover and eliminate. A more recent example of this type of individual is former Central Intelligence Agency (CIA) Analyst Edward Snowden, who covertly accessed sensitive government information and reprinted this classified information to the public using outlets such as newspapers and websites like WikiLeaks (Andress & Winterfeld, 2014). Viruses infected targeted computers and often manipulated or modified files to cause harm and sometimes render the computer useless. Even with anti-virus software written to reduce the chances of hacker involvement, viruses continue to find ways to disrupt the technologic universe and have become a serious worldwide issue.

As technology evolved, cybersecurity became an international concern and experts suggest there is a growing need for emergency management training to include cybersecurity classes (Kessler & Ramsay, 2013). Emergency management personnel include first responders such as emergency medical technicians, firefighters and members of law enforcement. The "opportunity to bridge the gap between cybersecurity defense and the emergency management community is in order to manage the potential catastrophic physical consequences of a successful cyber-attack" (U.S. Department of Homeland Security [DHS], 2013, p. 2). Cyber-attacks on United States civilian government contractors such as Lockheed Martin increased from 28 attacks in 2010 to 43 in 2014 (Drinkwater, 2014).[40] Another large cyber-attack against the Office of Personnel Management (OPM) in the United States compromised the personal and security clearance information of 22 million previous, current and potential federal employees' personal information. The result of this intrusion costs millions of dollars in federal funds to provide identity protection to all victims. OPM maintains large databases of personally identifiable information and includes security clearance information; therefore, this breach has the potential for serious consequences for those at risk (U.S. Office of Personnel Management, 2015).

The United States is not the only country that has suffered information breaches initiated by cyber-criminals. In 2014, India reported in its National Crime Bureau report that there were 9,600 instances of cyber-crimes. However, it is believed that most of these crimes go unreported; and the actual incident count could exceed 300,000 (Desai, 2016). Africa also reported an increase of 30 percent of cyber related crimes since 2013 (ISC Africa, 2015). It has also been noted that South Africa, due to its wealth, has become a target for ransomware which will be discussed in the next section.

Types of Cyber-Crime
Cyber-criminals have adapted and evolved as quickly as the technology they infiltrate. The North Atlantic Treaty Organization (NATO) (2010) suggests that the Internet will become the next battleground as it is the instrument of contemporary life. Cyber-crime has also evolved from the basic desktop computer to countless electronic devises utilized in every aspect of business and personal activity. For example, these devices include the mechanisms in a vehicle, a cellular telephone, or can be integral to the infrastructure of electric companies or nuclear power plants that service many lives (Peterson, 1998a). It is important to remember that the cyber environment not only facilitates crimes such as child pornography fraud, ID napping , and stalking, but can also be the target of crime, including interception of data, phishing, doxing and ransomware.

---

[40] Lockheed Martin provides security and aero defense for the United States military.

Unauthorized Use and Phishing

There are many crimes assisted by computer systems; they are the principal gateway for shopping, social media, email and information gathering. Because there are an abundance of access points, crimes such as unauthorized use and phishing are commonly seen. Phishing is the act of acquiring private or sensitive data by sending emails which appear to come from credible sources that require users to put in personal data such as a credit card number or other private information. This information is then transmitted to the hacker and utilized to commit acts of fraud (Andress & Winterfeld, 2014). Companies are interested in what the consumer purchases, therefore, phishing is often thought of as a victimless crime because companies send specific information or advertisements to search engines regarding their web pages simply to entice similar buyers.

- **Proactive control of unauthorized use:**

One method of mitigating unauthorized use and phishing can be achieved by limiting access points. Removing access points for social media and other potentially hazardous websites will reduce the chances of phishing schemes within an organization. The fewer access points available to employees, the less opportunity there is to lose valuable company information both internally and externally. Restriction of access also allows the organization to control the flow of information and limits employees wasting time on social media sites such as Facebook, Twitter and Instagram (King, 2016). Additional ways to mitigate unauthorized use include but are not limited to layering of access points such as passwords, hardware tokens, smart cards, temporary access numbers, and biometrics (Singleton, 2010). The multi-layer access allows another level of security into systems to reduce the chances of unauthorized use within an organization.

ID napping

Unauthorized use of email is considered ID napping. In 2013, *Time Magazine* suggested that one's personal identity on the black market was valued at $5.00 USD (Docketerman, 2013). Hackers often steal keystrokes then hack into email, bank accounts, credit card accounts, etc. The cyber thief can also send emails to all contacts with malicious intent and the recipients of those messages then click on a link to start a virus and/or malware. This type of crime is combated by installing virus control programs such as McAfee or Norton Anti-Virus on computers and file servers.

Virus control is the primary line of defense against ID napping. The main concern for any organization is the uncertainty of malicious infiltration. Cyber security contractors are often used to mitigate circumstances where deficiencies are identified and can assist private companies and government agencies in securing network systems that need these specialized services.

Interception of data

There are two types of data interception: monitoring and collection of data (Ward & Horne, 2015). Both forms of data interception can be devastating to an organization or governmental agency. These types of attacks usually involve someone in the background reviewing information as a covert observer until enough information can be collected to create collateral damage. There are two focuses when it comes to law enforcement in this area: protection of data and being able to use interception to collect data.

Intelligence communities are often concerned with interception of data since information gathering, policy adherence and intelligence are their main focus. As intelligence is used to gather information about targets, counterintelligence is ensuring that the enemy doesn't know that they are the focus of intelligence gathering efforts. If cyber-criminals have the ability to intercept important strategic intelligence information, many lives are potentially at risk. This can be seen on a battlefield or in a terrorist community. An example is the interception of an arrest warrant communication wherein the target is warned of the pending arrest and successfully flees. There are many scenarios where such an interception of data can cause both short and long term consequences.

There are varied tactics that can be used for interception of data but Casey (2011) suggests four main types. These include:

o   Reconnaissance- which mainly relies on the process of obtaining a target for observation.

o   Attack- which entails the actual implication of the target system which can include access and denial-of-service.

o   Entrenchment- is the ability of the interception to be hidden for a long period of time without detection.

o   Abuse- which is the goal of the attacker for the system that they chose as a target system.

Once analysis is done on the potential interception or collection of an agency's data, there are several methods to investigate the breach. The techniques used by intrusion investigators follow specific steps to resolve and correct the intrusion. Host agencies should have an incident response plan prepared for remediation of the intrusions to include future goals to reduce these risks. It is in risk reduction that intelligence-led policing comes into play.

Doxing

"Doxing is the process of retrieving, hacking and publishing other people's information such as names, addresses, phone numbers and credit card details. Doxing may be targeted toward a specific person or an organization. There are many reasons for doxing, but one of the most popular is coercion" (technopedia.com, 2017). One notable example of this was the hacking of the U.S. Democratic National Committee's servers and having over 44,000 emails published in what some claim was an effort by Russian cyber specialists to influence the 2016 U.S. Presidential election (*NY Times*, 2016).

Child Pornography, Sexual Predators

Shareware software allows individuals to download applications or links to their computers to connect with others of similar interests. These programs may also provide sexual predators a gateway to find potential victims. Many agencies have taken proactive measures to create undercover profiles and/or act as children on sites known to be frequented by these types of predators. The Internet is also a vehicle for child pornography distribution and illegal peer-to-peer file sharing.

Digital forensics has helped law enforcement to proactively identify possible suspects who use peer sharing programs to distribute pornographic pictures of children. Law enforcement agencies also use sting operations that include police officers posing as children in chat rooms to identify adults attempting to lure children into inappropriate communications. Technology has created an open entry of anonymity wherein children can become victims if they are not aware of the reprehensible intent of these predators.

Child pornography has been a concern for decades and many countries have protection policies in place to help protect children. Some examples would be:

- Lanzarote Convention in the Netherlands which expanded criminalization for anyone intentionally obtaining child pornography by means of a computer or communication service (Lanzarote Committee, 2016).

- In England the Cybercrime Convention was updated to include the distribution or taking of photos in an indecent manner to include data stored on a computer (Holder, 2012).

With the evolution of the Internet, nations around the world have made policy changes to incorporate the use of electronic means of distribution of materials that would involve the protection of children. Previously, electronic shareware issues would not have been a concern however, these policies are becoming increasingly complex as the use of technology increases.

Anonymous online games such as Second Life also promote a potentially harmful cyber environment for children. In Second Life, users create avatars to represent themselves as people of unknown background. Children can pretend to be adults and participate in sexually suggestive relationships with real adults. The use of caricatures in these games creates difficult circumstances for law enforcement, as intent on the part of the participants is not clear; thus, the activity may not be considered criminal. The role and capabilities of law enforcement must continue to grow with this ever-changing online environment.

The Role and Capabilities of Law Enforcement in Combating Cyber-Crime

The evolution of the Internet brings with it the need to be able to combat cyber-criminals and their actions. With these evolving changes the law enforcement community needs additional knowledge, skills and training to combat future attacks. This poses a challenge for law enforcement agencies as they must attempt to keep pace with the latest technology available to cyber-criminals and often fall far behind that technology.

The Internet has not only provided us with new methods of misconduct and new types of criminals, it has also provided new methods to commit traditional crimes (Johnston, 2001). Some of these crimes include fraud, child sexual exploitation, stalking, trafficking of drugs, prostitution and entry into restricted (cyber) areas (Johnston, 2001). Johnston mentions in his article that law enforcement agencies must protect "our critical infrastructure in this information age" as it presents new issues for law enforcement bodies (Johnston, 2001). This was written in 2001, there were approximately forty million users on the Internet. Today there are 3.7 billion users on the Internet (Internet World Stats, 2017) and a multitude of social network sites.

As the Internet expands and becomes more sophisticated, law enforcement organizations must implement regular training programs and if necessary, contract with private companies to accomplish this goal. Technical computer training is needed to gain the expertise required to combat cyber-crime. There are also many companies that sell computerized solutions that can assist law enforcement in the collection and dissemination of data. Private companies that specialize in the analysis of big data can likewise help train law enforcement and assist in the potential backlog of jobs.

Law enforcement agencies now often adapt private sector business intelligence methodologies to proactively obtain criminal intelligence information. One such technique is data mining large repositories of information. Proactive data mining is a tool that helps analysts to find patterns and/or identify outliers in their data, test hypotheses, and develop actionable intelligence. The results of data mining can help analysts and investigators to draw conclusions and test these hypotheses, patterns or conclusions (Loh, 2015). In doing so, law enforcement personnel are able to model certain behaviors, trends, and patterns. They can then apply their findings to cases that are presented to them which will in turn speed up investigation turnaround time. Organizations such as Wynyard Group which create analytic software used for fighting traditional and cyber-crimes; or Geofeedia which creates location based social media analytic software, are two companies that law enforcement agencies are using to assist in their investigations (Geofeedia, 2016). Utilizing these types of analytical platforms to mine data requires training and some technical knowledge, but they are effective in combating cyber-crimes as there is too much data to search through without the assistance of software to quickly and efficiently find the right evidence.

Fighting cyber-crime requires traditional criminal investigation knowledge combined with experience in technology. Just as a crime scene leaves traces of the suspect's DNA, a digital device such as a cellular phone or computer hard drive provides ample evidence that remains within the devise even after data has been deleted; thus, providing a kind of DNA or fingerprint that allows investigators to be able to gather useful intelligence information and/or evidence. Law enforcement is also challenged with maintaining evidence on cellular telephones or computers that are obsolete within a year (Pearson, 2015); but the concern of cyber-crime raises issues beyond evidentiary preservation. Companies such as Cellebrite are paving the way with technology that allows law enforcement investigators to quickly, efficiently, and effectively, access cell phones to analyze data that was once limited to computer experts (Cellebrite, 2017). Similar types of forensic programs are also utilized on computers (Encase) and vehicles (Berla Corporation).

Many departments now have cyber-crime divisions and/or forensic laboratories; however, it is still a challenge to keep pace with the multitude of attacks reported and devices seized. Perhaps the most serious breaches reported are complex network attacks. These incidents can put entire countries at risk. Cyber-attacks can occur on power grids, hospitals, and defense facilities, among others. These may rise to the level of cyber-warfare or cyber-terrorism and should be considered a priority by law enforcement and intelligence agencies.

In the United States, a National Cybersecurity Protection System (NCPS) has been created by the Department of Homeland Security, known as the EINSTEIN program (DHS, n.d.) It includes four areas of intelligence-based proactive measures: detection, analytics, information sharing and prevention. It provides analytic insights into potential cybersecurity threats and vulnerabilities to federal, state and local government agencies, private sector partners, infrastructure owners and operators and the public (DHS, n.d.).

Govtech.com suggests there are five steps to a cyber-security risk assessment:

1. Identify information assets

2. Locate information assets

3. Classify information assets (e.g., a rating scale, 1-5 of public, internal, sensitive, compartmentalized, and regulated information)

4. Conduct a threat modeling exercise using Microsoft's STRIDE method: looking for evidence of: Spoofing identity, Tampering with data, Repudiating transactions, Information disclosure, Denial of service, and Elevation of privilege in key system areas.

5. Finalize data and start planning (govtech.com, 2017).

Early cases of cyber-crimes with international implications failed in most cases to result in prosecution and penalties due to jurisdictional hurdles (Urbas, 2012). However, successes are on the rise due to international law enforcement collaboration, aided by efficient understanding of legal frameworks and the use of cross-border systems such as extradition (Urbas, 2012). There are also countries where it is difficult to obtain information. These raise issues such as obtaining evidence close to real time, language barriers, and so on. One body, the Asia Pacific Economic Cooperation, has requested additional work to create laws and systems that assist investigations and prosecutions of cross jurisdictional cyber-crime (Broadhurst, 2006).

Mutual legal assistance (MLA) treaties are utilized between agencies in varied countries to acquire materials that cannot be acquired with cooperation between police (James & Gladyshev, 2016). The problem lies in where data is stored, and in cyber related attacks, it may be impossible to ascertain the origin of the attack (Mena Report, 2016). To be able to work closely with other law enforcement bodies in the fight against cyber-crime, cooperation needs to be at a federal level.

The former Attorney General of the United States, Eric Holder, spoke about MLA in cyber cases, specifically within the Justice Department, at the Singapore Academy of Law. He stated that international law enforcement endeavors have been raised to the next level by augmenting exchange programs for judges, prosecutors, and investigators (Department of Justice, 2012). Holder also pointed out the global collaboration in the fight against cyber-crime, that being the Budapest Convention on Cyber Crime, which has a mutual legal assistance framework to insure countries have the means to fight cyber-crime.

Law enforcement and governments working in cooperation and collaborating is one way to combat cyber-crime. Governments are recognizing this and some have implemented plans with this goal in mind: to combat cyber-crime; such as, the plan implemented in Australia by the Attorney General's Department. Part of the plan put in place in Australia is the Australian Cyber Crime Online Reporting Network (ACORN). This reporting network was created to make it easy to report cyber-crime and obtain information to safeguard one's personal information and computer systems (Australian Attorney General's Department, 2016).

One issue within cyber investigation is that of "attribution." *Wired Magazine* commented that "a fundamental concept in cybersecurity…is the fact that it is sometimes extremely difficult after a cyberattack to definitively name a perpetrator. Hackers have a lot of technical tools at their disposal to cover their tracks. And even when analysts figure out which computer a hacker used, going from there to who used it is very difficult. This is known as the attribution problem" (Newman, 2016, p.1).

Analytic Methods Within Cyber Crime Investigations

But intelligence-led policing is not solely dependent upon information sharing. Analysis is a key component and numerous types of analysis are used while investigating cyber crimes. Among these are communications analysis, timelines, and network analysis.

Communications analysis, elsewhere described in Chapters 5 and 9, compiles and analyzes communication events that occur. These may include phone calls, texts, instant messages, emails, or web site visit logs. The latter might reflect an individual's gathering information from sites that show how to commit a cyber attack or could show visits to child pornography sites. The type of data that is used in communication analysis include dates, times, lengths of visit, URL visited, etc.

Timelines (described in chapter 6) are universal forms of analysis that allow us to show past and present activity in a chronologic manner. They reflect activity, but can also show gaps in activity and possible correlations of activities if patterns of activities recur.

Network analysis, including social network analysis, reflect the connections between individuals using the computer and other individuals, web sites, and other locations (See Chapter 5 and Chapter 10 for additional information). This may show the existence of a group of conspirators or uncover the motivation behind a cyber attack.

While these forms of analysis assist in investigating cyber crime and cyber attacks, the most common form of analysis designed to prevent cyber attacks are risk, threat and vulnerability assessment.

A risk assessment evaluates "the anticipated vulnerabilities and predisposing conditions affecting the confidentiality, integrity, and availability of information systems in the context of the planned environments of operation. Such assessments inform risk response, enabling information system owners/program managers, together with mission/business owners to make the final decisions about the security controls necessary based on the security categorization and the environment of operation" (NIST, 2012, p. 19 -- National Institute of Standards and Technology).

Threat analysis looks to "provide a clear and thorough articulation of assets, threats and attacks to facilitate business mission-relevant dialog and decision-making actions regarding risk level determination and risk management practices" while vulnerability analysis attempts "to select, implement, evaluate and determine gaps in security controls at the application, system, infrastructure and enterprise levels" (Muckin and Fitch, 2016, p. 6).

According to the NIST,"Vulnerability is a weakness in an information system, system security procedures, internal controls, or implementation that could be exploited by a threat source. Most information system vulnerabilities can be associated with security controls that either have not been applied (either intentionally or unintentionally), or have been applied, but retain some weakness" (2012,

p. 9). Thus a key component of preventing cyber attack is an honest appraisal of the systems in use and their potential vulnerabilities.

This appraisal may include three phases. Wentzel stated, "analysts attempt to identify information of value through... indications...indicators and evidence" (2016, p.7). Indications are "a sign, symptom or suggestion" (p. 8) while indicators are "known or theoretical steps an adversary should take in preparing to conduct an attack" (p. 9). Finally, evidence is a "collection of...known facts and information resulting from an action" (p. 10). The difficulty lies in having the first two types of data providing actionable intelligence before the event ("evidence") occurs; that is, to prevent the attack rather than having to mitigate its effects.

Cyber-Crime and the Future for Law Enforcement

Cyber-crimes are important enough to be a national security issue, now and in the future, in many countries. However, the consequences of many cyber-crimes are so multifaceted that they require detailed knowledge to better understand the changing nature of the risks as well as to create new methods to investigate them (Lemieux, 2012).

Intelligence led policing depends upon co-operation between law enforcement agencies and intelligence sharing. This is especially critical in the fight against cyber-crime (Lemieux, 2012). To date, large scale cyber-attacks have been largely denial of service attacks limited to computers, websites, software, and emails. However, things changed when state sponsored attacks such as the malicious computer worm Stuxnet began attacking industrial computer systems in physical locations (e.g. Iran) to purportedly safeguard against threats to national security. In another recent example, published by *The New York Times,* former U.S. President Barack Obama reportedly ordered officials in the Pentagon to step up their cyber-attacks against North Korea's missile program (Sanger and Broad, 2017). Unfortunately, this type of technology based threat will eventually fall into the hands of cyber-criminals, potentially jeopardizing critical infrastructure such as hospitals and power grids.

According to Wentzel, the future of cyber malware may be "onion bots" which use "privacy infrastructures to evade detection, measurement, scale estimation, observation and... all IP-based current mitigation techniques" (2016, p. 13). Thus, it is imperative for law enforcement to keep up with emerging technology so as to create a level playing field.

Lemieux noted (2012), one of the major issues for law enforcement agencies in investigating cyber-crime is the availability of resources due to budgetary constraints. He stated that annual budgets determine the number of agents employed and the amount of resources at its disposal. Agencies are devoting more time and resources to the development of a variety of cyber-crime interdiction strategies. Due to the highly technical and complex investigative responsibilities involved in detecting cyber-crimes, law enforcement agencies are greatly challenged to stay ahead of cyber-criminals (Lemieux 2012).

When investigating cyber-crime, law enforcement agencies are faced with applying technical methodologies, co-operating with concerned parties, and frequently operating between varying legal frameworks in international investigations. Hunton (2011) suggested the need for a cyber-crime investigation framework. His framework uses a wide range of traditional law enforcement investigation techniques combined with technical investigative skills. The premise behind this framework and others (for example by Katos and Bednar (2008)), is that investigations into cyber-crimes involve numerous individuals with differing skill sets who need to communicate and share intelligence gathered across many jurisdictions and agencies (Lemieux 2012).

Going forward, the need for consistent cyber-crime legislation and framework on a global scale, (through entities such as Interpol or the United Nations), is important (Alkaabi, 2010). Similarly, by integrating cyber-crime investigation processes into traditional criminal investigation methods of action, evaluation, and decision (Stelfox, 2009); established investigative activities will work closely with the complex challenges of investigating cyber-crime (Hunton, 2010).

Conclusion

Cyber-crime is a complex phenomenon that will continue to be a challenge for intelligence led policing far into the future. Fighting cyber-crimes requires funding, additional resources, and technical expertise to proactively address the complexity of these crimes. There needs to be co-operation between jurisdictions investigating cyber-crimes and the implementation of frameworks to assist in the investigation process. Future research should be concerned with the growing technological advances and how they relate to law enforcement's response to rapid changes in this environment. Many questions and decisions remain, to include: agency investment in staffing, training and technology, jurisdiction, legislative and legal actions, and the use of private contractors in intelligence investigations.

Chapter 8: Financial Intelligence Applications

By Alison Callery and Anne Walton

Introduction

The role of analysis in intelligence led policing cannot be overstated. "Intelligence-led policing (ILP) is the model which brings intelligence and analysis to the forefront of police operations"(Peterson, 2005, p. 3). Financial analysis is part of the intelligence process and fits squarely into the goals of ILP. Dr. Scott Phillips said ILP involves the "application of evidence to a more structured analytic framework to solve problems and reduce crime..."(2012, p. 41). Financial intelligence is at the forefront of this framework. It is useful in identifying patterns and crime trends, developing investigative leads and providing valuable information to guide decision makers in formulating effective police strategies. This chapter will discuss what financial intelligence is, sources of financial data and will offer an overview of the types of financial analyses that can be used to maximize intelligence-led policing efforts.

The Role of Finance in Criminal Activity

Groups involved in illegal activities, even those designed to make money, must generate and utilize a substantial amount to sustain operations, maintain administrative responsibilities, and pay for supplies, transportation and other forms of operational expenses. Perhaps the most common way of ensuring criminal activity continues is through the laundering of illicit proceeds of crime (money laundering).

Money laundering, a common way to move money and finance illicit activity, is the movement of currency that has been generated illegally, through accounts and businesses in an effort to disguise its source and make it available for expenditures by those who generated it (Peterson, 1998b). The three stages of money laundering are: (1) placement, in which illicit proceeds are introduced into the financial system; (2) layering, in which the criminal attempts to separate the proceeds from the crime through a series of transactions; and (3) integration, where the illicit funds re-enter the economy disguised as legitimate funds (Treasury, 2015). It is estimated that $300 billion is generated annually in illicit proceeds much of which are profits from drug trafficking and fraud (Treasury, 2015).

The global financial system provides many opportunities for criminals and terrorists to launder money and raise, move, store and spend money by way of many different types of products and services from a basic bank account to Bitcoin, a type of decentralized virtual currency (Treasury, 2015). Because of its value and relative safety, the U.S. dollar is the preferred currency in international commerce, particularly for trade finance and other business transactions. Methods of money laundering include:

- transferring funds (a wire transfer) to an offshore bank account
- purchasing of real estate and other commodities
- moving money through multiple bank accounts (continually creating layers between the originator and beneficiary)
- providing funds to relatives and friends for investments thus concealing the true owner
- using shell companies to hide the ultimate beneficiaries (Peterson, 1998b).

Rapid technological advances within the financial sector have further increased the speed with which individuals and businesses can transact with one another and avail users of the opportunity to anonymize many aspects of financial transactions. Further, many mobile devices enable the user to create many layers between the originator and the recipients of transactions, thereby concealing the source of the funds.

Despite the many ways in which criminals and terrorists can and have exploited the financial system to sustain operations and move illicit money, many opportunities exist for law enforcement to identify accounts, assets, front or shell companies and additional members of the network. Therefore, any investigation into criminal activity should include a financial component and should seek to obtain available financial intelligence and information in order to generate useful leads. By following the money, law enforcement has the opportunity to disrupt and dismantle criminal and terrorist networks, while also using actionable intelligence to prepare sound policing strategies. One way to do this is looking to "reverse engineer" money of unknown origin which might be found through reviews of financial records. "When large, unexplained profits are found to be going through offshore centers, money service businesses, or financial institutions, then criminal activity is strongly indicated. Following the trail of money back to the criminal source is challenging, but necessary. Without a predicate crime, money laundering charge cannot be laid. However, in some countries, only money derived from narcotics is considered as laundered, while in others, there is a wider range of predicate criminal activity" (Peterson, 1999b, p. 2).

What is Financial Intelligence?

Financial intelligence refers to financial information about individuals and businesses that has been collected, evaluated, collated and analyzed. Raw data showing financial activity can include bank accounts, travel details, wire transfers, transaction dates, amounts, times, and counterparties. Financial institutions monitor this activity in real time and maintain entire departments that are solely focused on analyzing and investigating financial activity to determine if it is indicative of money laundering, fraud, and/or terrorist financing. The data can sometimes be obtained via a series of reports filed by financial institutions as required by federal law or gleaned from other sources. Analysis of this and other forms of financial data and intelligence can be used to provide leads for investigations and/or supports the development of recommendations, or helps to identify indicators to assist in crime detection and prevention (Schussler, 2011).

Sources of Financial Information

Bank Secrecy Act Data

Certain financial reporting is a requirement of the Bank Secrecy Act (BSA). The BSA, passed in 1970, was designed to deter money laundering and the use of secret foreign accounts, create an investigative paper trail on currency transactions, impose civil and criminal penalties for non-compliance, and improve detection and investigation of violations (Peterson, 1998a). At the time the BSA was passed, Congress sought to arm law enforcement with tools to fight the war on drugs and tax evasion. It believed creating a paper trail of money placement and movement (i.e. layering) would be extremely effective in combating these offenses. Suspicious Activity Reporting (SAR) began in 1996 to provide visibility into non-cash activities that might relate to varied criminal undertakings (12 *C.F.R.*, Part 21.11). The USA

PATRIOT Act, passed in 2001, amended the BSA and contained provisions on international anti-money laundering efforts and modifications to the BSA reporting requirements for financial institutions (Cassara & Jorisch, 2010). Together this legislation provides law enforcement with valuable financial information and infrastructure by way of reporting requirements and targeting powers to identify, disrupt and dismantle criminal and terrorist organizations.

The BSA requires that financial institutions file a report should a transaction or incident exceed a dollar threshold or meet a series of criteria. BSA information is ultimately a record of a financial transaction or series of transactions that involved one or more financial institutions and was identified through surveillance, due diligence and/or investigative action by any one of the financial institutions (Walton, 2013). BSA reports may contain personal identifying information, account details, dates, times, dollar amounts, and transaction history. Another key requirement of the BSA is that financial institutions maintain adequate compliance programs to protect against money laundering and terrorist financing through the global financial system. Key components of the compliance programs are divisions such as financial intelligence units (FIUs), transaction monitoring and suspicious activity response teams; all of which are responsible for analyzing financial activity and customer profiles and reporting financial activity to the U.S. government. Figure 8.1 below provides a detailed explanation of the most common BSA forms.

The Role of FinCEN

The Financial Crimes Enforcement Network, (FinCEN) established in 1990, was created to "safeguard the financial system from illicit use and combat money laundering and promote national security through the collection, analysis and dissemination of financial intelligence and strategic use of financial authorities" (www.fincen.gov). As part of its mission, FinCEN analyzes the information acquired through the BSA to support financial criminal investigations and can assist law enforcement with 314(a) requests to financial institutions to locate accounts and transactions of persons that may be involved in terrorism or money laundering.[41] Law enforcement can access financial information and BSA data via FinCEN, Office of Law Enforcement Support (OLE) and through direct access to the BSA Database (www.fincen.gov).   Figure 8.1 below summarizes the more common reports that can be obtained via FinCEN and includes the criteria for the filing of each. Another avenue law enforcement can pursue to identify BSA data or get assistance with financial information is through the High Intensity Financial Crime Area program (HIFCAs). HIFCAs are designated high risk geographic regions that concentrate law enforcement efforts at the federal, state and local levels (HIFCA). As of 2017, there are seven designated regions: California Northern District and Southern District, Southwest Border, Chicago, New York and New Jersey, Puerto Rico and South Florida.

---

[41] FinCEN regulations under Section 314(a) of the USA PATRIOT Act enable federal, state, local and foreign law enforcement, via FinCEN, to reach out to more than 43,000 points of contact at more than 22,000 financial institutions to locate accounts and transactions of persons involved in terrorism or money laundering; see FinCEN 314(a) Fact Sheet, https://www.fincen.gov/statutes_regs/patriot/pdf/314afactsheet.pdf .

Figure 8.1 Common BSA Reports

Currency Transaction Report (CTR) Form 112	Report of a cash transaction over $10,000. Financial institutions are required by law to complete the CTR form, properly identify persons conducting transactions, submit the form to the FinCEN, and maintain appropriate records of financial transactions.
Report of International Transportation of Currency or Monetary Instruments (CMIR) Form 105	<ul><li>Required when a person physically transports, mails, or ships, or causes to be physically transported, mailed, or shipped currency or other monetary instruments in an aggregate amount exceeding $10,000 at one time from the United States to any place outside the United States or into the United States from any place outside.</li><li>Or when a person is the recipient of other monetary instruments in an aggregate amount exceeding $10,000 that have been transported, mailed, or shipped to the person from outside the United States.</li></ul>"Monetary instruments" are documents readily convertible to cash such as checks made out to cash, traveler's checks or money orders.
Foreign Bank Account Report (FBAR) Form 114	If a U.S. person has a financial interest in, or signature authority over, at least one financial account located outside of the United States; and the aggregate value of all foreign financial accounts exceeded $10,000 at any time during the calendar year, this account must be reported to the Department of the Treasury. (Report of Foreign Bank and Financial Accounts (FBAR))
Suspicious Activity Report (SAR) Form 111	Suspicious Activity Reports are filed:<ul><li>If insider abuse of the financial institution in any amount is suspected.</li><li>In violations aggregating $5,000 or more where a suspect can be identified.</li><li>In violations aggregating $25,000 or more regardless of a potential suspect being identified.</li><li>In transactions aggregating $5,000 or more that involve potential money laundering or violations of the Bank Secrecy Act.</li><li>If a computer intrusion has occurred.</li></ul>
Report of Cash Payments Over $10,000 Received in a Trade or Business Form 8300	<ul><li>Must be filed with the Internal Revenue Service (IRS) within 15 days of the transaction if a person engaged in a trade or business receives cash in excess of $10,000, in any 12 month period, in a single transaction or in two or more related transactions. (Form 8300 History and Law: IRS)</li></ul>

(Source: Financial Crimes Enforcement Network, 2017)

Bank Secrecy Act records can significantly assist in using proactive approaches to financial crime. "The use of financial transaction reports to identify targets includes the review and analysis of these reports for the purpose of pro-actively identifying money launderers and money laundering facilitators. In the U.S., this is done through reviews of the data reported to FinCEN" (Peterson, 1999b, p. 2).

Other sources of financial information

In the event that no BSA data is identified on individuals or businesses it does not mean that the subjects have been cleared or are not involved in illicit activity. The lack of BSA filings may actually be an indicator of financial crime. In the case of a cash business, for example, the absence of CTRs at a financial institution would be suspect (Peterson, 2002). There are a number of other methods investigators can use to identify bank accounts, assets and other financial information. Figure 8.2 shows numerous sources of both personal and business-related financial records. A mail cover could provide information on banks that are sending statements to the residence or business. These can be requested through the local office of the U.S. Postal Inspectors (Peterson, 2002). Surveillance of an individual, a residence and/or business also might provide valuable information on finances, other properties, assets and co-conspirators that may be involved.

Gathering Financial Data

Obtaining financial records and data is a crucial step in developing good financial intelligence and positive investigative outcomes. "The data collection portion of the Intelligence Cycle is the 'lifeblood of the intelligence process' and contains a variety of components designed to provide relevant data for analysis" (Coambs, 2011, p. 67). Identifying what information is needed and making a plan as to how it will be collected is the first step (Peterson, 2011). Planning for collection should begin with a an examination of the case or problem presented, review of the investigation reports, crime data relating to the case and any other facts known to date. It is important to be mindful of what type of information is necessary, the nature of the case or problem, the scope of data sought (date parameters, for example) and to limit the request for data to reflect only the documents required. Some financial records, such as bank accounts, are considered private and must be obtained via subpoena or search warrant, depending on the policies and procedures of the law enforcement agency seeking the records. In addition, public records are a wealth of information and can provide important insights into a person's financial life. "The depth and scope of information that exists on people, businesses, and places is staggering"(Hetherington & Sankey, 2008, p. 3). This is because public documents that are noted or recorded indicate "major events in people's lives—from birth to the first car and house, to death, wills and probate" (Hetherington & Sankey, 2008, p. 3). Some examples of sources are listed in Figure 8.2 below.

Figure 8.2 Sources of Financial Information

	Documents
Bank Records (subpoena or search warrant required for most)	Account Applications and opening documents Signature Cards Bank Statements Checks Wire transfers Business ledgers and journals Invoices and receipts Financial statements Tax records (in the United States) Credit card records Money order and travelers' checks
Public Records	Real estate and mortgages Tax assessment records Plat books Registration for building permits Chattel mortgages Probate records Brokerage houses Civil court records (civil suits, judgments, settlements) UCC filings Liens and judgments Newspapers and trade publications Business registrations Bankruptcy Filings

	Divorce/Family Law Court Records
	Judgments or Liens
	Permit/Licensing Agencies
	Reports to Investors
	County Clerk's Offices
Other	Social media profiles (may contain pictures of assets, houses or associates)
	Facebook
	Instagram
	Twitter
	Snapchat
	Utility companies
	Immigration records
	Travel records
	Customs records (imports, exports, value of shipments)
	Reddit
	Ebay
	Craigslist
	Venmo
	Google

(Shussler, 2011, p.166)

Financial data can also be obtained through various database vendors that collect, compile and provide public information to law enforcement. An example of this type of vendor is LexisNexis. A list of software and some public information database vendors is shown in Appendix 2. Using an information vendor can facilitate identifying financial leads and therefore streamline the data collection process. The method of actually securing financial information will depend on the policies and procedures of the agency seeking the data. Regardless of the approach used to obtain records, a collection plan should be prepared collaboratively by the team conducting the investigation. Some things a collection plan should address include the education and experience of team members, the specific data to be secured, a time-line for data collection, compliance with local, state and federal laws, whether the plan focuses on criminal activity, what sources of information will be utilized, assignment of responsibility for collection tasks to each team member, and the detailed goals of the collection process (Coambs, 2011). Once collected, the financial data should be inventoried to check that all necessary information was received and to plan for additional collection should any gaps be present (International Association of Law Enforcement Intelligence Analysts, 2012).

Processing, Analysis and Synthesis

At this point, the financial data should be processed, analyzed and then synthesized. The processing or collation of financial data requires that it be organized and formatted so that intelligence personnel can retrieve data, sort, identify patterns, anomalies or gaps, and store the data (U.S. Dept. of Justice, 2012). This is most often done with the use of computer software. In some cases, the data will be provided in electronic format and, depending on the format it can be quickly imported to a software application. In other instances, paper documents are received and must be organized and then incorporated into a software program utilizing scanning technology. There are various software applications available to law enforcement to support the processing and analyzing of large amounts of financial data. They generally fall into five categories: spreadsheets, databases, text/data mining, visualization and mapping (U.S. Dept. of Justice, 2012). These programs facilitate organizing data for use in various analytical products. (See Appendix 2 for a listing of software to assist analysis).

Spreadsheets

Spreadsheet applications are often used to sort, tabulate, display and create graphs of financial data (U.S. Dept. of Justice, 2012). Financial data in a spreadsheet is sorted by rows and columns. "They are ideal for financial data storage and collation" (U.S. Dept. of Justice, 2007, p. 5). Spreadsheet programs include functions that perform mathematical and statistical calculations, as well as summarize data in graphs and charts. Document recognition software can be used to scan similarly formatted records into a spreadsheet and can save a great deal of time for intelligence personnel who might otherwise be entering data one transaction at a time. In addition, spreadsheets are often compatible with other software and can be imported into other programs to analyze financial data and summarize findings. Microsoft Excel ™ is the most commonly used spreadsheet software, although there are other choices available including Wordperfect Office ™, Quattro Pro ™ and Lotus 123™.

Databases

Databases are similar to spreadsheets in terms of data entry, but databases have the added ability to create relationships between several tables at once. "Relational database software allows the option of records/fields within a database to be related to other fields" (U.S. Dept. of Justice, 2007, p. 6), while also allowing different tables to be related through fields that are similar. For example, an intelligence analyst at a local police department may maintain three different tables relating to gang suspect information, bank accounts discovered and associations identified through bank accounts, with each table related to the others via a unique field (in this example a bank account). By relating each table to the others via this common field, queries and searches can be performed that will include results from multiple tables. An example of a relational database schema is shown in Figure 8.3.

Figure 8.3 Relationships between Tables in Databases

Table 1 – Bank Accounts

Field 1 – Bank Acct#

Field 2 – Name of Bank

Field 3 – Account Holder

Field 4 – Account Holder Address

Table 2 – Suspect Information

Field 1 – Suspect Name

Field 2 – Suspect Address

Field 3 – Suspect DOB

Field 4 – Suspect Height

Field 5 – Suspect Weight

Field 5 – Suspect Eye Color

Field 6 – Bank Acct#

Table 3 – Associates Identified

Field 1 – Associate Name

Field 2 – Bank Acct#

Field 3 – Associate Address

Field 4 – Details of Transactions

(Source: Carter, 2017)

Running queries and reports within a database, allows much more information to be extracted as the data is coming from multiple tables and sources. In addition, some database programs will accept the import of already created spreadsheets, thereby avoiding the necessity to duplicate the creation of new tables and data sets. Some examples of relational database software include Microsoft Access, dBase, IBM Lotus Approach, Microsoft SQL, Oracle and FileMaker Pro.

Data Mining/Text Mining
Software is often needed for the processing of very large amounts of unstructured data. The purpose of data mining software is to "automate the process of determining patterns and relationships in extremely large volumes of information" (U.S. Dept. of Justice, 2007, p. 9). These tools are useful in complex case management that includes multiple suspects and large amounts of financial data. Data mining software is also useful in analyzing and processing large amounts of information found on social media websites, including historical and real-time events. Examples of this type of software include Dataminr, Genesis, Voyager, Penlink PLX and CellHawk.

Visualization
Visualization programs are very effective in conveying complex information in easy to understand summary charts and dashboards. With 65% of the population being visual learners (Bradford, 2004), data visualization software in law enforcement is now commonly used to display financial and other complex information through charts and diagrams. Often these applications can be used in conjunction with spreadsheets, where financial data is imported and then automatically depicted in an easy-to-read format (U.S. Dept. of Justice, 2007). The visual products that result are often helpful in

understanding complex data, identifying patterns and trends and in making more informed decisions about investigative strategy. Some data visualization tools can be used to create timelines, flowcharts, link analysis and association charts, as well as commodity flow and transaction analysis. A number of examples of visualization software include Tableau, DrawPerfect, i2 Analysts Notebook, Microsoft PowerPoint, Wordperfect Presentations and RFFlow.

Geographic Mapping

Geographic Information Systems (GIS) software can be used to map and analyze areas related to crime and other patterns, including dates, times and locations of specific events (U.S. Dept. of Justice, 2007). In terms of financial analysis, when and where monetary transactions are occurring may be pertinent to crime identification and reduction. Software is available to law enforcement which can aid in the analysis and understanding of this type of data.

For all types of computer software discussed in this chapter, there are many for law enforcement to choose from. Refer to Appendix 2 for a list of available software applications. Each agency must decide which software applications work best, with considerations given for the agency's need, the cost, resources available, the training and ability of intelligence personnel who will use the applications, and the overall goals sought through the use of the software.

Analyzing Financial Data

Once the financial information has been organized and processed, it should be analyzed by examining each set of data individually, and by comparing and contrasting the data sets to one another (Peterson, 2011). One of the ways this can be done is comparing several sets of records to one another. In a Maryland case, for example, sales tax records collected by the state government were compared to other state records for the same businesses. This resulted in an investigation and prosecution of 11 video gaming machine distributors who had claimed $13 million in income while realizing $34 million in income (Cook and Sommers, 1987, p. 1). Not only did this result in a successful prosecution, but its success led to the deterrence of others who might have committed this type of crime.

Figure 8.4

**Notional Example of Financial Analysis:
Comparison of Financial Records**

8 Video Companies Sales Tax Filings

Actual Income	Reported Income
1981-84	1981-84
$34,000,000	13,000,000

Unreported income of $21,000,000

$2,224,000 in State taxes recovered

(Source: Peterson, 2017)

This example shows how investigative work can be turned into proactive approaches. The sales tax data is collected quarterly and thus the discrepancies can be noted earlier if a 'flagging' system is installed and investigators then begin pursuing those who are responsible before large amounts are missing.

A more in-depth review of the data will lead to the identification of patterns, trends and other common threads that may exist. "A pattern is something that occurs and re-occurs, grows or lessens, or happens in cycles" (Peterson, 2009, p. 27). Monetary transactions alone may yield some valuable information including the flow of money and investigative leads, but there are other important details that may be found as well. Financial data can assist in focusing on trends relating to events, associations between people and groups, as well as criminal behavior.

A trend is a pattern seen over time (Peterson, 2009). Data analysis to reveal trends in monetary activity is useful in helping to make predictions about future transactions, as well as to explain anomalies. For example, the financial records of a suspected drug dealer show a series of large cash deposits on the weekends between Friday and Sunday evenings, at a bank branch in an area known for drug activity. The cash deposits are almost always in round numbers ranging from $2,500 to $9,000 each. Based on the analysis, a trend is identified and a prediction could be formulated asserting that this pattern of financial activity will continue.

In one investigation, records from varied companies were collected, including sales tax records, annual reports, and employee wage tax reports and these were placed in a database. As a result, discrepancies were uncovered. "Some companies, for example, reported much higher income on sales tax reports than in their annual corporate filing. They presumed, correctly, that the different state agencies to which these reports were sent would not compare notes. In other instances, companies reported wages paid which nearly equaled, or even exceeded, their reported income for that period. Clearly, they may have been underreporting their income. Another point of comparison used was the amount of income generating property held vs. the amount of reported income. One company showed almost no property from which they ostensibly made hundreds of thousands of dollars of income" (Peterson, 1985, p.4).

Anomalies are events that do not follow a previously observed pattern or trend. In the example above, if the pattern of cash deposits ceases or changes, then further analysis of the financial records might explain why. The continued review that reveals debit card purchases conducted out of state at a time when cash deposits have ceased, suggests that the suspect was out of town and was not able to make his usual cash deposits. Alternatively, if the cash deposits cease altogether then other explanations must be sought. A supplementary review of the suspect's accounts may show money being transferred from another account at a different bank into the known account. Possible reasons for the change in pattern could be that a new account was opened at another bank, the known account was about to be closed or the base of operations was relocated. As a follow-up, additional information should be taken into consideration by synthesizing the financial data with other intelligence developed through surveillance, informants or other investigative steps to assist in explaining the patterns and anomalies.

Analysis of financial transactions is also useful in isolating trends relating to events. This is often accomplished by comparing financial data sets to one another. For example, in a case involving a hypothetical organized crime group called "Mobsters, Inc." multiple financial accounts were obtained and analyzed. Together with intelligence established through other investigative means, the analysis of accounts for five suspected mob leaders yielded the following information:

- The bank account for Mobsters, Inc. shows average monthly deposits of $1.5 million, consisting primarily of cash deposits.
- The associates of Mobsters, Inc. are suspected of running an illegal gambling operation, and using the main five suspects to launder money.
- Financial analysis shows that on the first Monday of each month, credit card purchases for all five suspects are made at various restaurants, bars and parking garages throughout New York City.
- Within two days after the first Monday of each month, each suspect makes an aggregate deposit of $500,000 to his individual account, consisting of multiple smaller deposit items.
- A confidential informant has advised law enforcement that the "money guys" meet once a month to divide profits, and then the money is distributed to others.

Based on the above information, a predictive hypothesis could be formulated: "The five suspects will meet again on the first Monday of the next month somewhere in New York City, and within a few days after the meeting large deposits will be made to their individual accounts." Using this information, investigators may decide to obtain additional details from their informant, set up surveillance or an undercover operation, or even prepare an operational plan for a search warrant and the arrest of suspects. In this way, intelligence extracted through financial analysis assisted in predicting future events and helping law enforcement develop a plan going forward.

Caution should be used in relying on trends to forecast future events (Peterson, 2009). While reviewing past financial activity is helpful and can produce important information, there are a multitude of reasons why a trend might change, including simple events of daily life. For this reason, trends in financial activity should be observed with a discerning eye, by employing critical thinking and by comparison of financial data with other investigative information and leads.

Commodity Flow Analysis

Money is frequently exchanged for goods or services, making financial analysis a key component of commodity flow analysis. Commodity flow analysis shows the movement of goods, currency or services between people, groups or businesses, with a view toward defining the significance of the movement. "It can show the movement of criminal profits (e.g. money laundering), or a trail of stolen goods, or a series of dealings in which contraband (e.g. narcotics or weapons) changes hands" (Peterson, et al., 1996, p. 8). Analysis of financial data helps to identify transactions where money has been moved or exchanged. For example, money that is moved between several accounts may be evidence of money laundering. Or, wire transactions that can be linked to the sale of weapons (through other investigative means) may be an indication of weapons trafficking. It is important to note that the information used in conducting a commodity flow analysis should be drawn not just from financial analysis, but from various sources of information within the investigation, including investigation reports, surveillance summaries, confidential information, witness statements and other documents (Peterson, 1998a). Flow charts are useful in depicting the results of commodity flow analysis, especially in complex cases or criminal network operations. Once complete, the chart should be examined to derive the meaning of the information, including the identity of those who receive the largest amount of currency, the originating source and location from which the commodity flows, the hierarchy of the persons and entities involved and what information about their relationships can be observed (Peterson, 1998a). An example of a commodity flow chart is shown in Figure 8.5.

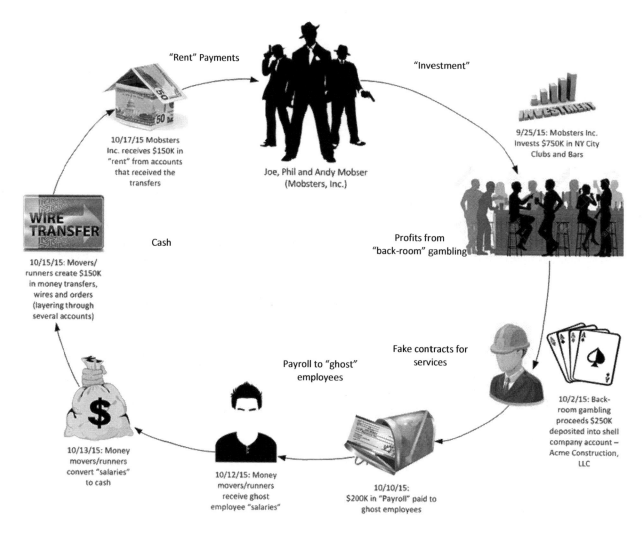

Figure 8.5 Commodity Flow Chart - (Source: Carter, 2017)

Indicator Analysis

Indicator analysis involves the gathering of information and the analysis of a particular activity in order to formulate a paradigm of what circumstances can be used to forecast the presence of that activity in another setting, location or time period (Peterson, 2009). Profiling of serial offenders often involves some aspects of indicator analysis, as the investigators try to formulate and understand an offender's method for carrying out his or her crimes. Similarly, it is possible to apply this analytical approach to financial analysis. For example, over time a list of indicators or "red flags" has been developed that may indicate money laundering is occurring. Some of those indicators include:

- *Smurfing* – breaking transactions up into smaller amounts to avoid BSA reporting
- Bank accounts in the name of shell companies, with no apparent purpose
- Lack of legitimate business expenses in account
- Use of cash payment for purchases ordinarily done by other means

- Purchases beyond apparent means
- Extra or unnecessary steps in an otherwise simple financial transaction (Association of Certified Fraud Examiners, 2008).

The indicators above might be used to flag certain individuals or businesses for further investigation. "Flagging systems are based on matching certain behaviors with previously known patterns of similar behaviors and their results" (Peterson, 2009, p. 31). In the realm of financial intelligence, if some or all of the indicators listed above are revealed as a result of analysis, it is possible that money laundering is occurring and should be further investigated. Identifying indicators may require the review of data over a period of time, with special attention given to similarities among the records; the indicators are then tested and refined (Peterson, 2009). Some indicators will be stronger than others. For example, the lack of business expenses reflected in a particular bank account may not be a valid indicator if the business has various other accounts from which expenses are or can be paid. In that case, an analysis of each data set (bank account), as well as all the business accounts together should be conducted in order to glean better insights into the financial relationships. Financial indicator analysis is a powerful tool for identifying possible crimes being committed as well as for expanding knowledge about the persons and entities involved.

Net Worth Analysis

Net worth analysis can provide information on whether a person has been living within his or her legitimate means. This analytic method was pioneered by the Internal Revenue Service in an effort to determine a taxpayer's income tax liabilities, primarily .where no books or records...have been maintained" (Nossen and Norvelle, 1993, p. 1). If the findings show substantial resources beyond reported income, it's possible the suspect obtained the surplus funds illegally. Thus, this is a pro-active method of determining participation in a criminal endeavor. It has been used to prove why assets should be seized and why a defendant was proven to be involved in an illegal activity.

To begin the analysis, a time frame should be established for the review of financial records. It is preferable to examine at least three consecutive years of finances to perform a net worth evaluation. (National White Collar Crime Center, 2011) In addition, the analysis requires the ability to obtain and review a substantial volume of financial data; the more information that is available for review, the more accurate the analysis will be. Total assets and liabilities should be established for the first year, also known as the base year. Assets consist of anything of value that is owned; liabilities are debts, financial obligations or liens. Examples of assets and liabilities are shown in Figure 8.6.

Figure 8.6 Examples of Assets and Liabilities

ASSETS	LIABILITIES
Personal Assets • Real Property • Cash (includes all bank accounts) • Personal Property (cars, furniture, jewelry, boats, motorcycles, clothing, antiques, etc.) • Stocks/bonds/retirement accounts	Personal Liabilities • Mortgages • Outstanding Loans (car loans, student loans, personal loans, etc.) • Liens against property • Credit card balances • Purchases made on credit (furniture, appliances, etc.) • Past due obligations (taxes, bills, alimony, child support, etc.)
Business Assets • Real Estate • Inventory • Equipment • Cash • Stocks/bonds • Vehicles • Accounts Receivable • Prepaid expenses (paid in advance)	Business Liabilities • Mortgages • Notes/Bonds payable • Accounts payable • Taxes Payable • Employee salary/wages (accrued expenses)

(Source: Callery, 2017)

The net worth for the base year is calculated using the formula:

TOTAL ASSETS
- <u>TOTAL LIABILITIES</u>
= **NET WORTH**

Once the net worth for the base year is calculated, the same should be done for each year that follows, while also determining the person's available income for each year. Legitimate sources of income include wages, rental property income, dividends/interest, pension and annuities, inheritance, gifts, and gambling or lottery winnings (National White Collar Crime Center, 2011). Any increase in net worth is noted from year to year and is considered income. A comparison should be made between the amount of the increase and the person's legitimate income for that year. If the increase in net worth exceeds the total legitimate sources of income for a particular year, then the difference could represent illegal sources of income received by the subject and further investigation is warranted.

One of the limitations of net worth analysis is ensuring that all financial records relating to the subject are identified and obtained for review. As shown in Figure 8.6, the types of records that document assets and liabilities can be extensive. For this reason, net worth analysis is more often used as an indicator of possible concealed income rather than an investigative tool. Even so, net worth analysis is considered an important approach in situations where there is no obvious and direct link between a target and illegal activity, wherein the target appears to be living a lavish lifestyle with a moderate income, or if corroboration of confidential information from an informant is needed (National White Collar Crime Center, 2011).

Source and Application Funds Analysis

A derivative of net worth analysis, source and application analysis examines the origins of available funds, while also comparing the amount of incoming money with the outflow of funds and how they are used. The difference between net worth and this type of analysis is that net worth examination focuses on changes in assets and liabilities, while the source and application approach studies how money is spent (Nossen and Norvelle, 1993). There are several advantages to using this method over net worth analysis, including:

- It is often easier to use and understand
- It can be used to verify the accuracy of other techniques
- It can be used when a subject has no net worth, but many cash expenditures
- The method is simple when there is minimal change in assets or liabilities (National White Collar Crime Center, 2011).

Financial records are reviewed to identify known sources of income for a specific time period. Some examples of sources of income include wages, bonuses, investment dividends, proceeds of a loan or the sale of an asset, inheritance money, gambling winnings, gifts or other windfalls (National White Collar Crime Center, 2011). Once sources of income are listed, financial records are examined to determine how funds were spent (or applied) during the same time period. Some examples of expenditures include living expenses, loan payments, credit card payments, purchases of assets (i.e. car, jewelry, etc.), and deposits to savings or retirement accounts. With knowledge of known sources of income and the application of the funds, the following formula is then applied:

TOTAL KNOWN SOURCES OF FUNDS
- TOTAL KNOWN APPLICATION OF FUNDS
FUNDS FROM UNKNOWN SOURCES

If the expenditures are greater than the known sources of funds (i.e. the end result is a negative number), then there is a question as to where the subject obtained the additional funds that were spent. The extra money represents funds from an unknown and potentially illegal source (National White Collar Crime Center, 2011). An example of Source and Application of Funds Analysis is shown in Figure 8.7.

**Figure 8.7 Source and Application Analysis Example**

Summary of Source and Application of Funds for Mario Thompson – Calendar Year 2002	
KNOWN SOURCES OF INCOME	
Wages/Salary	$65,000
Bonuses	$ 4,500
Interest on bank accounts	$ 210
Sale of 1995 Volvo	$10,000
TOTAL KNOWN SOURCES OF INCOME	$79,710
EXPENDITURES (APPLICATIONS)	
Personal living expenses	$45,000
Vacations	$ 5,500
Credit card payments	$23,400
Deposits to retirement/IRA	$35,000
Purchase diamond engagement ring	$22,500
College tuition payments (for child)	$42,800
TOTAL EXPENDITURES (APPLICATIONS)	$174,200
FUNDS FROM UNKNOWN SOURCES	
Total known sources of income	$ 79,710
- Total Expenditures	- 174,200
	($94,490)

(Source: Callery, 2017)

To avoid claims of bias, it is important to give a subject the "benefit of the doubt" and include every possible source and expenditure in the financial analysis, including any details or explanations obtained directly from the subject (National White Collar Crime Center, 2011).

Source and application analysis has many benefits over net worth analysis and is simpler to complete because only changes in sources and spending are considered for a single time period (National White Collar Crime Center, 2011).

Geographic Distribution Analysis
    The locations of criminal or other activities can often be determined through financial analysis. This approach known as geographic distribution analysis "looks at the occurrence of something over a particular geographic area to determine what can be concluded about the activity or group as a result" (Peterson, 1994, p. 46). Bank records in particular will show detailed information about the location of a deposit, a withdrawal or even a purchase made using a debit card (Peterson, 1998b). The location data

derived from financial records can then be plotted on a map (although summary form is acceptable also) where it can be examined and conclusions drawn about the activity or the persons conducting the activity. In the earlier example of the suspected drug dealer making cash deposits, we may be able to apply geographic distribution analysis. By reviewing the location of each cash deposit, we may conclude that drug activity increases in a certain area between Friday evening and Sunday afternoon. This type of analysis is similar to crime mapping and is useful in "identifying the hot spots where the policing strategies are best implemented" (Santos, 2014, p. 159). In this way, mapping financial activity can assist in identifying and understanding the "hot spots" where crime is occurring and plan appropriate police responses. In addition, by geographically mapping the locations of activity from a previously prepared commodity flow analysis, information may be obtained about the location of a group's base of operations. In fact, a geographic map or flow chart is very similar to a commodity flow chart as it can be based on the same analysis. Generally, a map is easier to read because it demonstrates the locations and distances relating to flow of money (Peterson, 1998).

   To illustrate, Figure 8.8 below is a sample of data derived from financial records which shows the dates, locations and amounts of transactions found in the account of a subject who is suspected of drug trafficking:

__Figure 8.8   Sample Financial Data__

Date	Description	Location	Zip Code	Amount
2/8/14	ATM Cash Withdrawal CVS	Heartville IL	62401	-$200
2/8/14	ATM Cash Withdrawal Walmart	Salem IL	62881	-$200
2/15/14	ATM Cash Withdrawal Pilot	Steele AR	63877	-$140
2/15/14	POS Purchase Pilot	Byltheville AR	72315	-$408
2/22/14	POS Purchase Exxon	Forest City AR	72335	-$408
2/22/14	POS Purchase McDonalds	Forest City AR	72335	-$17
2/23/14	ATM Cash Withdrawal	Carlisle, AR	72024	-$80
3/1/14	Cash Load	Arkedelphia AR	71923	$400
3/2/14	ATM Cash Withdrawal Pilot	Texarkana TX	75501	-$100
3/7/14	Cash Load	Chicago IL	60605	$450
3/8/14	ATM Cash Withdrawal	Hillsboro TX	76645	-$60
3/9/14	Cash Load	Chicago IL	60616	$650
3/9/14	POSPurchase	Waco TX	76701	-$608
3/9/14	ATM Cash Withdrawal	Waco TX	76701	-$60
3/21/14	Cash Load	Chicago IL	60608	$600
3/22/14	POS Purchase Walmart	San Antonio TX	78201	-$608
3/22/14	ATM Cash Withdrawal	Dilley TX	78017	-$100
3/23/14	ATM Cash Withdrawal Home Depot	Encinal TX	78019	-$20
3/23/14	POS Purchase	Botines TX	78045	-$17
3/25/14	POS Purchase Starbucks	La Presa TX	78046	-$17
3/30/14	POS Purchase Costco	Rio Grande City TX	78582	-$438
3/30/14	ATM CashWithdrawal	Rio Grande City TX	78582	-$120

(Source: Walton, 2017)

Using geographic mapping software, this data can be plotted to create an informative illustration of the information for law enforcement use. Figure 8.9 is the map created from the data presented.

Applying Critical Thinking

Critical thinking in financial analysis also requires drawing inferences from the data, using known information, applying common sense, and considering all possible explanations for the activities being analyzed. It should include a view toward developing alternate scenarios which might explain the behavior. Applying critical thinking to financial analysis will help to identify biases or mind-sets, while also exposing any weaknesses in the primary viewpoint. In examining the financial data, the transactions that support the primary viewpoint should be challenged; certain questions should be asked while also considering all the possible answers and explanations for the transactions. These questions may include:

- Why was the money paid?
- Who got paid?
- When was the money paid?
- Does the payment make sense?
- Why was the payment made that way?

Critical thinking is extremely valuable and should be employed in every financial analysis. When coupled with strong analytic techniques, it "will instill objectivity, imagination, and creativity in the process of analysis. It will improve the reasoning process and problem solving, challenge assumptions, help defeat bias, and overcome mind-sets in translating data into meaningful and actionable intelligence" (U.S. Department of Homeland Security, 2011, p. 55). Once armed with the skill of critical thinking and awareness of cognitive biases, the intelligence analyst or detective is ready to obtain records and fairly evaluate financial data.

Sharing Financial Data

A key tenet of intelligence-led policing is information sharing. Sharing information with investigative team members, as well as decision makers, is at the heart of using financial information to meet the goals of intelligence led policing. But presenting intelligence findings, either in report form or in an oral presentation, requires more than just restating financial facts and figures. It involves the explanation of complex information in simple form. "Sworn personnel and analysts, at all levels, must take complicated problems and investigations and put them into a form…that can be readily understood by both the specialist and generalist" (Cariens, 2011, p. 117). It is the task of intelligence staff to not only explain analytical findings but give them some context thereby providing key people with actionable intelligence.

Figure 8.9 Sample Geographic Mapping of Financial Data

3/7/14: Cash Load $450
3/9/14: Cash Load $650
3/21/14: Cash Load $600

2/8/14: ATM Cash Withdrawal CVS $-200
2/8/14: ATM Cash Withdrawal Walmart $-200

2/15/14: ATM Cash Withdrawal Pilot $-140   2/15/14: POS Purchase Pilot $-408

2/22/14: POS Purchase Exxon $-408
2/22/14: POS Purchase McDonalds $-17
2/23/14: ATM Cash Withdrawal $-80

3/1/14: Cash Load $400

3/2/14: ATM Cash Withdrawal Pilot $-100

3/8/14: ATM Cash Withdrawal $-60
3/9/14: ATM Cash Withdrawal $-60
3/9/14: POSPurchase $-608

3/22/14: POS Purchase Walmart $-608

3/22/14: ATM Cash Withdrawal $-100

3/23/14: ATM Cash Withdrawal Home Depot $-20
3/23/14: POS Purchase $-17

3/25/14: POS Purchase Starbucks $-17

3/30/14: ATM CashWithdrawal $-120
3/30/14: POS Purchase Costco $-438

(Source: Carter, 2017)

In the realm of ILP, the target audience will most likely be law enforcement leaders and decision makers. To support ILP, an intelligence assessment should focus on a relevant topic or issue with a view toward supporting a hypothesis and identifying any information gaps. "Assessments can be tactical or strategic, based upon a short-term problem and solving that problem; or a longer term analysis with recommendations for the future. They may assess current or future threats or predict future activity" (Department of Homeland Security, 2010, p. 54). A written report relating to *financial* intelligence should include the same components described above, with a focus on the allegation or hypothesis, a summary of the financial analysis, the financial evidence that supports the hypothesis, things that are still unknown and conclusions and recommendations for additional action. The format for writing an intelligence assessment may vary from agency to agency. Most formats are adequate as long as the key components are included and the report provides pertinent information to its audience. For more complex financial information, summary charts may be utilized to present information within a report. Charts should not replace the more detailed written information within a report, but may help the reader better understand financial information through visualization.

Summary/Conclusion

One of the primary goals of intelligence-led policing is crime prevention (Ratcliffe, 2011). Achieving this goal begins with developing actionable intelligence from which tactical and strategic policing decisions can be made. All forms of intelligence are vital to the goals of ILP. But financial intelligence holds a unique and essential place in this forum. Unlike many other types of analysis, examination of financial data has applications that cross over into various *other* types of criminal analysis. It can, therefore, be considered a global tool in identifying investigative leads, establishing offender associations, understanding the structure and location of crime groups and tracing the flow of commodities. Indeed, due to the monetary nature of most crimes, financial analysis is arguably the most critical piece of the intelligence process used by law enforcement professionals and leaders. By cultivating and considering sound financial intelligence, police officers and their leaders cannot only carry out the important task of identifying and apprehending offenders, but they will also have the ability to make more objective policy decisions and set policing strategies that truly address the needs of their communities.

Chapter 9 Gang Crime and ILP

By David Creagh and Alyssa Ryder

Introduction

Gangs and gang-related crimes are some of the most serious forms of violent crime in the United States today. During the 1990s, mainstream media popularized gangs to include the Bloods and Crips. Recording artists used their experiences on the streets to tell a story of their interaction with law enforcement and rival gangs while contending with the deteriorating economic situation as well as the increase in drug use.

The mysticism of gangs in the 90s has not decreased. Even today, sports icons like Serena Williams celebrated her victory on the world stage with her rendition of the "Crip-Walk." *Rolling Stone* magazine featured recording artist Little Wayne while he displayed the Piru hand sign and tucked a black and red handkerchief (colors predominantly used by the Bloods) in his back pocket.

These icons have reached audiences young and old. Children in elementary schools to adults dealing narcotics throughout U.S. inner cities aspire to be like their idols. They memorize song lyrics. They adopt behaviors portrayed in music as being socially acceptable.

Due to the popularization of gangs, law enforcement finds itself in a winless battle. Since the 1990s, gangs have become more ingrained in our society. No longer are law enforcement officers contending with the traditional Bloods and Crips, but are dealing with dozens of gangs, with memberships often relating to territory, ethnicit, crimes perpetrated, and/or criminal backgrounds.

Law enforcement officers now find themselves battling transnational gangs like La Mara-Salvatrucha, or MS-13. Prion gangs, including the Aryan Nation and Black Guerilla Family (BGF) lead a sophisticated network of drug trafficking inside the prison walls as well as the streets while employing correctional officers to smuggle contraband inside the prisons. The most notable example of this occurred in the Baltimore City Detention Center when self-proclaimed BGF leader Tayvon White alleged he ran the detention center. White had in his employ multiple female correctional officers, some of whom were pregnant, smuggling contraband to him

Outlaw motorcycle gangs (OMGs) like the Hells Angels and the Pagans still present a problem to law enforcement officers. While on the surface they may seem like a legitimate club of riders, their violent tendencies still surface to this day. On May 17, 2015, members of the Bandidos and Cossacks found themselves in a shootout in Waco, Texas leaving nine people dead. As a result of the violence, approximately 170 individuals were charged with engaging in organized crime (FoxNews, 2015).

The final classification of gangs, and probably the most difficult to target, are neighbor-hood based gangs. Just like their classification alludes to, these gangs comprise members of small neighborhoods. While these groups may be small and centralized, their violence and drug trafficking is not to be underestimated.

Unfortunately, the problem with gangs is that by the time they come to the public's attention, it becomes difficult for law enforcement to root them out of society. Eventually, law enforcement finds itself targeting them in a reactionary posture and it becomes difficult to take a proactive stance.

By utilizing intelligence-led policing (ILP) methods, law enforcement would be using a pro-active posture, rather than the reactionary posture it normally employs. Law enforcement officers and intelligence analysts would be more effective combating gangs through the use of geographic analysis, communications analysis and social media-based social network analysis. These techniques are just a few of the tools in law enforcement arsenal. As technology increases, so do the opportunities for law enforcement to reduce gang presence and violence before it can develop a stranglehold on a neighborhood.

Defining Gangs

Gang membership is not decreasing. In fact, it is growing in some areas. In the 2015 *National Gang Report*, 92 percent of the 109 agencies responding reported that street gang membership increased or remained the same over the previous two years (NGIC, 2015, p.11). Increases in motorcycle gang membership were also seen while prison gang membership has been increasing steadily over the period, with ties to domestic extremism (NGIC, 2015, p. 15).

While these numbers may be alarming to some and possibly represent a national trend, many jurisdictions could argue they do not have a gang problem. There are numerous reasons why a community may ignore the fact that gangs are present in their community. While some of the reasons may be political in nature, Barciz points out that in order to understand if a community has a gang problem, the first step is to define what a gang is. Not all gangs are going to be engaged in violence. He notes that many communities may see crime dramas depicting gangs in Chicago and Los Angeles and think their problem is, comparatively, not that bad (pp. 34, 37, 2014).

The biggest problem facing communities and law enforcement when defining gangs comes in the form of nomenclature. According to the National Institute of Justice (undated), there is no universal definition for a gang. To make matters even more problematic, the federal gang definition can differ to that of varying states' gang definitions. To compound the problem even more, different agencies, federal or state, may have adopted their own form of a gang definition.

While there may be no universal definition for gangs, many states adopted the following federal definition with minor changes:

"'Criminal street gang' means any ongoing organization, association or group of three or more persons, whether formal or informal, having as one of its primary activities the commission of one or more of the criminal acts…, having a common name or common identifying sign or symbol, and whose members individually or collectively engage in or have engaged in a pattern of criminal gang activity (National Institute of Justice, n.d.)".

The reason for the small changes in gang definition is largely due to the location and presence of gangs. Depending on an agency's location in rural America and its perceived gang problem, its definition will most likely differ to that of a major metropolitan city. Due to the uniqueness of the definitions facing the different jurisdictions, their methods to identify and validate an individual as a gang member also changes (National Institute of Justice, n.d.).

According to the National Institute of Justice (undated), they used the following criteria to classify someone as a gang member:

- The group consists of three or more members, generally between the ages of 12-24;
- Members share an identity, typically a name as well as a set of symbols;
- Members view themselves as a gang while others in the community also perceive them to be a gang;
- The group maintains some sort of permanence and an organizational structure; and
- The group is involved in some sort of criminal activity.

To fully understand why defining gangs and agreeing on a set of identifiers is important, we only need to look at two extreme ends of the spectrum when considering gangs. It should come as no surprise that the MS-13 gang is largely accepted as one. The gang is largely involved in drug trafficking, extortion and murder. When considering graffiti gangs on the other hand, major metropolitan centers may not even consider them as such.

According to the National Institute of Justice (2017), they used the following criteria to classify someone as a graffiti gang member:

"The association may also possess some of the following characteristics:

- The members may employ rules for joining and operating within the association.
- The members may meet on a recurring basis.
- The association may provide physical protection of its members from others.
- The association may seek to exercise control over a particular geographic location or region, or it may simply defend its perceived interests against rivals.
- The association may have an identifiable structure." (National Institute of Justice, 2017, p. 1).

To fully understand why defining gangs and agreeing to a set of identifiers is important, we only need to look at two extreme ends of the spectrum when considering gangs. It should come as no surprise that the MS-13 gang is largely accepted as such. The gang is largely involved in drug trafficking, extortion, and murder. When considering graffiti gangs on the other hand, major metropolitan centers may not even consider them as such.

If we use the National Institute of Justice's identifiers, then clearly some would argue a graffiti gang is a legitimate gang. It comprises three or more members between the proposed age range who have a set of symbols and identifiers associated with them. Members can place their "tags" on almost any fixed structure in an attempt to claim their territory and bring awareness to the public of their presence. Therefore, they display a sense of permanence while the community at large accepts them as a gang.

Ayres (1994) points out that "taggers" in Los Angeles views themselves as a gang although their objective was originally to claim territory through the use of their symbols. At times, rival graffiti gangs would meet to show off their artistic talent. Over time, however, some graffiti gangs turned to violence. As a result of claiming territories from rivals, taggers find themselves armed. Tagging in a rival gang's territory could result in violent assaults or murder. According to the Los Angeles Police Department, some of these gangs have escalated to burglary and robbery to add to the nuisance of vandalism.

Types of Gangs

The example in the previous section compared two opposite ends of the spectrum when attempting to understand the definition of gangs. Gangs use various methods to recruit members and advertise their criminal activities. To fully appreciate the difficulty facing law enforcement when attempting to define gangs, there needs to be a clear understanding of the different types of gangs. The basic underlying motive for all of these gangs is the furtherance of their organization through various criminal means. The uniqueness of their classification starts with whom they affect.

International Gangs

International gangs like MS-13 have taken root in numerous areas throughout the United States. Many may think of this organization as having a presences in major metropolitan cities, but the fact of the matter is MS-13 is present in almost every state. Currently, there are approximately 6,000 members in 46 states and the District of Columbia. The MS-13 gang was established in Los Angeles as immigrants fled El Salvador to escape a brutal civil war. Members of this gang were from Honduras, Guatemala, Mexico, and other Central and South American countries (CNN, 2017).

Today, MS-13, and many other Central and South American gangs routinely engage in numerous acts of violence, narcotics trafficking, and human trafficking. In September 2016, four MS-13 gang members were charged with the murders of two teenage Long Island girls. During one of their court proceedings, a federal judge informed the four they could likely face the death penalty for their crimes. While this should be alarming to the accused, one MS-13 member grinned as the family sobbed (Robbins, 2017). There have been 11 gang-related killings in central Long Island since mid-2016 (Conley, 2017). In Houston, TX, two MS-13 members were recently accused of murdering a 15year old woman in a "Satanic Ritual" (Sokmenseur, 2017).

These international gangs are not just made up of males. Many employ females to carry out duties for their organization. In Maryland, a female 18th Street gang member received approximately 25 years in federal prison for her criminal involvement with the gang. According to her plea agreement, Silvia Martinez and other fellow 18th Street members kidnapped and subsequently killed a 15-year-old who they believed to be a member of a rival gang in January 2009 (Federal Bureau of Investigation, 2012).

In February 2009, Martinez and two other gang members discussed plans to kill rival gang members in Montgomery County, Maryland. Martinez and the others eventually identified their target, approached, and shot their target dead (Federal Bureau of Investigation, 2012).

Prison Gangs

Prison gangs are another focus of law enforcement that is beginning to come into the forefront of violence and corruption. Prison gangs like the Aryan Brotherhood and the Black Guerrilla Family are easily able to run their criminal organization even under 24-hour watch. Much of this criminal activity could not be accomplished without some form of prison corruption. According to the National Gang Intelligence Center, corruption within correctional facilities continues to threaten the security and order of the U.S penal system. Inmates target vulnerable correctional officers to help facilitate their criminal enterprises. No group has taken advantage of their incarceration more than the Black Guerrilla Family (p.19, 2015).

Since 2013, it appears Baltimore has been in the spotlight for the Black Guerrilla Family as a result of the efforts of Tayvon White and his prison corruption conspiracy. However, the Black Guerrilla Family and other prison gangs throughout the country have been equally as active. In California, the leadership of the Black Guerrilla Family has been attempting to take over the cocaine distribution with Crips as their soldiers. Initially, prison gangs were formed in an effort to take over dominance inside the prisons. After members were paroled, however, their bonds with the gangs behind the walls never subsided. Instead, they would go on to continue their criminal activities to support those still behind bars (Lindsey, 1985).

In 2013, many throughout the United States awoke learning of the Black Guerrilla Family. Historically, the Black Guerrilla Family achieved their rise in the California Department of Corrections after they split from the Black Panther Army. Since that time, the organization has made its way across the United States to Baltimore in 1996. Since then, Baltimore has become synonymous with the Black Guerrilla Family (Gorilla Convict, 2015).

Throughout 2012 and 2013, it was revealed that the Black Guerrilla Family had taken control of the Baltimore City Detention by a self-proclaimed leader, Tayvon White. White and other co-conspirators had paid corrupt correctional officers to smuggle contraband into the facility. To make matters worse—and more embarrassing to the city of Baltimore—White had managed to impregnate four correctional officers during his stay at the detention center. It should not come to any surprise either that these four correctional officers were also assisting White in his scheme (Fenton, 2016).

During the course of the federal investigation, White had managed to coerce numerous correctional officers into smuggling cellular telephones, narcotics, and cigarettes into the correctional facility. Prior to the end of the case, White, in a recorded telephone conversation, stated the Baltimore City Detention Center "was his" jail (Fenton, 2016).

While much of the criminal activities surrounding White and his co-conspirators occurred in the lock up, White was able to direct other Black Guerrilla Family members to handle gang business on the streets of Baltimore. Black Guerrilla Family members on the streets of Baltimore worked in tandem with their incarcerated brethren. Those on the street earning for the gang were required to pay fees, sometimes through extortion. According to one former inmate, if a high-level earner was weak, the gang would take that individuals family for ransom until they received payment from the earner (Toobin, 2014).

Outlaw Motorcycle Gangs

Many Americans have been infatuated with the idea of the wind in their face and the freedom of the open road. Because of that, like-minded motorcycle riders have chosen to join the many motorcycle clubs throughout the country. According to Springer, motorcycle clubs were first established once Indian manufactured the first motorcycle in 1901. As time progressed for the motorcycle enthusiasts, so did the way their clubs operated. Today, the main questions for motorcycle clubs are whether motorcycle clubs happen to have criminals in their ranks or are they devoted to carrying out criminal acts (2014, p.1)

The motorcycle gang culture was widely popularized well before the television series "Sons of Anarchy." Problems with motorcycle gangs can be traced as far back as 1937 when Wino Willi Forkner joined the 13 Rebels Motorcycle Club. Following the United States entry into World War II, Forkner traded in his motorcycle for a .50 caliber machine gun aboard the B-24 Liberator. Following his service in the war, Forkner returned to 13 Rebels; however, he had more aggression in him most likely from the war. Forkner would eventually be arrested in San Diego during a race which authorities disrupted (Barker, 2010, p.3).

Following Forkner's arrest, he and three other fellow veterans went on to establish the Boozefighters Motorcycle Club. Soon after, clubs such as the Galloping Gooses, Satan Sinners, and the Pissed Off Bastards of Bloomington were created by veterans. This group of rowdy riders would give rise to the term "one percenters"[42] (Barker, 2014, p.4).

As the decades progressed, so did the expansion of motorcycle clubs—some more violent than others. According to Barker, biker experts agreed that five motorcycle gangs were to be considered criminal gangs. They included: Hells Angels, Pagans, Mongols, Bandidos, and the Sons of Silence (2014, p. 25).

As time marched on, so did the evolution of the motorcycle gangs. What was once a group of rowdy motorcycle enthusiasts evolved into a more violent type of gang. On May 17, 2015, members of the Bandidos and Cossacks found themselves in a shootout in Waco, Texas leaving nine people dead. As a result of the violence, approximately 170 individuals were charged with engaging in organized crime (FoxNews, 2015).

Membership initiation into these organizations is rigorous. According to William Queen (2015), aspirants fill out applications detailing every detail about their life, which could include family members and work history. Only after this membership form is filled out would groups then have private detectives, usually full patched members themselves, conduct a thorough background check.

---

[42] "One percenters" refer to the one percent of motorcycle gangs members who are determined to be violent and dangerous, while the vast majority (99 percent) of motorcycle riders are law-abiding citizens.

Neighborhood-Based Gangs

The National Gang Intelligence Center, states that neighborhood-based gangs and national-level based gangs are the biggest threat to communities throughout the United States. These types of gangs vary in size as well as ethnicity. Gangs are opportunistic and seek out many different ways to earn money and gain notoriety. The biggest source of income for gangs is narcotics distribution. In order to corner the market on the drug trade, gangs often resort to violence against rival gang members (NGIC, 2015, p.11).

When not engaged in a gang war, gangs may form the unlikeliest of alliances in order to further their criminal enterprises or take advantage of a public relations angle. As long as both gangs are profiting from the alliance, it would be far more beneficial to cooperate and earn money than be feuding. Following the death of Freddie Gray in Baltimore, enraged Baltimoreans took to the streets of the western district and rioted. Since "Black Lives Matter" was the central issue of the riots, members of the Bloods, Crips, and the Black Guerrilla Family declared a truce in order to protect their community (Khimm, 2015).

In fact, the National Gang Intelligence Center reported that 43 percent of jurisdictions with gang problems saw rival gangs forming alliances. In San Diego, members of the Black MOB, Skanless, Neighborhood Crips, Lincoln Park, and West Coast Crips allied and trafficked female prostitutes in 46 cities across 23 states (2015, pp. 12-13).

One of the major misconceptions about neighborhood-based gangs is the perception that they are not in almost every community. Even in the most rural communites gangs can be formed. The problem with many communities, however, is that they do not want to admit they may have a gang problem. This could largely be the result of not having enough knowledge and understanding of gangs. It could also be the result of not wanting to have a stigma associated with their community. The fact of the matter is, gangs are everywhere.

In 2011, a Baltimore grand jury handed down 35 indictments for members belonging to the South Side Brims. The South Side Brims was a Bloods based gang out of Frederick, Maryland and had a foothold throughout all of Maryland. According to the indictment, members of this faction engaged in murder, home invasions, robberies, shootings, and drug distribution. What made this investigation unique, however, is that many of the members of the South Side Brims broke away from the traditional stereotype of being an all-black gang. Many of its members were white, most likely causing the community to feel they did not have a gang problem (Federal Bureau of Investigation, 2011).

Proactive Gang Policing

Up until now, much has been described in the various gangs that plague our communities, however, not much has been said on how intelligence-led policing can be used to combat these criminal organizations

Intelligence analysts use geospatial analysis to develop creative ways to track emerging trends and provide realistic warning analysis to policy-makers. Through the use of various sophisticated geospatial information systems (GIS), analysis can produce intelligence to help direct investigations. One major aspect of gang activity is its geographic spread.

Geospatial intelligence, or GEOINT, can trace its roots back to George Washington as well as Meriweather Lewis and William Clark's exploration of the Northwest Territory. Fast forward to the John F. Kennedy administration, GEOINT was pivotal in the discovery of Soviet missiles in Cuba sparking 13 days of fear which were soon referred to as the Cuban Missile Crisis (National Geospatial Intelligence Agency, undated).

During the late 90s, GEOINT was crucial in Kosovo in uncovering ethnic cleansing atrocities and providing much-needed analysis after Hurricane Katrina. That said, while GEOINT provides valuable intelligence in wartime and natural disasters, how could it be used to aid law enforcement in their venture to combat violent crimes (Murrett, 2007)?

According to analysts at Crime Tech Solutions, understanding where and when crimes occur can assist in preventing future crimes. Using GEOINT to further geospatial criminal mapping can allow an agency to better focus on particular neighborhoods experiencing an influx of gang-related crime. In doing so, it allows the agency to dedicate more resources to said neighborhoods to respond to the problem areas in the short-term, while analysts and law enforcement officers use various intelligence-led policing approaches, to include community-oriented policing, to understand the root causes of the problem (Crime Tech Solutions, 2015).

Geospatial intelligence provides more than just density maps to law enforcement executives when determining where to increase patrols. Analysts can use this method of intelligence to combat drug trafficking, auto theft, and other forms of crime in which violent gangs engage. By understanding where and when certain crimes are occurring, analysts can use these indicators to anticipate future crimes and ultimately become proactive in prosecuting violent gangs (esri, 2011).

Gangs are known to defend their territories to the death. The map below, created by the Los Angeles Police Department, is reflective of the territories of over 40 gangs in that city. This map shows jurisdictions in Southern California creating the nation's first gang injunctions—civil court orders against alleged members of a gang. The injunctions prohibit alleged gang members within set geographic areas ("safety zones") from engaging in otherwise legal activities, such as associating with other alleged members, being in public at night, and/or carrying a cell phone. This is one aspect of using known data on gangs to reduce the level of criminal activities in which they are engaged in a proactive manner (University of Southern California, 2014).

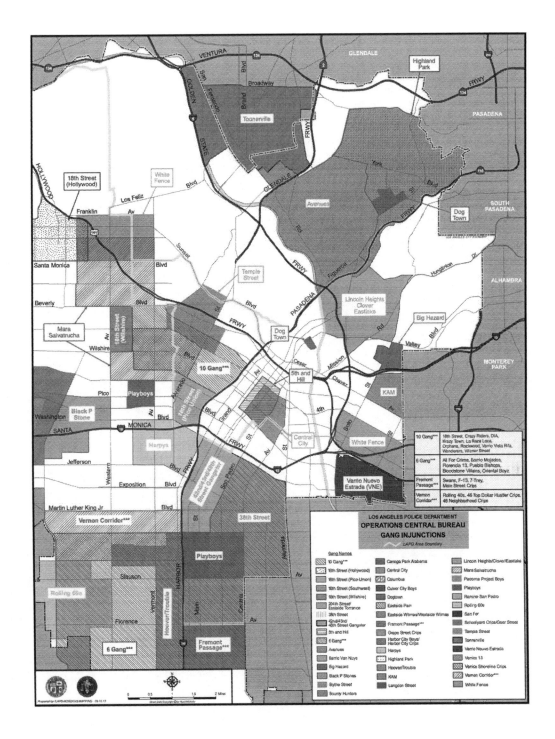

Figure 9. 1: Los Angeles Gangs (Source: Los Angeles Police Department, 2017)

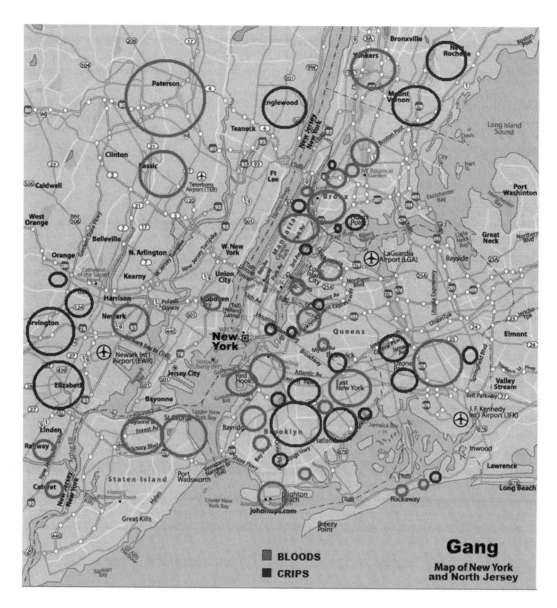

Figure 9.2: Gang Map of New York and North Jersey.
(Source: https://sites.google.com/site/redgangsandblue/the-bloods-and-the-crips/home, 2017)

This second map shows Bloods and Crips territories in the New York City area. The sizes of the circles involved are reflective of the size of gang membership in that area. The largest circle appears to be in Paterson, NJ, which is counter-intuitive to the belief that the strongest gang membership areas should be in the most urban area (the five boroughs of New York).

The third map depicts gangs in Chicago, IL. It includes the locations of five major gangs in that city, with representation of other, smaller gang activity not identified by name.

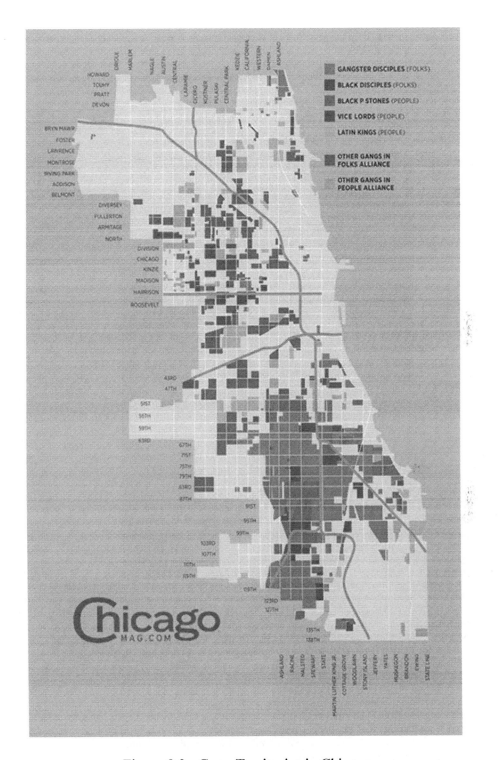

Figure 9.3: Gang Territories in Chicago
(Source: https://www.reddit.com/r/chicago/comments/5mpasz/map_of_gangs_in_chicago/, 2017)

Using such maps to determine areas of gang occupation, police can proactively determine what areas are likely to spark disputes over territory. For example, the Gangster Disciples appear to occupy a great deal of territory in southern Chicago, while the Vice Lords appear to be a dominant force in parts of northern Chicago. The Latin Kings occupy a middle space between them. However, in some areas, there appear to be pockets of opposing gangs in the middle of broader dominant gang space. How likely is there for violence or opposition to be appearing in those pockets?

Intelligence-led policing looks at those types of examples, as well as others. If we had maps reflecting block control by quarter or half-year for several years, the movement of the gangs could be more clearly seen. If their direction of control were determined, proactive measures could be taken to impede their march into new territories.

Social Networks, Social Media and Gangs

Regardless what type of gang is being investigated, the approaches to becoming proactive should be similar. When investigating these criminal organizations, it is essential for investigators and analysts to construct the organizations's hierarchy and leadership. This can be accomplished in myriad ways; however, telephone record analysis and social media analysis are becoming key to uncovering the social construct.

According to Heuer and Pherson, "network analysis is the review, compilation, and interpretation of data to determine the presence of associations among individuals, groups, businesses or other entities; the meaning of those associations to the people involved; and the degrees and ways in which those associations can be strengthened or weakened" (2015, p. 68).

Not only can network analysis establish the hierarchy for a criminal organization, but it can also establish an individual or an organization's pattern of behavior. This too can reveal, but is not limited to, travel, financial transactions, and other interactions not readily available from one single source of information (Heuer and Pherson, 2015, p. 78).

Communications Analysis

One way to construct an organization's network is through the use of communication analysis. Communications analysis is a broad term; however, it yields the same results. It not only uncovers an organizational structure, but it can also reveal certain calling patterns which can allow law enforcement to become more proactive. Whether an analyst or law enforcement officer is exploiting an individual's cellular call detail records or their online exchanges, a network of communication patterns emerge. (See Chapter 5 for more detail on communication analysis.)

While this method of analysis provides information on patterns and connectivity, it does have one major limitation. While a network chart can show you the hierarchy of an organization and show calling patterns, it will not divulge the intentions of the criminal group. That is not to say that communications analysis should be ignored. Through the use of this analytical method, investigators can identify those individuals of a criminal conspiracy that can have a long-lasting effect on dismantling the organization or severely hindering it. This is accomplished through eigenvector centrality, a term used in social network analysis.

Understanding how eigenvector centrality works can assist intelligence analysts and law enforcement officers in making the best educated choice in targeting a criminal enterprise. Without a clear understanding of this concept, unnecessary time can be used targeting low-level drug dealers while, with a little more effort, an individual on the organization's next level might have a more effective impact.

What does it mean to an analyst to identify someone in a social network with a high eigenvector score. According to Newman, the eigenvector system acknowledges that not all nodes or connections are equal, unlike a measure of centrality. Centrality focuses solely on how many connections a vortex has. Eigenvector on the other hand looks as the central node and determines how much influence it has on surrounding connections (2008, p. 4).

To put this theory into practice, one respondent in a Nix, Smith, Petrocelli, Rojek and Manjarrez study found he had the highest eigenvector score since he was closely linked to nine associates (2016, p 410). A law enforcement professional educated and armed with this concept can have a detrimental effect on a criminal organization.

Social Media Intelligence

While numerous efforts allow law enforcement to become proactive in targeting gangs, constructing a social network of a gang is key. Prior to the creation of social media sites like Facebook and Instagram, law enforcement was already using various methods to understand a gang's organizational structure. Thanks to the advances in social media, law enforcement now has the ability to outsmart gangs due to the arrogance of gang members.

Additionally, social media exploitation allows us to understand which nodes of the organization to target in order to have the greatest affect in dismantling the organization. While it is critical to understand how an organization is structured and functions, it is equally important to understand which nodes of the organization to target to have the highest potential of dismantling the organization. Not only does this method of analysis provide investigators with vital organizational information, it is probably the first method of analysis that results in intent and actionable intelligence.

Since their advent, gangs have sought out different ways to project their image and recruit. This advantage allows law enforcement to retain social media postings necessary to secure convictions when it comes time for trials. Another advantage to social media is it allows law enforcement officers and intelligence analysts to uncover a deeper social network within these criminal organizations.

Criminal organizations have always looked to technology to increase their awareness and prominence. During the early days of social media, these were somewhat limited but today there are a plethora of social media sites at their disposal. This was largely due to the number of social media platforms, nimble wireless and mobile technology. That, coupled with the creation of smart phones and tablets, social media are now limitless as new and improved applications are created every day (Nix, Smith, Petrocelli, Rojek and Manjarrez, 2016, p. 397).

Social Media as a Recruiting Tool

During a 2007 study, it was reported that approximately 45 percent of gang members used the Internet. Fast forward to 2011, that number increased to 82 percent. Of that 82 percent, 71 percent of respondents were actively using Facebook or Myspace. Numerous studies, however, found that social networking sites were not actively used as a recruitment tool. Instead, gangs would use these sites to advertise their strength and prominence as well as brag about criminal activities (Nix, Smith, Petrocelli and Manjarrez, 2016, p. 397).

This can be argued, however, as these posts are still a means to recruit members. Many times, gangs target vulnerable members with a sense of family and success. Some gangs will resort to fear when recruiting new members, while others will provide cigarettes, alcohol, and drugs to the potential gang members. Additionally, social media allows vulnerable youth to see the good side to being in a gang. Many times, the youths are shown the successes of being a member of a gang and given a sense of family and unity. For some growing up in an urban environment without strong positive role models in the home this may appear to be a promising solution. While many of these studies claim social media was not a recruitment device and gangs do not actively address recruitment in social media posts, social media posts displaying violence, unity, and wealth, thereby serving as a de facto recruitment tool for impressionable and vulnerable youth (Office of the Attorney General of Florida, 2009).

Social Media's Role in Intelligence

With the advances of social media, law enforcement can develop a better understanding of gangs and potentially be in a position to thwart criminal activities. Berhman argued that while social media can be used retroactively and provide prosecution valuable evidence needed for a conviction, this method of exploitation should not be overlooked for its proactive approaches. As an example, law enforcement officers and analysts who rely on social media may uncover a gang's willingness to participate in a violent plan (2015, p. 321).

Not only is social media valuable for gangs to use as a recruitment tool, but social media provides a platform for violent gang members to coordinate and plan their criminal activities. Violent individuals and gang members living inside violent neighborhoods rely on social media to fuel conflicts between individuals and other gangs. These individuals use social media as a means to advertise their violence while insulting or threatening rivals. This harassment has been termed "Internet banging" (Paton, Lane, Leonard, Macbeth and Smith-Lee, 2016, p. 2).

Gakirah Barnes was affectionately known as the "teen queen of Chicago's gangland." Barnes was a model youth for recruitment into a gang. Barnes grew up fatherless in the Woodlawn neighborhood of Chicago. Her father was shot and killed prior to her first birthday. In fact, Barnes was routinely exposed to violence. Barnes eventually met a group of Gangster Disciples. From the age of 14 to 17 years old, Barnes established herself as a prominent gang member (Paton, Lane, Leonard, Macbeth and Smith-Lee, 2016, p. 4).

On March 29, 2014, a close friend of hers was shot and killed during an encounter with the Chicago police. Following the shooting death of her friend, Barnes changed her Twitter name to

@TyquanAssassin to honor her friend. In April, Barnes carelessly posted a photo to her account showing herself and other gang members sitting in front of a residence frequented by other Gangster Disciples members. Following her post, Barnes was murdered close to this location (Paton, Lane, Leonard, Macbeth and Smith-Lee, 2016, p. 4).

Armed with this knowledge, law enforcement officers could have identified the area as a known Gangster Disciple location. This intelligence could have allowed the area to be more closely watched. If law enforcement had responded quickly, they may have been in the position to stop Barnes' murder.

In 2015, the social media group Geofeedia alerted the Baltimore Police to an increase in social media activity prior to the Baltimore riots following the death of Freddy Gray. In April of that year, Freddy Gray was detained by Baltimore Police officers. Subsequent to his arrest, Gray suffered injuries that ultimately led to his death. In response to Gray's death, western Baltimore erupted in a violent riot. Thanks to social media, the Baltimore Police and city officials were alerted well in advance. Geofeedia uncovered a high volume of chatter where Baltimore's youth planned to protest following the conclusion of their school day. What resulted was anything but a protest. Baltimore Police officers took the information and were able to intercept many youths who were armed with rocks and bricks heading toward the area of Mondawmin Mall in Baltimore's western district (Cush, 2016).

Since the days of Myspace, social media analysis significantly evolved. Much of the social media analysis that was conducted focused on keyword searches. While keyword searches still provide vital intelligence, early on analysts missed the opportunity to use social media to build a social construct of criminal organizations. That is what Nix, Smith, Petrocelli, Rojek, and Manjarrez pointed out. Their analysis of social media focused on the network (2016, p. 399).

They revealed that collecting on someone's publicly available social media site could yield a wealth of knowledge. Analysts and law enforcement officers could uncover an individual's travel pattern, residence, and rank within the gang. According to their study, Nix, Smith, Petrocelli, Rojek, and Manjarrez found that 63 percent of gang members indicated their rank and/or occupation. A number of these members openly identified themselves as 'sicarios', or 'hitmen' (2016, p.405).

Armed with this information, law enforcement could establish and maintain databases housing vital information on gang members. This information would be at the investigators fingertips and allow immediate access to last known addresses and familial relationships in the event the gang member is wanted. Additionally, tattoos can provide proof of someone's gang affiliation (Behrman, 2015 p. 321).

Conclusion

No matter which gang, or type of gang a law enforcement agency may be investigating, intelligence-led policing should be at the forefront of every investigator's and analyst's mind. In past investigations, law enforcement officers may have partially been using intelligence-led policing. Constructing social networks through common call analysis or social media could be seen as the first step in the equation. Understanding how to have a bigger impact on a social network through the use of eigenvector centrality would allow investigators and analysts to make a more calculated decision on who would have a crucial impact in the dismantling of a gang.

With the evolution of social media, it has become easier for investigators and analysts to identify these social networks, understand a gang's hierarchy, and become proactive. While an investigator can use social media as a basis to establish his case reactively, he or she could immediately transition to a proactive stance as was the case for Baltimore Police Department during the Freddie Gray riots.

No matter what type of gang is being investigated, social media can be used. As law enforcement professionals, we are taught to maintain a very low persona on line. Many in the law enforcement community see this as away to not be targeted themselves. This mindset must change, however. As social media advances, so too do the gangs. In order to become proactive, we must embrace social media smartly and understand how we can exploit it to become intelligence led.

From the birth of the United States, geospatial intelligence has provided analysts in all disciplines with another means to view daily problems. While some in the law enforcement community may view crime mapping as nothing more than density maps to allocate resources to problem areas, it can allow analysts to better understand shifts in gang crime and use those indicators as a means to forecast have a positive impact on gang crime trends.

Chapter 10: National Security and Intelligence

By David Gervais

Introduction

On April 15, 2013 the iconic Boston Marathon forever changed when the Tsarnaev brothers placed two pressure cooker bombs near the start line (O'Neill, 2015). On December 2, 2015, Syed Rizwan Farook and Tashfeen Malik killed and injured their colleagues at a San Bernardino County, California Department of Public Health holiday party (Schmidt and Perez-Pena, 2015). On November 28, 2016, one Ohio State University student was killed and 11 were wounded by a Somali student, Abdul Razak Ali Artan (Smith, Perez-Pena and Goldman, 2016). On January 6, 2017, an attack at the Ft. Lauderdale, FL, airport killed five. Esteban Santiago said he carried out the Florida attack for ISIS (Sanchez and Conlon, 2017).

These incidents reflect a national security issue that requires support of both federal and local law enforcement agencies as well as both national security and law enforcement intelligence. Although the prevention of all incidents such as these may not be possible, decision makers and operational elements of law enforcement applying the right resources and with proper support from both national and law enforcement intelligence can prevent most from occurring. This chapter discusses national security issues and the differences and similarities between both national security intelligence and law enforcement intelligence. The chapter also discusses how national security intelligence and law enforcement intelligence support each other through various information sharing systems. The primary purpose of this chapter is to provide analysts with an overview of analytic techniques used by both national security intelligence and law enforcement intelligence in support of national security issues. Security issues such as terrorism affect countries globally, not just the United States, with the November 13, 2015 Paris attacks, the March 22, 2016 Brussels Airport attack and the May 22, 2017, Manchester, UK attack as grim examples. The analytic techniques described in this chapter may be utilized by law enforcement intelligence analysts internationally. This chapter however will look at the application of the analytic techniques from the perspective of the United States.

National Security Issues that Require Law Enforcement Intelligence Support

Across the United States, federal, state and local law enforcement agencies coordinate on multiple criminal issues including organized crime, narcotics trafficking, smuggling, fugitive tracking, etc. At times, criminal investigations are entwined with national security threats requiring coordination amongst law enforcement agencies, as well as intelligence support to investigations. There are a multitude of threats that are deemed by the United States as national security threats. National security issues that require law enforcement intelligence support at various levels are counter-terrorism (CT), counterintelligence (CI), weapons of mass destruction (WMD) and counter-proliferation (CP), smuggling, and counter-narcotics. The Federal Bureau of Investigation (FBI) is the primary federal agency tasked with counter-terrorism, counterintelligence and weapons of mass destruction and counter-proliferation. Immigration and Customs Enforcement (ICE) is the primary federal agency tasked with investigating smuggling. Smuggling issues range from humans, bulk cash, firearms, explosives, ammunition, and possibly counterfeit goods.   The Drug Enforcement Administration (DEA) is the primary federal agency tasked with counter-narcotics. The integration of law enforcement intelligence with national security investigations is an important component in addressing national security threats. The coordination of law enforcement agencies and law enforcement intelligence in support of national security intelligence assists in driving investigations, identifying threats, allocating resources and enhancing information sharing.

Defining National Security Intelligence

Prior to understanding the types of analytic techniques and tools available for law enforcement intelligence analysts in support of national security intelligence (NSI), we must first have an understanding of what national security intelligence is and the similarities and differences between both NSI and Law Enforcement Intelligence (LEI). Intelligence is the analysis and assessment of information collected by various means utilized to inform customers and decision-makers. In terms of national security, intelligence is utilized to protect United States' sovereign principles from threats that emerge from foreign governments, organizations or individuals who seek to undermine or destroy the United States and/or the pillars that support United States sovereignty (Carter, 2012). Issues such as terrorism, narcotics, and proliferation that pose a threat to national security are associated with various crimes. However the Intelligence Community, with the exception of portions of the FBI, DEA and DHS, are not always concerned about criminal prosecution and utilize intelligence to support policy and security actions that protect the United States from threats (Carter, 2012). Now that we have a baseline understanding of what national security intelligence is, let's examine some of the similarities and differences between national security intelligence and law enforcement intelligence.

Similarities of National Security Intelligence and Law Enforcement Intelligence

Although national security intelligence supports United States foreign and security policies while law enforcement intelligence supports criminal investigations, there are some similarities between the two. One similarity is that both types of intelligence support the identification of homeland and national security threats. Both produce analysis and assessment products that are utilized by the customer to make key and timely decisions. There are analytic standards that ensure that products are completed in an ethical manner. They have an intelligence process/cycle to manage the collection and flow of information and use a scientific approach to problem solving for intelligence analysis (Carter, 2012). When information is collected from sources for both national security and law enforcement intelligence, there are practices in place to protect the sources of the information. Both types of intelligence utilize databases to store information and for analysts to obtain and share that information. Perhaps the most important similarity is that both national security and law enforcement intelligence seek to provide security to the United States and its communities (Carter, 2012).

Differences between National Security Intelligence and Law Enforcement Intelligence

National security and law enforcement intelligence share similar factors in definitions of terms, however there are differences in how both types of intelligence are obtained and utilized. There are significant differences in the mission, priorities, permissible processes, constitutional restrictions and roles of LEI and NSI (Carter, 2012). Perhaps two key factors that separate both national security intelligence and law enforcement intelligence are authority and civil liberties. Law enforcement legally utilizes intelligence activity based on their statutory authority to enforce the criminal law (Carter, 2012). The other, and one of the most important and controversial aspects of law enforcement intelligence, is significantly less of an issue to the Intelligence Community: the protection of privacy, civil liberties and civil rights (Carter, 2012). Terminology is also a differentiating factor between national security intelligence and law enforcement intelligence. Though both types of intelligence may use similar terminology or vocabulary, those terms or words will have different meanings based on their usage.

Another factor that differentiates national security intelligence from law enforcement intelligence is their differing goals. Within the Intelligence Community, there are multiple intelligence agencies that use varying types of intelligence collection, analysis, assessment products and dissemination methods. However, all of it comes together for one common goal, which is the support of decision makers to rely heavily on products from Intelligence Community agencies to make important decisions about U.S. national security (Carter, 2012). Law enforcement agencies share a common goal of minimizing or preventing criminal threats across communities. However, these goals differ based on the agency and its priorities. Intelligence collection in support of national security and law enforcement is another key difference between the two entities. The Posse Comitatus Act of 1867 effectively prevents U.S. military entities from engaging in domestic law enforcement (Bayer, 2010). The National Security Act of 1947, which created the Central Intelligence Agency (CIA), along with the Foreign Intelligence Surveillance Act of 1978, the Church/Pike Committee hearings, the Levi Guidelines, and United States Signals Intelligence Directives all effectively preclude intelligence agencies from conducting intelligence activities in the United States or targeting U.S. citizens (Bayer, 2010). At the same time, law enforcement agencies have been restricted to the domestic arena (Bayer, 2010).

How intelligence is utilized in support of law enforcement and national security is another area that separates the two. Law enforcement intelligence provides support and products based on an analytic process that provides an integrated perspective to disparate information about crime, crime trends, crime and security threats, and conditions associated with criminality (Carter, 2009). Intelligence in support of national security is the collection and analysis of information concerned with the relationship and homeostasis of the United States with foreign powers, organizations, and persons with regard to political and economic factors as well as the maintenance of the United States' sovereign principles (Carter, 2009). One final difference that separates both national security intelligence and law enforcement intelligence is constitutionality. Law enforcement intelligence in support of criminal investigations has constitutional restrictions applied in terms of information collection, records retention, and use of information in a raw capacity, that do not apply to the Intelligence Community where there is no criminal investigation (Carter, 2009).

Law Enforcement in Support of National Security Intelligence

Given the differences between both law enforcement intelligence and national security intelligence, as well as the role of both law enforcement agencies and Intelligence Community agencies, how can law enforcement intelligence support national security investigations into security threats? There are two ways that LEI can support NSI, one is through collection and the other is through prevention and planning.

The first way that law enforcement intelligence can support national security intelligence is through collection. There are multiple police agencies at the federal, state and local level with officers interacting with the community on a daily basis. In the course of performing their daily duties, officers are exposed to a vast amount of information. Untold, untapped quantities of information exist within their reports that, if analyzed, could help solve many crimes, help direct efforts to prevent crime, and possibly help find and/or connect some of the dots to help prevent terrorist acts in the United States (Bayer, 2010). Officers know their respective communities, which places them in a unique position to gain awareness of the citizens and citizen lifestyles. They have an understanding and working knowledge of their respective functional areas, therefore making them well suited for spotting suspicious activity.

The second way is through prevention and planning. Law enforcement intelligence, in a similar fashion to national security intelligence, provides intelligence products that support decision-making at the strategic, operational and tactical levels. Prevention involves gaining or developing information related to threats of terrorism or crime and using it to apprehend offenders, harden targets, and use strategies that will eliminate or mitigate the threat (Carter, 2009). Operational and tactical level intelligence products produced by law enforcement intelligence can assist decision makers in prevention plans and policies. Operational level intelligence products provide actionable intelligence about long-term threats that is used to develop and implement preventive responses (Carter, 2009). Tactical level intelligence products provide actionable intelligence about imminent or near-term threats that is disseminated to the line functions of a law enforcement agency for purposes of developing and implementing preventive, and/or mitigating, response plans and activities (Carter, 2009). Along with prevention, decision makers rely on intelligence products for planning purposes. Planning and resource allocation provides information to decision-makers about the changing nature of threats, the characteristics and methodologies of threats, and emerging threat idiosyncrasies for the purpose of developing response strategies and reallocating resources, in order to accomplish effective prevention (Carter, 2009). Intelligence produced by law enforcement at the strategic level assists decision makers with planning processes. Strategic level intelligence products provide an assessment of the changing threat picture to the management of a law enforcement agency for purposes of developing plans and allocating resources to meet the demands of emerging threats (Carter, 2009).

National Security Intelligence in Support of Law Enforcement Intelligence
One primary way that national security intelligence can support law enforcement intelligence is through information sharing. Intelligence agencies in the Intelligence Community have access to information via their collection capabilities and authorities that law enforcement agencies do not. After the September 11, 2001 attacks on the United States, a principal recommendation by the 9/11 Commission was information sharing between intelligence agencies and law enforcement. The Intelligence Reform and Terrorism Prevention Act (IRTPA) mandated the creation of an Information Sharing Environment (ISE) that provides the technologies, procedures, policies, and standards for sharing terrorism related information among federal, state, and local jurisdictions (AFCEA, 2007). As a result of the USA PATRIOT Act, there now exist elements and procedures through which this information can be evaluated and shared (Bayer, 2010).

To assist with information sharing between the Intelligence Community and law enforcement agencies, the National Counterterrorism Center (NCTC) was established, the FBI expanded Joint Terrorism Task Forces (JTTFs) and the DHS increased funding towards the creation of fusion centers. The NCTC was created to help assure the flow of information to law enforcement agencies (AFCEA, 2007). Within the FBI's JTTFs federal, state, and local agencies have assigned officers to the JTTFs to help coordinate intelligence and law enforcement operations across bureaucratic lines (Waxman, 2009). The Department of Homeland Security funds state-operated fusion centers to synthesize law enforcement and investigative information (Waxman, 2009). Unlike the JTTFs, which help manage operations of participating agencies, the fusion centers operate as information clearinghouses (Waxman, 2009). Programs such as the JTTFs, centers like the NCTC and fusion centers in support of strategic, operational and tactical level intelligence, enable effective information sharing in support of national security threats.

Federal agencies that perform national security intelligence with the intent of mitigating threats have multiple resources for law enforcement agencies and law enforcement intelligence analysts to utilize. The FBI operates the Terrorist Screening Center with the Consolidated Terrorist Screening Database, Law Enforcement Online, Guardian and E-Guardian. Along with the supporting fusion centers, the DHS also has the Homeland Security Information Network (HSIN) and the Homeland Security State and Local Intelligence Community of Interest. The U.S. Congress appropriates funds to the Regional Information Sharing System (RISS) which operates an intelligence database (RISSNET) and the Automated Trusted Information Exchange. The DEA sponsors the El Paso Intelligence Center (EPIC) and, in the past, the National Drug Intelligence Center which provided National Drug Threat Assessments. The U.S. Congress as part of the Anti-Drug Abuse Act of 1988 created High Intensity Drug Trafficking Areas (HIDTAs). The Federal Protective Service (FPS) sponsors Secure Portal in support of threat and risk assessments to facilities. The Department of the Treasury operates the Financial Crimes Enforcement Network (FinCEN) with databases such as the financial records database, commercial databases and a law enforcement database. Another resource of FinCEN is the High Intensity Financial Crime Areas (HIFCAs). The ATF sponsors the National Field Office Case Information System with two databases, N-FORCE and N-SPECT, which are case management databases in support of law enforcement investigations for firearms, explosives, ammunition and arson.

Types of Analysis Techniques Utilized for National Security Issues and Intelligence
Intelligence analysts, whether for law enforcement or for national security, have a wide range of analytic techniques available to them in order to produce assessments. Analytic techniques utilized by analysts for national security intelligence are the same as those techniques and tools utilized by law enforcement analysts. Techniques such as threat, link and flow analysis are utilized by both national security intelligence and law enforcement intelligence. With the exception of why it is being applied and for what it is being applied too, these analytical techniques are similar in function. Some analytical approaches including denial and deception analysis or indications and warnings analysis are used by national security intelligence analysts; however they can be applied to law enforcement intelligence. There are some analytical techniques such as financial analysis and commodity flow analysis that are utilized by law enforcement intelligence; but they have now been integrated into national security intelligence. The rest of this chapter will list analytic techniques that can be applied by law enforcement intelligence analysts in support of national security threats. Some techniques have been referenced in

previous chapters, therefore this chapter will provide a quick overview for analytic techniques previously mentioned, and focus on analytic techniques that have not.

Analytic Techniques Used by Both National Security Intelligence and Law Enforcement Intelligence

Threat Analysis: Two types of analytic techniques that are of great value to law enforcement intelligence analysts involved in anti-terrorism investigations are threat analysis and vulnerability analysis. Vulnerability analysis will be covered in a following section. Threat analysis assesses the scale of risks posed by individual offenders or organizations to individual potential victims, the general public, and to law enforcement agencies (Carter, 2009). Threat analysis and threat assessments can benefit decision makers at the tactical, operational, and strategic level; but are primarily conducted in support of strategic level planning. Intelligence analysts conducting threat analysis assess the potential of a terrorist or criminal organization to conduct a terrorist/criminal act against a likely target. This in turn helps decision makers at the strategic level to develop policies, prioritize law enforcement requirements and allocate resources. Upon completion of a threat analysis, an assessment can be produced that helps decision makers at the tactical, operational, and strategic level form plans to prevent or minimize the threat occurring from terrorism. Analysts can perform threat analysis for singular events or for recurring threats, such as annual threat reports on terrorist organizations. When conducting threat analysis, common factors for an analyst to examine are the intentions, past activities and current capabilities of a terrorist or criminal organization. Data that an analyst will want to gather in support of threat analysis is information on the possibility of the threat occurring, a projected time frame for the threat, and possible target(s) (Peterson, 1994).

During the course of analysis, analysts will want to be aware of indicators that will affect the threat assessment. Indicators to evaluate are political, economic and social data that affect the likelihood of a terrorist organization wanting to commit a violent act. Information from analytical techniques such as financial analysis, trend analysis, statistical analysis, as well as data from link charts, timelines, open source and police files can be incorporated into threat analysis (Peterson, 1994). The following checklist can assist an analyst in conducting threat analysis and forming a threat assessment:

1. List identified targeted groups, members and incidents.
2. Report results from checking websites and publications, report target and suspect analyses.
3. Initiate a link analysis.
4. Provide link charts and matrixes, sort based on numerous variables.
5. Provide results of reviewing against other link charts and older data.
6. Report data search results on victims, suspects, groups, and targets.
7. Identify specific details: groups, member's targets and geographical limitations.
8. Verify leads and information.
9. Report results of site file reviews and visits.
10. Determine posture of the site's physical security status.
11. Report results of briefing conducted.
12. Identify all splinter groups.
13. Identify all supporter groups (active and passive).
14. Identify financial links.

15. Continually update all links and information without delay.
16. Perform final analysis review of all available data (Ronczkowski, 2007).

When an analyst concludes the threat analysis, a product that is formulated is a threat assessment. Mentioned previously, threat analysis and threat assessments primarily assist decision makers at the strategic level. A threat assessment looks at a group's propensity for violence or criminality, or the possible occurrence of a criminal activity in a certain time or place (Peterson, 1994). The threat assessment report contains an introduction to the type of threat, a description of the possible target(s), assessment of the threat, related threat activity and a conclusion. Conclusions about the probability that the threat will materialize into action must be made, along with recommendations for countermeasures or (if prior action is impossible) response to the threatening action once it occurs (Peterson, 2007). Within the conclusion, analysts rank the possibility of the threat occurring as either low, medium or high. A low designation means the threat has little to no probability of occurring. A medium designation means a threat exists; but it is not imminent. A high designation means that threats are evident and distinctive. These recommendations presume some knowledge of the analyst of what actions are available to the agency and the feasibility of those actions (Peterson, 2007). Based on the designation by the analyst, law enforcement makes decisions on which resources to apply, as well as how and where to apply those resources in response to the threat. Examples of threat assessments are the FBI's National Gang Threat Assessment and Daily Threat Reporting from the National Counterterrorism Center.

Vulnerability Analysis: Another analytical technique for analysts performing anti-terrorism analysis is vulnerability analysis and its product, the vulnerability assessment. Where threat analysis and assessment looks at terrorist and criminal organizations, vulnerability analysis and assessment looks at potential target(s) and assesses its vulnerability. It focuses on measuring the potential vulnerabilities of a certain targeted individual, location, or event (Wells, 2011). Law enforcement agencies, in coordination with local businesses and government organizations, perform vulnerability analysis and assessment on all types of structures, facilities, utilities, and various network systems that could be potential terrorist targets. Vulnerability analysis and assessments can also be performed for special events such as sporting events and dignitary visits. The objective of a vulnerability assessment is to identify weaknesses in potential targets in order to develop plans and policies to ensure the safety and security of the target.

The vulnerability analysis process is similar to conducting threat analysis. Analysts gather applicable data and information and then identify gaps in information that needs to be collected. This information may range from informant data, data from other departments, scientific data, and public record data within the community (Peterson, 1994). When the analysis is completed, the analyst writes the vulnerability assessment. The assessment includes potential threats to the target, how the target is vulnerable and recommendations to lessen the risk of threat to the target. The assessment can also include applicable charts, timelines, and other analytical products by the analyst as it relates to the vulnerability of the target. An example of a vulnerability assessment is the Department of Homeland Security's (DHS) Critical Infrastructure Vulnerability Assessment. Analysts may refer to the DHS Protective Security Coordination Division for survey and assessment tools that can assist in conducting vulnerability analysis and assessment.

Association Analysis: When conducting investigations against terrorist or criminal organizations, investigators and leadership want to know which people are connected, along with how and why they are connected. Association analysis, also known as link or network analysis is an analytical technique that assists in connecting the dots between people and networks. Association analysis is the collection and analysis of information that indicates relationships among varied individuals suspected of involvement in criminal activity and providing insight into the criminal operation and which investigative strategies might be the most effective. Analysts gather applicable information for association analysis with information from police reports, corporate records, public record data and other various types of sources. The information is reviewed to find and determine associations between people and networks. When building a database of associations, analysts enter names, the type of relationship between people and networks, and timeframe of the relationship. Upon completion of gathering and organizing information, association charts are created to reflect the connections. The following process (Figure 10.1) can be utilized to assist analysts in conducting association analysis.

Figure 10.1 Steps to Complete Association Analysis

1. Collect the material and mark it for reliability of the source and validity of the data.
2. Number each page or use pre-numbering for tracking.
3. Organize the case information.
4. Extract the association material.
5. Place the data into an association database.
6. Prepare an association matrix.
7. Count the associations of each individual or entity.
8. Create a diagram based on the association database or matrix.
9. Complete background research on entities to fill in knowledge gaps.
10. Produce biographic summaries on each entity on the chart.
11. Review the relationships shown for density, betweeness, closeness, information bottlenecks, degree of centralization, peripheral players, and so forth.
12. Ask critical questions of the data in the chart.
13. Summarize the chart.
14. Establish what necessary information is present and what is missing.
15. Draw interim hypotheses and analyze them for the best hypothesis.
16. Make recommendations for further action.
17. Present findings and written report to management.

(Source: Peterson, June 2007)

The association chart is created with information gathered from reports by the analyst or with the use of an association database. The formatting of an association chart is based on the number of connections between people and networks. People and networks with significantly more connections are placed in the center. People and networks with fewer connections are placed on the outside. Standard symbols for association charts are circles, boxes, solid lines and dotted lines. Circles depict people, boxes depict businesses, solid lines depict strong relations and dotted lines depict weak/suspected relations. Other symbols and/or icons may be utilized by analysts, as long as they are explained in a legend. A legend at the bottom of the association chart is utilized to denote the meaning of symbols used on the chart. The final product is used to provide investigators and law enforcement leadership with information on the overview of a network and how people within that network relate to each other. Once a chart is completed, the analyst must summarize what it says, interpret it, and draw inferences about its meaning (Peterson, 1994).

Along with the association chart, analysts conclude their findings from the analysis in a report. The report includes interpretation by the analyst of the individuals with known information and analyst presumptions, provided they can be supported. The summary, conclusions, and recommendations may include information on the organization - its hierarchy, its strong and weak points, and the strength of the relationship among the people or entities and possible members who could be used to infiltrate the group - and requests for data on additional suspected relationships (Peterson, 1994).

Social Network Analysis: Terrorist organizations are structured where they operate as cells within networks. Each cell within the network is structured for specific responsibilities, such as the recruiting cell, financing cell, targeting cell, operations cell, etc. and these cells maintain limited contact with each other, either directly or indirectly. For law enforcement, this type of organization structure can pose a challenge when conducting investigations and determining which individuals or cells to target. Association (link or network) analysis assists analysts with connecting the dots between individuals or networks. To go a step further, social network analysis can assist analysts and in turn the investigators with who to target. Social network analysis is the mapping and measuring of relationships and flows between people, groups, organizations or other information/knowledge processing entities. Analysts contend that law enforcement can better mitigate threats posed by criminal networks – whether composed of individual criminals, criminal organizations, or some other criminal entities – by identifying and targeting central network actors (Schwartz and Rouselle, 2008). Through social network analysis individuals within the network are analyzed to determine their strength, longevity, and connectedness to determine key individuals who play interconnecting roles and/or central roles (Peterson, 2011).

Terrorist organizations such as Islamic State (ISIS) or Al-Qaeda (AQ) or criminal organizations such as the MS-13 Gang or drug cartels grow and become expansive and more complex, consequently there are more individuals for analysts to examine. This is where determining who the central figures are can help prioritize intelligence and investigation resources. For analysts conducting social network analysis, it begins with a similar process like association/network analysis. Analysts gather necessary information through various police reports, public records and other source material to start creating a network chart. Analysts then go a step further and gather information on how individuals communicate with each other, how often they communicate with each other, the purpose of the contact and use this information to determine the human organization and social interactions of the network. This is then analyzed to determine who the central nodes are and how those central nodes affect the rest of the network. Identifying the central nodes is accomplished by analyzing an individual's importance in the overall system, their roles, level of involvement, and relationship to the rest of the network. Three measurements are used to determine an individual's centrality within the network. The three measurements are degree, betweenness and closeness. Degree gauges how many connections a particular node possesses, betweenness measures how important it is to the flow, and closeness indicates how quickly the node accesses information from the network (Johnson, Reitzel, Norwood, McCoy, Cummings, Tate, 2013).

A model of social network analysis that analysts can use for investigations into terrorism is Steve Borgatti's key player measurement. He uses two measurements, fragmentation and reach, to determine which central nodes to target for investigations and for intelligence (Schwartz and Rouselle, 2008). Using this model of social network analysis can help analysts determine which individuals in a network to target for either disruption purposes or for intelligence collection. Fragmentation is used to determine which individuals for enforcement purposes to target that will disrupt the network. Reach is used to determine which individuals, for intelligence purposes, have a high degree of connectedness, or "reach." Those with more reach are preferred to those with less, because the former can potentially yield more information on other network actors (Schwartz and Rouselle, 2008).

A key component of social network analysis is that it is highly quantitative in nature. Multiple tools and database programs are available for analysts who use social network analysis. Analytic tools such as Social Network Visualizer and Gephi, Pajek and UCINet, which are web-based programs for conducting social network analysis are available.

Matrix Analysis: The analytic technique of matrix analysis can be used as a stand-alone technique or in conjunction with other analytic techniques such as threat analysis or association analysis. One example of a matrix analysis utilizes charts with two axes, one axis with categories deemed by the analyst or agency as important capabilities to an organization. The second axis lists organizations that the law enforcement agency is comparing. The analyst then ranks the organizations by the capability categories as high, medium, low, or unknown based on available information in a pre-determined color code system. Based on the input into the matrix, analysts and law enforcement agencies then rank the terrorist/criminal organizations to determine where to focus and prioritize resources with the organization(s) that pose(es) the greatest or most immediate threat. The matrix is periodically reviewed and re-assessed based on the outcomes of investigations and intelligence collection. A benefit of this matrix for analysts is that the unknowns in the matrix assist in identifying gaps that can be utilized to drive information collection requirements. An example of a matrix is in shown in Figure 10.2. This matrix is the Sleipnir Matrix used by the Royal Canadian Mounted Police (RCMP) that produces a framework for setting priorities by comparing the groups' capabilities, limitations, and vulnerabilities (RCMP, 2007). The matrix is the basis for systematically comparing groups in order to present and explain the relative threat they pose (RCMP, 2007).

Figure 10.2 RCMP Organized Crime Threat Matrix

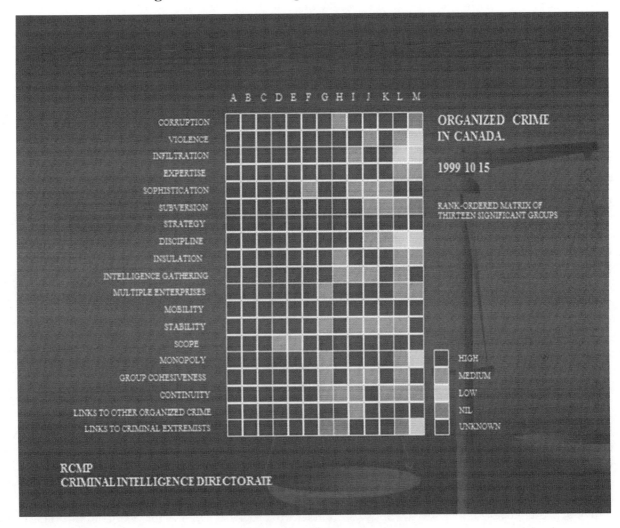

(Source: RCMP, 2007)

Indicator Analysis: The structured analytic technique of indicator analysis is the analysis of events or activities that occur within a larger activity or events that are then utilized to assess patterns that may be useful to investigations in determining possible activities in the future or other locations. This type of analytic technique assesses a terrorist/criminal organizations' or individuals' previous behaviors and activity. Indicator analysis is useful with financial crimes, crime patterns, and determining potential terrorist acts. Assessment products from indicator analysis are produced for strategic level decision making by law enforcement agencies that are applied to support operational and tactical level plans and investigations. For further information on indicator analysis, refer to Chapter 8: Financial Intelligence Applications.

Timeline Analysis: When events occur, such as the September 11, 2001 attacks and the San Bernardino County, CA December 2015 Department of Public Health attack, the activities in the event occur across a time spectrum. Timeline analysis involves the analysis and assessment of the timeline as the events occurred. Through analyzing the timeline of the event, analysts are able to identify patterns, gaps, or anomalies that can be further investigated or assist in information collection requirements. This type of analytic technique is useful for aiding crime pattern analysis, financial intelligence and geospatial analysis. For further information on timeline analysis, refer to Chapter 6: Proactive Approaches to White Collar Crime.

Geospatial Analysis: Geospatial analysis is the utilization of maps and mapping programs (geographic information systems) to track, analyze and assess criminal and terrorist activity in support of investigations and other analytical techniques. Chapter 9: Gang Crime and ILP discusses geospatial analysis; therefore this chapter will discuss how geospatial information systems can benefit other analytical techniques as well as plans and policies for responses to threats. Geographic information systems assist analysts in collecting, displaying and analyzing information. There are multiple geographic information systems applications available for agencies to utilize. One program that is in use by most law enforcement and government agencies is ARCGIS. There are five benefits of geographic information systems in support of analysis and plans, which are detection, preparedness, prevention, protection and response and recovery (Ronczkowski, 2007).

The first benefit, detection, supports threat analysis, vulnerability and crime analysis by adding a spatial and temporal background for analysis. By linking and analyzing temporally and spatially associated information in real time, patterns may be detected that lead to timely identification of likely modalities and targets (Ronczkowski, 2007). The second benefit, preparedness, provides planners and first responders with real-time information in support of emergency responses. Real-time geospatial information supports responses to terrorist attacks and natural disasters. The third benefit, prevention, provides geographic information that is useful in supporting vulnerability analysis. It allows analysts to look at geographic information to analyze patterns in threats and attacks in conjunction with infrastructure, utility systems, and transportation systems. This can help analysts make recommendations for planners establishing policies to disrupt or prevent terrorist attacks. The fourth benefit, protection, also supports vulnerability analysis. Geospatial information is an important component in the analysis of critical infrastructure vulnerabilities and in the use of decision support technologies such as visualization and simulation to anticipate and protect against cascading effects of an attack on one system as it relates to other interdependent systems (Ronczkowski, 2007). The last benefit, response and recovery, is the use of geographic information in support of responses to attacks, natural disasters, and the possible long-term recovery operations that follow large scale events.

Document Exploitation: Materials seized by law enforcement, both document and media sources, at crime scenes for further analysis and assessment of information is known as document exploitation. Data analyzed and assessed through document exploitation provide law enforcement decision-makers with information on possible threat capabilities, limitations, and intentions of terrorist and criminal organizations that is beneficial towards establishing plans and policies. The analyzed and assessed information can also provide support to aid current or follow-on investigations.

Two categories of information in document exploitation are document and media sources. Document sources are materials that can be handwritten, printed, engraved or photographic. Figure 10.3 provides examples of various types of document sources.

Figure 10.3   Examples of Document Sources

	Identity Documents	
Passports Driver's Licenses Identification Cards Nationality or Citizenship Cards	Military, police or civilian ID cards Residence cards Employee cards Union affiliation cards	Coalition issued ID cards Voter registration cards Food ration cards
	Personal Documents	
Letters and notes Books	Diaries Newspapers	Photographs
	Official Documents	
Overlays Field Orders Maps Tactical and Technical Manuscripts and instructions Maintenance records Blueprints	Code Field Manuals Reports Service records Logbook Payrolls Engravings	Informal documents such as hand-written sketches, diagrams and drawings Shipping and packing slips and lists Weather and terrain data

(Source: U.S. Army ATP 2-91.8, May 2015)

Media sources are items such as computers, hard drives, compact discs, cell phones, and printers that contain information. Figure 10.4 provides examples of various types of media sources.

Figure 10.4: Examples of Media Sources

	Hardware	
Computer workstations Desktop computers Laptop computers Computer tablets Printers Fascimile machines Personal digital assistants Network attached storage stations	Digital cameras Wristwatches Servers Answering Machines Close circuit television systems Global Positioning System Locators Copy machines Caller identification devices	Routers Voice recorders Switches Scanners Modems Portable media players Tape/disc duplicators Video recorders
	Solid State (Electronic) Data Storage	
Read only memory (chips) Random access memory (chips) Universal serial bus and thumb drives	Flash multimedia cards (such as secure digital cards, extreme digital picture cards, and memory sticks)	Solid state drives Integrated circuit smart cards
	Magnetic and Optical Storage	
Compact discs Digital video discs Internal hard drives (spinning) External hard drives (spinning)	Audio tapes Digital tapes Video tapes	Zip and jaz disks Floppy disks
	Communications Equipment	
Mobile phones Smart phones Landline phones Hubs	Internet protocol phones Pagers Antenna systems	Radios Radio transcievers Handheld radios

(Source: U.S. Army ATP 2-91.8, May 2015)

Document exploitation analysis consists of three basic steps. Step 1 is the processing of collected information sources in accordance with established law enforcement evidence procedures. Step 2 is the analysis and assessment of information discovered in either document or media sources. Step 3 is the reporting and dissemination of assessed information through appropriate intelligence reports and which is then disseminated to those who require it. Document exploitation is an analytic technique that provides support to intelligence production, targeting, indications and warning, criminal prosecution, and collection of forensic and biometric data. (U.S. Army 2015)

Conducting analysis of information involves the following steps: Identify and extract reportable information; Assess source reliability and information accuracy; Analyze information; and Assess reporting (U.S. Army, 2015). Document and media sources contain information that may be useful for investigations or filling information gaps for other analytic techniques. Extractable information from documents includes organizational composition, support, plans, resources, and information about current and proposed activity. After extracting information from documents and media, analysts then assess the reliability of the source and the accuracy of the information. Assessing the reliability of the source is dependent on the source itself and where law enforcement obtained the information. The accuracy of the information assists law enforcement in assessing if the information is useful in aiding current or future investigations. Once information is determined to be reliable and accurate, analysts process the information for analysis and reporting.

Law enforcement intelligence analysts conducting document exploitation analysis have a few resources to assist them through the following federal agencies: The National Media Exploitation Center (NMEC); Joint Document Exploitation Center (JDEC) Operations Division; the FBI; and the Joint Intelligence Task Force for Combating Terrorism. The National Media Exploitation Center is a federal center established by the Office of the Director of National Intelligence (ODNI) and executively controlled by the Defense Intelligence Agency (DIA). They support document exploitation needs for the intelligence community, law enforcement and homeland security. The Joint Document Exploitation Center Operations Division is a branch within the NMEC. The FBI has a Digital Media Exploitation Unit that supports computer, forensic and fingerprint analysis in regards to document exploitation.

Visual Investigative Analysis: This analytic technique analyzes the procedural steps during the course of an investigation or the steps taken during a criminal act. Analyzing the steps taken prior to the conclusion of the investigation allows investigators to determine what to conduct in order to ensure they do not overlook anything. For criminal acts, it allows analysts and investigators to reconstruct the criminal act in order to visualize the activity, again so that they do not overlook anything. An analytic tool to aid visual investigative analysis (VIA) is a visual investigative analysis chart. The chart provides a graphic depiction of the specific steps taken or remaining within a criminal occurrence or criminal investigation (Peterson, 1994). VIA charts use a standardized charting format where symbols appear (numbered and dated) along a line and depict the actions taken, and appear in chronological order (Peterson, 1994). Radiating from symbols are lines with recordings of the nature of the action and its results (Peterson, 1994).

Analysis of Competing Hypothesis: Analysis of competing hypothesis (ACH) is a structured analytical technique which aids the judgment of analysts when they consider alternate explanations or conclusions for analytic assessments. ACH assists analysts in overcoming or minimizing their thinking limitations as they go through the analytic process. In terms of law enforcement intelligence, the ACH tool can help analysts when they form hypotheses during association analysis and forming judgments on the linkages of people, organizations, activity and the resources involved in the terrorist/criminal activity. It is an eight step process where an analyst evaluates all possible alternatives and weighs those alternatives at the same time. Figure 10.5 lists the eight step process for ACH.

Figure 10.5 ACH Eight Step Process

1. Identify the possible hypotheses to be considered. Use a group of analysts with different perspectives to brainstorm the possibilities.
2. Make a list of significant evidence and arguments for and against each hypothesis.
3. Prepare a matrix with hypotheses across the top and evidence down the side. Analyze the "diagnosticity" of the evidence and arguments—that is, identify which items are most helpful in judging the relative likelihood of the hypotheses.
4. Refine the matrix. Reconsider the hypotheses and delete evidence and arguments that have no diagnostic value.
5. Draw tentative conclusions about the relative likelihood of each hypothesis. Proceed by trying to disprove the hypotheses rather than prove them.
6. Analyze how sensitive your conclusion is to a few critical items of evidence. Consider the consequences for your analysis if that evidence were wrong, misleading, or subject to a different interpretation.
7. Report conclusions. Discuss the relative likelihood of all the hypotheses , not just the most likely one.
8. Identify milestones for further observation that may indicate events are taking a different course than expected.

(Source: Heuer, 1990, p. 97)

Target Profile Analysis: When analysts want to identify an individual(s) in a terrorist or criminal organization for further investigation, an analyst may utilize the analytic technique of target profile analysis. Target profile analysis is an analytic technique that describes criminals, their criminal activity, lifestyle, associations, the risk they pose, and their strengths and weaknesses to give focus to the investigation targeting them (Carter, 2009). Analysts can utilize target profile analysis to identify intelligence gaps and aiding decision makers with how to allocate resources during the investigation of a target(s). When conducting target profile analysis the following information can aid an analyst in the type of data needed to select which target(s) to focus on for further investigation: personal records; criminal records; financial profile; network/associations report; communications report; and surveillance reports (United Nations, 2011).

Analytic Techniques used by National Security Intelligence

Denial and Deception: Denial and deception is a tool utilized by criminal and terrorist organizations to deceive law enforcement. When used correctly, law enforcement may utilize denial and deception as an analytic tool in planning operations to target organizations or individuals. In order for an analyst to know if terrorist or criminal organizations are using denial and deception, they must first have an understanding of the organization they are analyzing. Denial and deception involves concealing the true intentions or goals of the deceiver and the effort to cause an adversary to believe something that is not true (Godson and Wirtz, 2000). When terrorist or criminal organizations use denial and deception, it poses an immediate threat, with law enforcement investigation and intelligence resources squandered against fake or insignificant issues (Godson and Wirtz, 2000). Through education, case studies, and analysts' understanding the organization(s) and individuals(s), analysts can detect and monitor for denial and deception techniques.

Indications and Warnings: Indications and warnings is an analytic tool utilized with predictive intelligence or with the analytic technique of indications analysis. Indications are generally defined and observable actions that, based on an analysis of past known behaviors and characteristics, collectively suggest that a person may be committing, or preparing to commit, an unlawful act. Warning is an assessment of potential danger to a particular area or target formed by discovering certain indicators or emerging trends. Analysts, upon thorough analysis of information or indications, utilize indications and warnings to brief decision makers that allow them to plan and initiate appropriate actions for protection measures of events. Warning products, used in both crime analysis and strategic analysis, take the form of a crime bulletin, crime alert, or the conclusions drawn at the end of an assessment of threat or vulnerability. (Peterson, 1994)

Center of Gravity Analysis: An analytic technique that can determine a terrorist or criminal organization's weakness(es) for development into targeting for investigators is center of gravity analysis. Analysts using center of gravity analysis first look at an organization's capabilities and determine what the critical capabilities are. Critical capabilities are components of the organization, such as financing operations or information operations, that without it, the organization will suffer effects from its loss. After determining the critical capabilities, analysts look at those selected critical capabilities and determine the critical requirements. Critical requirements are resources and means essential for making a critical capability function. For example, if it is determined that financing operations are a critical capability of a terrorist organization, a critical requirement might be the control of drug smuggling routes to earn money to finance terrorist operations. Upon determining the critical requirements, analysts then determine critical vulnerabilities. Critical vulnerabilities are components of critical requirements, that without it, that requirement and therefore that capability would fail to be successful for the terrorist or criminal organization. Analysts then determine the critical vulnerabilities which is the center of gravity, or the one critical vulnerability that investigators can focus on that will ultimately lead to the organization's neutralization or arrests. For further information on center of gravity analysis refer to Chapter 5: Strategically Combating Organized Crime.

Analytic Techniques used by Law Enforcement

Communications Analysis: The analytic technique of communications analysis involves the analysis and assessment of various forms of communications ranging from cell phones, telephones, texts, e-mails, and social media platforms. Analysts determine how individuals communicate, how often they communicate, with whom they communicate, and analyze why the communication is occurring. From this, analysts can determine patterns in communications between individuals or networks. Advancements in today's forms of communications, such as social media, allow terrorist and criminal organizations to pass messages about certain activity while hiding it from the general public. Therefore analysts must be vigilant in new forms of communications and how it affects the ability to mask the true intent of messages passed between individuals and networks. (See also Chapter 5.)

Financial Analysis: Financial analysis is a review and analysis of financial data to ascertain the presence of criminal activity. It can include bank record analysis, net worth analysis, financial profiles, source and application of funds, financial statement analysis, and/or bank secrecy record analysis. It can also show destinations of proceeds of crime and support prosecutions. The analytic technique of financial analysis, as it implies, involves the analysis of financial transactions of terrorist and criminal organizations and businesses/banks related to these organizations. The intent is to document transaction trends of intelligence targets (both individuals and organizations) and identify discrepancies or suspicious financial activities (Carter, 2009). Given that virtually all crimes have some form of financial element, financial analysis is an important tool (Carter, 2009).

When analysts utilize financial analysis, a product that they can put their findings into is a financial summary. A financial summary can depict findings for a given period from financial accounts expressed in a combination of table or graph formats with written assessments (Peterson, 1994). The purpose of financial analysis for terrorist organizations and other national security issues is to determine the source of illegal funds in order to target and freeze those financial assets. This minimizes the amount of funds available to individuals or organizations and helps investigators find means to target those individuals or organizations. For further information on financial analysis refer to Chapter 8: Financial Intelligence Applications.

Commodity Flow Analysis: The analytic technique of commodity flow analysis involves the assessment and movement of market goods, services and currency. Terrorist and criminal organizations utilize goods and services, legally and illegally, to either mask illicit funds or to provide means of financial support. An example is in Iraq where the Islamic State sells oil to Turkey to raise funds for operations and sustainment. Commodity flow analysis may give insights into the nature of a conspiracy, a hierarchy of a group, or the workings of a distribution network (Peterson, 1994). When utilizing commodity flow analysis, the type of information to gather is persons, businesses, commodity type and purpose of the commodity, direction of the commodity, and dates and times. Assessment products analysts can utilize to translate findings are market profiles, directional matrix, and commodity flow charts.

A commodity flow chart depicts how a type of commodity is moving from point A to point B, who moves it, and locations where the commodity is flowing to and from. Market profiles are assessments, updated on a periodic basis, on commodities in relation to the criminal market, such as drugs, guns, and cars. A directional matrix shows the relationship between a commodity and money and how each one flows in accordance with the transactions. To accompany each of these products, analysts put their findings into a written assessment. The written assessment provides facts and conclusions about the activity or organization involved and recommendations for investigative action, and further information collection needs and/or prosecution (Peterson, 1994). For further information on commodity flow analysis refer to Chapter 6: Proactive Approaches to White Collar Crime.

Activity (Event) Flow Analysis: Activity flow analysis depicts the general steps needed to complete a particular process to allow for an analysis or understanding of how that process works. This analytic technique assists analysts in gaining insight into organizations and how they operate and how activities connect. A product with this analytic technique is an activity flow chart. The activity flow chart provides a visual overview of activity. The chart along with a written assessment explains the general process of how the activity occurs, conclusions and recommendations. For further information on activity flow analysis refer to Chapter 6: Proactive Approaches to White Collar Crime.

Conclusion

Although national intelligence and law enforcement intelligence differ in terms of purpose, support and mission, there are similarities between both in terms of processes and analytic standards. Analytic techniques such as threat analysis, association analysis, financial analysis and geospatial analysis are techniques used by analysts in support of both national intelligence and law enforcement intelligence. Information sharing platforms provided by the FBI, Department of Homeland Security and the National Counter Terrorism Center allows analysts to access information in support of analysis and investigations. National security issues, primarily counter-terrorism, as well as counter-narcotics and counter-proliferation requires cooperation amongst federal, state and local law enforcement. Therefore law enforcement intelligence analysts have an important role to play in providing timely, accurate assessments for investigators and decision makers.

Appendix 1: Glossary of Intelligence and Intelligence-Led Policing

Definitions without attribution were contributed by Marilyn Peterson.

Activity Flow Analysis – "Activity flow analysis is used to provide a generic view of a set of criminal actions, or modus operandi, to determine what the key actions were and provide an overview of the crime…(It) can also be used to compare to other crimes, to see if there may be a connection between them" (Peterson, 2011, p. 97).

Analysis - The evaluation of information and its comparison to other information to determine the meaning of the data in reference to a criminal investigation or assessment. Or "that activity whereby meaning, actual or suggested, is derived through organizing and systematically examining diverse information and applying inductive or deductive logic for the purposes of criminal investigation or assessment" (Global, 2007).

Analytic Writing - Written communication focusing on distilling and summarizing factual information to provide concise and clear reports for managers and other customers (Global, 2012).

Assessments - Strategic and tactical assessments are used to assess the impact of a crime group or a criminal activity on a jurisdiction, now or in the future. These may include assessments of threat, vulnerability, or risk (Global, 2012).

Association Analysis/Network Analysis - Collection and analysis of information that indicates relationships among varied individuals suspected of involvement in criminal activity and providing insight into the criminal operation and which investigative strategies might be the most effective (Global, 2012).

Association Matrix – the arrangement of data on relationships among people, places, activities, and entities into a triangular format. Can be used as a mid-level array of data in support of an association chart or analysis (Peterson, 2016).

Briefing – The oral presentation of pertinent facts and conclusions regarding an investigation or assessment (Peterson, 2016).

Case Analysis - **(UK)** examination of the cycle of data-decision-action-new data-new decision that is the essence of investigative management …Provides a useful resource for detailing the what, when and why' of management decisions, and thus justifying every state of the process and policy of an investigation. **(US)** an approach used to manage the analysis of varied data in support of current or historical investigations (Peterson, 2011, p. 98).

Center of Gravity (COG) - Primary sources of moral or physical strength, power and resistance. (Eikmeier, 2007).

Collation - The process by which information is assembled and compared critically (Global, 2012).

Collection - The directed, focused gathering of information from all available sources (Global, 2012).

Collection Plan - A plan directing the collection of data on a particular topic with a specific objective, a list of potential sources of that data, and an estimated time frame (Global, 2012).

Commodity Flow Analysis – The compilation, review and analysis of data relating to goods, services, or currency moving from one entity to another (Peterson, 1998).

Communications Analysis - The review of records reflecting communications (telephone, e-mail, pager, text messaging, etc.) among entities for indicators of criminal associations or activity. Results may recommend steps to take to continue or expand the investigation or study (Global, 2012).

Conclusion – a definitive statement about a suspect, action or state of nature based on the analysis of information (Global, 2007).

Content Analysis - the review, analysis and attribution of meaning to oral or written communications (Peterson, 1998).

Content Validity - An evaluation scale generally represented from 1 to 5 or 1 to 4 reflecting the level of accuracy of the content of a raw data report. The scale ranges from "known to be true" to "truthfulness unknown" (Global, 2012).

Crime Analyst – In the U.S., crime analysts are generally found in municipal police departments and analyze criminal incident data to arrive at trends and forecasts of future crimes of that nature. In Europe and some other countries, the term 'crime analyst' refers to all those who analyze criminal data.

Criminal Investigative Analysis – an analytic process that studies serial offenders, victims and crime scenes in order to assess characteristics and behaviors of offenders with the intent to identify or aid in the identification of the offenders (Global, 2007).

Crime-Pattern Analysis - A process seeking links between crimes and other incidents to reveal similarities and differences to help predict and prevent future criminal activity (Global, 2012).

Criminal Analysis - The application of analytical methods and products to raw data to produce intelligence within the criminal justice field (Global, 2012).

Criminal Business Profile - A product detailing how criminal operations or techniques work, including how victims are chosen, how they are victimized, how proceeds of crime are used, and the strengths and weaknesses in the criminal system (Global, 2012).

Criminal Intelligence - Information compiled, analyzed, and/or disseminated in an effort to anticipate, prevent, or monitor criminal activity (Global, 2012).

Critical Capabilities (CC) - Primary abilities which merit a centre of gravity to be identified as such in the context of a given situation (Eikmeier, 2007)

Critical Requirements (CR) - Essential conditions, resources and means for a critical capability to be fully operative (Eikmeier, 2007).

Critical Vulnerabilities (CV)- Critical requirements or components thereof which are either deficient or vulnerable to neutralization, interdiction or attack in a manner achieving decisive results (Eikmeier, 2007).

Critical Thinking - The objective, open, and critical cognitive process applied to information to achieve a greater understanding of data, often through developing and answering questions about the data (Global 2012).

Customers - Consumers of intelligence products who may be within the analyst's agency or in other agencies or organization (Global, 2012).

Data - Raw facts or variables used as a basis for reasoning, discussion, or calculation (Global, 2012).

Deductive Reasoning – the process of arriving at a conclusion using only the facts at hand

Demographic/Social Trend Analysis - An examination of the nature of demographic changes and their impact on criminality, the community, and law enforcement (Global, 2012).

Dissemination - The release of information, usually under certain protocols (Global, 2012).

Dissemination Plan - A plan to show how an intelligence product is to be disseminated, at what security level, and to whom (Global, 2012).

Estimate - A numeric forecast of activity based on facts but not able to be verified or known (Global, 2012).

Evaluation - An assessment of the reliability of the source and accuracy of the raw data (Global, 2012).

Event-Flow Analysis – the review of raw data to determine the sequence of events or interactions that may reflect criminal activity (IALEIA, 2004).

Feedback/Reevaluation - A review of the operation of the intelligence process and the value of the output to the consumer (Global, 2012).

Financial Analysis - A review and analysis of financial data to ascertain the presence of criminal activity. It can include bank record analysis, net worth analysis, financial profiles, source and application of funds, financial statement analysis, and/or bank secrecy record analysis. It can also show destinations of proceeds of crime and support prosecutions (Global, 2012).

Flow Analysis - The review of raw data to determine the sequence of events or interactions that may reflect criminal activity. It can include timelines, event-flow analysis, commodity-flow analysis, and activity-flow analysis and may show missing actions or events needing further investigation (Global, 2012).

Forecast - An evaluation of what has happened or what may happen, based on what is known and verifiable, suspected and not verifiable, and unknown. Likelihoods or probabilities of future activity are usually included, with suggested steps to protect against criminal activity (Global, 2012).

Frequency Distribution – the number of times a given event has occurred

GIS – Geographic Information System

Geographic Analysis - An evaluation of the locations of criminal activity or criminals to determine whether future criminal activity can be deterred or interdicted through forecasting activity based on historical raw data (Global, 2012).

Geographic Profiling – "an investigative methdology that uses locations of a connected series of crimes to determine the most probable area of offender residence. It is applied in cases of serial murder, rape, arson, robbery and bombing…" (Rossmo, 2000 ,p. 1)

Homeland Security Analysis – The application of analytical methods and products to raw data to produce intelligence within the homeland security field

Hypothesis - A tentative assumption to be proven or disproven by further investigation and analysis (Global, 2012).

Indicator – generally defined and observable actions that, based on an analysis of past known behaviors and characteristics, collectively suggest that a person may be committing, or preparing to commit, an unlawful act (Global, 2007).

Indicator Analysis - A review of past criminal activity to determine whether certain actions or postures taken can reflect future criminal activity. It can result in the development of behavioral profiles or early warning systems in computerized environments (Global, 2012).

Inductive Reasoning – the arrival at a conclusion that goes beyond the facts at hand (Peterson, 1998). **Information** - Facts, data, or knowledge that has not been subjected to analysis. Often referred to as "knowledge in raw form" (Global, 2012).

Intelligence - the product of the analysis of raw information related to crimes or crime patterns with respect to an identifiable person or group in an effort to anticipate, prevent, or monitor possible criminal activity (Global, 2007).

Intelligence Assessment – a comprehensive report on an intelligence issue related to criminal or national security threats available to local, state, tribal, and federal law enforcement agencies (Global, 2007).

Intelligence Cycle - The criminal intelligence cycle includes planning, collection, collation, evaluation, analysis, dissemination, and feedback. The national security intelligence cycle begins with requirements and continues on with the mentioned phases (Global, 2012).

Intelligence Gap - A topic requiring additional information collection and analysis (Global 2012).

Intelligence-Led Policing- .The collection and analysis of information to produce an intelligence end product, designed to inform police decision making at both the tactical and strategic levels (Global, 2012).

Logic - the use of reasoning to arrive at a fact-based conclusion.

Market Profile - An assessment surveying the criminal market around a particular commodity in an area for the purpose of determining how to lessen that market (Global, 2012).

Models - Hypothetical sets of facts or circumstances developed to test the likelihood of a hypothesis (Global, 2012).

Modus Operandi – The habitual way in which one commits a crime (Peterson, 1998).

Multi-dimensional Analysis - "The analysis of a set of data using temporal, geographic, associational and/or other aspects of the data and layering the results upon each other to have a more contextual view of the information" (Peterson, 2011, p. 100)

National Security Analysis – The application of analytical methods and products to raw data to produce intelligence to inform decision-makers within the national security field.

Network Analysis - See Association Analysis.

Net Worth Analysis – The compilation, review and analysis of data relating to an entity's income and expenditures

Profile – A description of an individual's background and habits that are often reflected in their criminal activity

Problem Profile - Identifies established and emerging crimes or incidents for the purpose of preventing or deterring further crime (Global, 2012).

Raw Data - Data collected by officers or analysts not yet subjected to the intelligence process, thus it is not intelligence (Global, 2012).

Recommendations – a set of suggestions for courses of action provided by an analyst after completing an examination of the facts in an investigation or inquiry.

Requirements - The details of what a customer needs from the intelligence function (Global, 2012).

Results Analysis - An assessment of the effectiveness of police strategies and tactics as used to combat a particular crime problem. May include suggestions for changes to future policies and strategies (Global, 2012).

Risk Analysis/Assessment - An evaluation of untoward outcomes from an incident, event, or occurrence. Assesses the likelihood of risks and consequences posed by individual offenders or organizations to potential victims, the public at large, and law enforcement agencies. It generally includes preventative steps to be taken to lessen the risk (Global, 2012).

Social Network Analysis –The mapping and measuring of relationships and flows between people, groups, organizations...or other information/knowledge processing entities" (orgnet.com, 2006).

Source Reliability - A scale reflecting the reliability of information sources; often shown as A–D or A–E. It ranges from factual source to reliability unknown (Global, 2012).

Spatial Analysis - See Geographic Analysis.

Statistical Analysis – The review and interpretation of numeric data to provide further information in an inquiry.

Strategic Intelligence – An assessment of targeted crime patterns, crime trends, criminal organizations, and or unlawful commodity transactions for purposes of planning, decision-making, and resource allocation; the focused examination of unique, pervasive, and/or complex crime problems (Global, 2007).

Tactical Intelligence - Information regarding a specific criminal event of immediate use by operational units to further a criminal investigation, plan tactical operations, and provide for officer safety (Global, 2012).

Target Profile - A person - or organization - specific report providing everything known on the individual or organization that is useful as the investigation is initiated. Based on the data, a best course of action regarding the investigation may be recommended (Global, 2012).

Telephone Record/Toll Analysis - See Communications Analysis.

Threat Assessment - A report that evaluates a natural or man-made occurrence, an individual, an entity, or an action which has harmed or could harm life, information, operations, the environment, and/or property. Assesses the present or future threat and recommends ways to lessen the impact (Global, 2012).

Timeline Analysis – The compilation, review and analysis of a series of events, in chronologic order, that can result in the identification of patterns in activity, gaps in patterns, and potential causal relationships among events.

Time Series Analysis – The analysis of a series of crimes and their relationship to time.

Victimology – The analysis of the attributes found in a series of victims that can be used to discern patterns or trends.

Visual investigative Analysis - The compilation, review and analysis of data relating to investigative steps taken (Global, 2012).

Vulnerability Assessment - A report evaluating physical features or operational attributes that render an entity, asset, system, network, or geographic area open to exploitation or susceptible to a given hazard. Often recommends ways to lessen or eliminate the vulnerability (Global, 2012).

Warning – An assessment of potential danger to a particular area or target formed by discovering certain indicators or emerging trends.

Appendix 2: Technology Supporting ILP[43], Sean Tolbert and Paula Carter

Web-Based Resources

Today's intelligence analysts have the ability to easily and expeditiously gather large amounts of relevant data. Thanks to the Internet, an analyst can log into web based systems and access classified law enforcement and open source information, social media posts, and public information from around the world in a matter of minutes. Many of these data resources offer their own proprietary analytical tools (network analysis, geospatial analysis, etc.). It is imperative that intelligence analysts know what data sources are available to assist them in their research and analysis.

Application Name	Description
Accurint	LexisNexis' Accurint tool is offered as a solution for multiple industries. In the Government and Law Enforcement industries Accurint enables users to conduct in-depth searches of their "databases, which include both public and proprietary information (Accurint for Law Enforcement, n.d.)." Accurint's analytical tools allow users to: "locate and identify both people and businesses; quickly uncover assets; discover links between people, businesses, assets and locations; and fight fraud (Accurint for Law Enforcement, n.d.; Accurint for Government, n.d.)." http://www.accurint.com
Babel X	Babel Street is a company that offers tools that enable users to "collect, analyze, monitor, and report on information from online and private electronic sources (Babel Street, n.d.)." Babel X is the most powerful tool that Babel Street offers. Babel X allows users to conduct searches in over 200 languages and utilize geo-fencing across social and traditional media sites. Babel X offers a "dynamic user-friendly interface (Babel X, n.d.)" that includes graphical and geospatial dashboards for analysis. www.babelstreet.com/Product_Babel_X.aspx
Business Watch International	Business Watch International has R.A.P.I.D., the **R**egional **A**utomated **P**roperty **I**nformation **D**atabase. BWI technology facilitates Intelligence Based Policing, which on a fundamental level is having the most comprehensive, timely information when it matters. Business Watch International has developed best-in-class electronic transaction reporting and investigation tools that provide real time an historical transaction data, and tools to query and report on that data. Electronic Pawn Transaction Reporting is one of the newest data sources to be leveraged by police across North America to help solve property crime, drug crime and violent and domestic crime. BWI's RAPID products and services are designed in collaboration with police officers from across North America, to reflect their specific investigative need. http://www.bwirapid.com
CarFax for Police	Allows partial license plate search, alerts on VIN activity, VIN scanning, search and viewing of accident report, etc. http://www.carfaxforpolice.com

---

[43] This appendix is a sampling of solutions available, not a complete list. Inclusion of these programs and web pages is not an endorsement of their use by the authors or IALEIA.

CLEAR	CLEAR is an online investigative tool that was developed by Thompson Reuters to enable users to search public records and proprietary databases for information about companies, people, and their assets. Additionally, CLEAR has the ability to conduct "integrated Web searching of social networking sites, news, watchlists, and more (CLEAR Investigation Software, n.d.)." Analysts utilizing CLEAR also have the ability to "Visualize, detect, and analyze patterns and trends (CLEAR Investigation Software, n.d.)" in the data that their queries return. http://legalsolutions.thomsonreuters.com
Consumer Sentinel Network	"Consumer Sentinel is the unique investigative cyber tool that provides members of the Consumer Sentinel Network with access to millions of consumer complaints... based on the premise that sharing information can make law enforcement even more effective. To that end, the Consumer Sentinel Network provides law enforcement members with access to complaints provided directly to the Federal Trade Commission by consumers, as well as providing members with access to complaints shared by data contributors." https://www.ftc.gov/enforcement/consumer-sentinel-network
Cutting Edge,C.A.	Cutting Edge provides network security, network vulnerability and cyber threat analysis and mitigation services. http://www.cuttingedgeca.com
CyberCop	"CyberCop is a grassroots Law Enforcement movement designed for efficient and effective information sharing among Law Enforcement, First responders, Homeland Defense and Law Enforcement related professionals. The CyberCop Portal is open to all law enforcement, first responder, homeland defense and related individuals, subject to verifi- cation by a sponsoring authority." www.officer.com/company/10028767/cybercop-software
Dataminr	Dataminr offers "real-time information discovery … from Twitter and other public sources … (Dataminr, n.d.)" The purpose of Dataminr is to identify "the most relevant information in real-time for clients in Finance, the Public Sector, News, Corporate Security and Crisis Management (Dataminr, n.d.)." Dataminr allows users to monitor and instantly analyze Twitter activity via location based key word searches and alerts. https://www.dataminr.com/
DigitalStakeout	DigitalStakeout offers "Software as a Service (SaaS) that performs analysis of social, deep and dark web data to detect unknown threats and vulnerabilities (DigitalStakeout, n.d.)." DigitalStakeout allows users to search and monitor social media utilizing location based key word searches and alerts. DigitalStakeout offers four main interfaces for public safety professionals: real-time social intelligence; automated incident detection; location based search; cluster and link analysis (DigitalStakeout Public Safety Intelligence, n.d.). https://www.digitalstakeout.com/
Echosec	Echosec is "a location-based search platform that provides public safety, security, journalism, and intelligence professionals actionable knowledge based on social media and other information (Echosec, n.d.)." Echosec offers tools that enable users to: "monitor key locations for social media activity (Echosec Public Safety Intelligence, n.d.);" monitor persons of interest for social media activity; "establish a timeline, generate a new lead, recognize a pattern, visualize a routine, or dismiss a misleading tip (Echosec Public Safety Intelligence, n.d.)."

	https://www.echosec.net/
El Paso Intelligence Center	"The El Paso Intelligence Center (EPIC) was established in 1974 in response to a study by the Justice Management Division of the U.S. Department of Justice entitled, 'A Secure Border.' The initial focus of the Center was to assist in the identification of drug traffickers and alien traffickers along the U.S. - Mexico border. EPIC's vision is to continue to provide timely and expeditious support to Federal, State, local, tribal, and international law enforcement agencies and to remain the premier tactical operational intelligence center in the nation." https://www.epic.gov/
Financial CrimesEnforcement Network (FinCEN))	FinCEN's mission is to safeguard the financial system from illicit use and combat money laundering and promote national security through the collection, analysis, and dissemination of financial intelligence and strategic use of financial authorities. Most FinCEN data is available to law enforcement agencies in the U.S. https://www.fincen.gov/
Foreign Military Studies Office (FMSO)	"The Foreign Military Studies Office (FMSO) at Fort Leavenworth, Kansas, is an open source research organization of the U.S. Army…FMSO maintains this research tradition of special insight and highly collaborative work. FMSO conducts unclassified research of foreign perspectives of defense and security issues that are understudied or unconsidered but that are important for understanding the environments in which the U.S. military operates. FMSO's work today is still aimed at publication in unclassified journals and its research findings are taught in both military and civilian venues in the United States and around the world." http://fmso.leavenworth.army.mil/
Geofeedia	Geofeedia is an intelligence platform that enables users "to predict, analyze and act on real-time social media content from anywhere in the world (Geofeedia, n.d.)." Geofeedia allows users to conduct location based social media discovery. Geofeedia offers users multiple analytical tools including: keyword trends; time-based activity; influential posters; activity trends; social media sources; sentiment analysis; image recognition (Geofeedia, n.d.). https://geofeedia.com
Homeland Security Information Network (HSIN)	"The Homeland Security Information Network (HSIN) is the trusted network for homeland security mission operations to share Sensitive But Unclassified information. Federal, State, Local, Territorial, Tribal, International and Private Sector homeland security partners use HSIN to manage operations, analyze data, send alerts and notices, and in general, share the information they need to do their jobs." (U.S.) https://www.dhs.gov/homeland-security-information-network-hsin
Information Sharing Environment (ISE)	"The Information Sharing Environment (ISE) consists of the people, projects, systems, and agencies that enable responsible information sharing across the national security enterprise. The ISE was established by the Intelligence Reform and Terrorism Prevention Act of 2004 and a direct result of 9/11 Commission recommendations. Law enforcement, defense, and intelligence personnel rely on timely and accurate information to keep America safe." https://www.ise.gov

Infragard	"InfraGard is a partnership between the FBI and the private sector. It is an association of persons who represent businesses, academic institutions, state and local law enforcement agencies, and other participants dedicated to sharing information and intelligence to prevent hostile acts against the U.S." InfraGard is an information sharing and analysis effort serving the interests and combining the knowledge base of a wide range of members. https://www.infragard.org/
Intelink	"Intelink is both an architectural framework and an integrated intelligence dissemination and collaboration service providing uniform methods for exchanging intelligence among intelligence providers and users. The Intelink service was patterned after the Internet model in which a variety of institutions have come together in the context of a global network to share information. The Intelink intelligence network links information in the various classified databases of the US intelligence agencies (e.g. FBI, CIA, NGA, DIA, DEA, NSA, USSS, NRO) to facilitate communication and the sharing of documents and other resources." https://www.intelink.gov/ (Access limited to those with specific federal credentials)
Law Enforcement Enterprise Portal (LEEP)	"The Law Enforcement Enterprise Portal, or LEEP, is an electronic gateway that provides law enforcement agencies, intelligence partners, and criminal justice entities with centralized access to many different resources and services via a single sign-on. These resources strengthen case development for investigators and enhance information sharing between agencies. LEEP accounts are available to personnel affiliated with the criminal justice system, intelligence community, and the armed forces." (U.S.) https://www.fbi.gov/services/cjis/leep
Media Sonar	Media Sonar is "an innovative platform that helps organizations from the Corporate, Security, Entertainment and Education markets identify relevant data to help gain knowledge and perspective through a variety of online networks. Media Sonar allows users to search and monitor social media utilizing location based key word searches. Media Sonar enables users with numerous built-in analytical tools such as: "qualitative data visualizations; quantitative data visualizations; volumetric data visualizations (MediaSonar, n.d.)." https://www.mediasonar.com/
National Crime Information Center (NCIC)	The National Crime Information Center, or NCIC, is "an electronic clearinghouse of crime data that can be tapped into by virtually every criminal justice agency nationwide, 24 hours a day, 365 days a year. It helps criminal justice professionals apprehend fugitives, locate missing persons, recover stolen property, and identify terrorists. It also assists law enforcement officers in performing their duties more safely and provides information necessary to protect the public." https://www.fbi.gov/services/cjis/ncic
National Data Exchange (N-DEx) System	"The N-DEx system provides criminal justice agencies with an online tool for sharing, searching, linking, and analyzing information across jurisdictional boundaries. A national repository of criminal justice records submitted by agencies from around the nation, N-DEx enables users to "connect the dots" between data on people, places, and things that may seem unrelated in order to link investigations and investigators.... Additionally, N-DEx provides visualization tools to graphically depict associations between people, places,

	things, and events either on a link-analysis chart or on a map. For ongoing investigations, the subscription and notification feature automatically notifies analysts/investigators if other users are searching for the same criteria or if a new record concerning their investigation is added to the system." (U.S.) https://info.publicintelligence.net/FBI-NDEx-Overview.pdf
National White Collar Crime Center (NW3C)	"NW3C offers, free of charge, a number of tools to assist our law enforcement partners in the prosecution of economic and high-tech crime: **PhotoHunter** is a software product that is distributed free of charge to law enforcement that allows the user to view and plot images and their associated EXIF information. **Report Generator** is a software product that is distributed free of charge to law enforcement that allows the user to generate an HTML-based report from separate data files. **PerpHound** is a software product that is distributed through the NW3C Cyber-Investigation 105 Cell Phone Mapping and Analysis (CPMA) course." http://www.nw3c.org
Open Source Center (OSC)	"OpenSource.gov provides timely and tailored translations, reporting and analysis on foreign policy and national security issues from the Open Source Center and its partners. Featured are reports and translations from thousands of publications, television and radio stations, and Internet sources around the world. Also among the site's holdings are a foreign video archive and fee-based commercial databases for which OSC has negotiated licenses. OSC's reach extends from hard-to-find local publications and video to some of the most renowned thinkers on national security issues inside and outside the U.S. Government. Accounts are available to U.S. Government employees and contractors." http://www.opensource.gov
ProMonitor	LexisNexis developed ProMonitor to assist law enforcement agencies in locating persons or interest. ProMonitor is an automated tool that LexisNexis' databases for information about persons of interest that are identified by the user. ProMonitor automatically alerts users when relevant information (e.g. "significant identity variables in a profile change or items such as arrest and unusual patterns suggesting unexplained affluence (ProMonitor for Law Enforcement, n.d.)") is discovered. www.lexisnexis.com/risk/products/government/promonitor.aspx
Regional Information Sharing Systems (RISS)	"RISS is a U.S. federally funded program that maintains a network of six multistate centers to assist law enforcement officials to combat illegal drug trafficking, identity theft, human trafficking, violent crime, and terrorist activity both regionally and on a nationwide scale. RISS also operates the RISS Secure Cloud to facilitate law enforcement information sharing. Hundreds of thousands of law enforcement officers and criminal justice personnel access RISSNET to share intelligence and coordinate efforts across jurisdictions." (U.S.) https://www.riss.net/
Snaptrends	Snaptrends is a location based social media solution that enables users to "monitor, analyze and visualize this public data quickly and easily so users can make informed decisions and implement effective strategies (Snaptrends, n.d.)."

	Snaptrends allows users to conduct searches of social media platforms utilizing key words, and geo-fencing. Snaptrends offers users an analytical dashboard that includes geospatial tools, as well as data visualization and manipulation through dynamic charts and graphs of activity (Snaptrends for Law Enforcement, n.d.). https://www.getapp.com/business-intelligence-analytics-software/a/snaptrends
Whooster.com	Whooster delivers investigative data solution tools to law enforcement, government agency and private sector clients who need real-time delivery of accurate data on the location, phones and background of individuals and businesses. Through SMS/Text MessagingWeb Based, Batch, Direct Connect and Integrated SaaS Solutions Whooster Data Fusion technology delivers the fresh, reliable data needed for enforcement, regulatory, and private concerns. http://www.whooster.com/products
World-Check	World-Check is a risk management solution for organizations that are concerned about "Know Your Customer (KYC), Anti-Money Laundering (AML), organized crime, sanctions, Countering the Financing of Terrorism (CFT), and Politically Exposed Persons (PEPs) (Thompson Reuters World-Check, n.d.)." World-Check gives users access to a "strictly monitored risk database, with: Data collated by more than 350 research analysts based in 11 research centers across 5 continents; A research team that speaks more than 60 languages, contributing 750,000 man hours of research a year; Specialist research units monitoring 100,000s of reputable information sources." Additionally, World-Check enables users to identify and visualize relationships between entities in their search results and other entities of interest in the database (Thompson Reuters World-Check, n.d.). https://risk.thomsonreuters.com/en/products/world-check-know-your-customer.html

Data Management

Every intelligence analyst needs to understand data management and the tools that are available to assist them in managing their data. These tools allow analysts to consolidate data or information from multiple sources into one location where it can be standardized for tracking and analysis. Good data management tools also enable intelligence analysts to directly import information from the tool's format into analytical tools (e.g. ESRI's ArcGIS, IBM's i2 iBase). Analysts that understand and can use these tools will be much more efficient and accurate.

Application Name	Description
dBASE PLUS 11	Published in 1980, dBase was one of the first database management systems for personal computers. dBASE's underlying file format, the .dbf file, is widely used in applications needing a simple format to store structured data. "The new dBASE PLUS 11 builds on the prior releases of the product. The updated product includes a modern object oriented programming language (dBL) that runs on 32 and 64-bit versions of Microsoft Windows operating systems." www.dbase.com/
FileMaker Pro	FileMaker Pro "is powerful, easy-to-use database software that helps you and your team gets any task done faster on Windows, Mac, and the web. Tackle any task - Get more than 30 professionally designed templates to help manage your tasks in

	minutes. Create custom databases - Build a database tailored for your unique needs." www.filemaker.com/products/filemaker-pro/
IBM DB2	"DB2 V11.1 is powerful multi-workload database software that powers the next generation of applications including mobile, advanced analytics, cognitive and highly available transactions. IBM DB2 offers a security-rich environment required for the hybrid world, designed to protect data both in flight and at rest. It also scales to new heights of performance by enabling its in-memory technology to be easily deployed across a massively parallel processing architecture and helping to dramatically improve response times." https://www.ibm.com/analytics/us/en/technology/db2/
IBM Informix	IBM Informix has "new capabilities, giving you a way to combine unstructured and structured data in a smart way. IBM Informix offers a "hybrid" database system that is capable of supporting relational and non-relational data, giving you the ability to store JSON (sometimes JavaScript Object Notation) and relational tables in the same storage engine." https://www.ibm.com
IBM Netezza	Netezza is IBM's Data Warehouse technology system. "Obtaining insights from the massive volumes of data is mission-critical. Yet many companies lack the resources and technology to manage today's big data analytic challenges. The IBM PureData System for Analytics - Powered by Netezza technology - part of the IBM PureSystems family, can help your organization simplify the delivery of critical insights." https://www.ibm.com/software/data/puredata/analytics/nztechnology/analytics.html
Infobright	"Infobright is a commercial provider of column-oriented relational database software with a focus in machine-generated data…. Infobright's database software is integrated with MySQL, but with its own proprietary data storage and query optimization layers." Http://www.dbms2.com/category/products-and-vendors/infobright-brighthouse/
Interbase	Interbase features "Change Views" a "new approach to tracking data changes (with field level granularity) in server as well as personal computer/tablet/mobile databases. It is designed for today's mobile centric world." https://www.embarcadero.com/products/interbase
Microsoft Access	Microsoft Access is a tool that enables users to create custom databases from templates or from scratch in order to catalog large amounts of relational data. Relational data is data with a commonality (e.g. a name [Bob Smith]) that would typically reside in multiple separate spreadsheets / tables (e.g. addresses associated with the investigation, phone numbers associated with the investigation, people associated with the investigation). Access is set-up to make queries around related data points easier than in Excel. For example, Access is a better tool than Excel to identify and depict all information associated with cell phone numbers identified in toll record analysis that are located within a set sector of a cell tower. https://products.office.com/en-us/access
Microsoft Excel	Microsoft Excel is a tool that enables users to maintain and analyze data in spreadsheets while introducing limited relationships between spreadsheets. Excel is a very versatile tool for two main reasons. First, Microsoft Excel's file formats are commonly accepted by most databases and analytical software suites for import /

	export purposes. Second, Excel allows users to utilize formulas to clean, normalize, and analyze data. Most people do not understand the Excel's analytical capabilities; for the most part users are limited only by their dataset. Excel allows analysts to identify trends in time (e.g. year, month, day of the month, day of the week, time of day), trends in location (e.g. country, state, county, city, neighborhood, street), trends in activity (e.g. assault, larceny, fraud) and trends by entity (e.g. criminal, victim, location). All of this can be accomplished expeditiously with tools such as pivot tables, and easily visualized using charts and graphs. https://products.office.com/en-us/excel
Microsoft SQL Server	The most commonly used data storage system, Microsoft SQL Server, "continues to evolve and stay ahead of organizational data needs. Customers have responded to this evolution by showing confidence in using SQL Server to manage their mission-critical data. Industry analysts have also responded positively... SQL Server has consistently added groundbreaking functionality over the last 15 years." https://www.microsoft.com/en-us/sql-server/sql-server-2016
MySQL by Oracle	"MySQL is the world's most popular open source database for cost-effectively delivering reliable, high-performance and scalable e-commerce, online transaction processing, and embedded database applications... MySQL delivers the ease of use, scalability, and high performance, as well as a full suite of database drivers and visual tools to help developers and DBAs build and manage their MySQL applications." https://www.oracle.com/mysql/
Oracle	Oracle Database is an object-relational database management system produced and marketed by Oracle Corporation. https://www.oracle.com/database/index.html
Quattro Pro	"Corel Quattro Pro is a spreadsheet application that is available as part of the WordPerfect Office suite. Quattro Pro is very similar to Microsoft Excel in the way it looks, feels, and functions. There is a formula bar where you can write formulas that will be used in cells. There are also formatting options such as font, cell color, borders, and size. Quattro Pro can open many of the formats that Excel can as well." http://www.corel.com/
SAP Hana	SAP HANA is an "in-memory computing platform available to power SAP Business One. The software allows businesses to capture and analyze information across all applications, unleashing the potential of big data unprecedented insight across your business." https://www.sap.com/products/hana.html
SAP Adaptive Server Enterprise (Sybase)	SAP Sybase, now known as SAP Adaptive Server Enterprise, is "Designed to meet the demands of the digital economy, this high-performance SQL database server uses a relational model to power transaction-based applications – on premise or in the cloud." https://websmp106.sap-ag.de/~sapidp/011000358700001121852012E/index.htm
Sintelix	Sintelix Incorporated offers a solution for the analysis and visualization of unstructured data. It is highly user friendly and enables users to extract entities, identities, relationships, geo-locations, events, languages and many other facts from unstructured data.

Visualization and Analysis

There are numerous ways to analyze and visualize data for intelligence purposes. Visualization and mapping programs can prove invaluable in intelligence analysis, especially in criminal analysis. Robust network association diagrams and geospatial intelligence products are not only extremely useful to investigators, they are invaluable to prosecutors.

Application Name	Description
ACISS TAP	ACISS TAP is a web based application that scales from the single user to the largest agency. It can handle multiple DNRs and wiretaps at the same time. It analyzes information using the entire database. A telephone number input in a case is immediately linked to that number, even in a case closed months before. http://www.aciss.com
Agnovi REX	Investigation and Criminal Intelligence Database Software - "REX was designed with small teams of police and law enforcement in mind. Its' easy-to-use interface helps you manage investigation and intelligence information. You can easily document, search and report law enforcement activities (e.g. statements, tactical operations) and subjects (e.g. suspects, offenders, informants, places and things). REX uses the MySQL relational database for storing structured investigative information, advanced searching and instant collaboration. Other REX benefits include scalability, attachment support, and report generation." This program also includes system generated entity relationship charting. https://www.agnovi.com/
Analyse-it	This tool is a "statistical add-in for Excel. Describe and visualize data, uncover the relationships hidden in your data, and get answers to the important questions so you can make informed, intelligent decisions." https://analyse-it.com/
Analytics 10	Expert Solutions delivers the solution for your data analysis, We work with the best suppliers of BI technology tools at the forefront of the market. Our applications are specially designed for the requirements of your industry, optimizing the analysis of your data for the needs of your company and improve your business. http://www.analytics10.com
IBM i2 Analyst's Notebook	"IBM i2 Analyst's Notebook is a visual intelligence analysis environment that can optimize the value of massive amounts of information... It allows analysts to quickly collate, analyze and visualize data from disparate sources while reducing the time required to discover key information in complex data. IBM i2 Analyst's Notebook delivers timely, actionable intelligence to help identify, predict, prevent and disrupt criminal, terrorist and fraudulent activities" (Analyst's Notebook, n.d.). http://www.ibm.com/i2
ArcGIS	ArcGIS is a robust and versatile geographic information system (GIS) that is used by numerous industries for their mapping and geospatial analysis needs. ArcGIS gives users the ability to import points, lines, and polygons in numerous formats (ranging from .txt files to .shp files). ArcGIS also allows users to import imagery and text files that correlate to locations of interest. Additionally, ArcGIS has numerous tools for analyzing data geospatially. For

	example, cell phone metadata can be analyzed in ArcGIS to identify where calls were made by highlighting areas based on the cell tower, the sector of the tower, and the strength of the connection (ESRI for Law Enforcement, n.d.; ArcGIS for Law Enforcement, n.d.). http://www.esri.com
Cell Hawk	CellHawk loads over 1000 Call Detail Records per second. This data is then presented in a point&click, graphical user-interface so you can quickly & accurately find answers in minutes … (without becoming an expert in Excel pivot tables). Most users are up and running with less than an hour of informal training. Online help & unlimited support are available to ensure your success. Hundreds of federal, state & local agencies trust their analysis and court room presentations to CellHawk. Several top users participate in our Law Enforcement Advisory Panel that helps guide product features & direction. https://support,hawkanalytics.com
CFIS	Comprehensive Financial Investigations Solution (CFIS) by Advanced Investigative Technology. CFIS is a standard investigative tool in use by Federal, State and Local, Prosecutors, Law Enforcement, Regulatory Agencies and forensic accountants to investigate financial crimes. By automatically importing data, it provides an increase in productivity. Standardized reports allow immediate access to a range of financial outputs. http://www.aitcfis.com/about
CrimeNtel	CrimeNtel allows the analyst to organize, analyze, and manage data and create alerts in Web, Windows and Mobile versions. Search capabilities are almost unlimited with the help of "fast find", ad-hoc query and report builder features. http://crimentel.com
CrimeView	The Omega Group developed CrimeView to be a law enforcement specific GIS tool. The Omega Group is partnered with ESRI and CrimeView is based on ArcGIS, therefore a lot of the functionality is the same (e.g. import / export data, spatial analysis) (CrimeView Desktop, n.d.). http://www.theomegagroup.com/police/crimeview_desktop.html
DataWalk	DataWalk is a next-generation analytical platform for intelligence-led decision making. DataWalk easily connects many large data sources for fast visual analysis and collaborative investigations. Analyze data using visual queries, maps, time-series analysis and link analysis. www.datawalk.com
DrawPerfect	DrawPerfect was developed by Corel but is now defunct. Some aspects of it can be downloaded now as freeware. https://winworldpc.com/product/drawperfect
Genesis	Genesis develops programs to support: Web-Based Home Banking Systems; Check Imaging Systems; Web-Based Account Statement Presentation Systems; Asset and Portfolio Management Systems; Leasing and Equipment Finance Management Systems; Web-Based Online Auction and Bidding Systems; Inventory Management Systems;Broadcast Faxing, Emailing and CRM solutions; Order Fulfillment Systems; ACH and Payment Processing Systems;

	Web-Based Paperless Office Solutions; HIPAA, FFIEC, NCUA Compliancy; and Claims Processing Systems. http://www.genesisys.com/software
GeoTime CRT	The Geo Time Call Records Tool allows the analyst to automatically clean Call Data Recorders (CDRs), create top calls, pattern of life, automated summaries, visible date ranges, 3D mapping and courtroom presentation data. It supports all carrier reporting formats. http://geotime.com
Google Earth	Google Earth is a free geospatial tool for analysts. It allows users to import points, lines, and polygons in numerous formats (ranging from .txt files to .shp files). Google Earth also allows users to import imagery and text files that correlate to locations of interest. While Google Earth does not have the spatial relationship analysis capabilities of some other tools, it enables analysts to visually depict data geospatially, create geospatial timelines to show change or movement over time, and measure distances. http://www.google.com/earth/index.html
IBM Watson	"Watson Analytics is a smart data analysis and visualization service you can use to quickly discover patterns and meaning in your data – all on your own. With guided data discovery, automated predictive analytics and cognitive capabilities such as natural language dialogue, you can interact with data conversationally to get answers you understand. Whether you need to quickly spot a trend or you have a team that needs to visualize report data in a dashboard, Watson Analytics has you covered." http://www.ibm.com/Watson
Lumen – a product of Numerica Corp.	Lumen provides for integratable data sources including CAD, RMS, Fire, Jail, GIS Shaefiles, MS Word, and Intel files. It is scalable, CJS compliant with two-factor authentication, and supports varied databases. www.numerica.us/lumen
Microsoft Visio	Microsoft Visio can be used for manually creating charts and visualizations. "Microsoft made Visio 2013 for Windows available in two editions: Standard and Professional. The Standard and Professional editions share the same interface, but the Premium edition (discontinued) has additional templates for more advanced diagrams and layouts, as well as capabilities intended to make it easy for users to connect their diagrams to data sources and to display their data graphically." https://products.office.com/en-us/Visio/microsoft-visio-pro-for-office-365?wt.srch=1&wt.mc_id=AID522514_SEM_4xYGC7RC
NCSS	"NCSS software provides a complete and easy-to-use collection of hundreds of statistical and graphics tools to analyze and visualize your data." https://www.ncss.com
Netmap	"NetMap Data Mining identifies emergent groups within myriads of individual data items and utilizes special algorithms that aid visualization of 'emergent' patterns and trends in the linkage. It complements conventional data mining methods, which assume the independence between the attributes and the independence between the values of these attributes. These techniques typically flag, alert or alarm instances or events that could represent anomalous behaviour or irregularities because of a match with pre-defined patterns or rules. They serve as 'exception detection' methods where the rules or definitions of what might constitute an exception are able to be known and

	specified ahead of time." http://netmap.com/au
Palantir	"Palantir Law Enforcement features an intuitive, user-friendly interface that allows any agent, detective, or investigator to quickly access all available information in one place. Instead of logging in to separate systems, users can conduct one search for a suspect, target, or location through a single portal and return data from all relevant systems. Palantir Law Enforcement supports existing case management systems, evidence management systems, arrest records, warrant data, subpoenaed data, RMS or other crime-reporting data, Computer Aided Dispatch (CAD) data, federal repositories, gang intelligence, suspicious activity reports, Automated License Plate Reader (ALPR) data, and unstructured data such as document repositories and emails." In addition to the crimes mentioned here, the software has been used with cases involving national security, consumer fraud, public corruption, drug and human trafficking, and gang violence. https://www.palantir.com
PowerPoint	Design like a professional in seconds with PowerPoint Designer. To help you maximize the visual impact of your presentation, it provides design options like Morph, which creates fluid, cinematic motion in one click. Just duplicate two slides that you want to morph together, move objects in them based on how you want to animate them, and click Morph. https://products.office.com/en-US/powerpoint
PENLINK	PENLINK products include PLX, XNET and DATA SCIENCE. The products assist law enforcement to collect and analyze large sets of communications data. https://www.penlink.com
Tableau	"Tableau helps people transform data into actionable insights. Explore with limitless visual analytics. Build dashboards and perform ad hoc analyses in just a few clicks. Share your work with anyone and make an impact on your business. From global enterprises to early-stage startups and small businesses, people everywhere use Tableau to see and understand their data." http://www.tableau.com
UCINet	UCINET 6 for Windows is a software package for the analysis of social network data. It was developed by Lin Freeman, Martin Everett and Steve Borgatti. It comes with the NetDraw network visualization tool. https://sites.goole.com/site/ucninetsoftware/home
Vigilant	Vigilant specializes in facial recognition software that allows the analyst to identify the image, apply data filters to a search, run the search, verify the choice and have the possible match as an investigative lead. It also provides license plate recognition and data sharing. https://www.vigilantsolutions.com/
VisuaLinks	VisuaLinks helps analysts sit through volumes of data to find targets of interest using filtering, drill-down and link analysis tools. VisuaLinks can zero in on, or isolate, specific targets in the data, and then, step-by-step, build relationships that show patterns of activities or behaviors. Applying a combination of these tools and techniques enables analysts to perform reactive and proactive (strategic and tactical) analysis in a fraction of the time a manual analysis

	would take. http://www.numerical-analytics.com/visual-link
Visual Network Analytics	Centrifuge Analytics includes the following four key functional areas: 1: Data Unification: Simply point Centrifuge Analytics at one or more data sources, glue them together to define a Centrifuge problem space and you are ready to go. 2: Integrated BI Visualizations: Centrifuge Analytics comes with a full suite of visualizations including: properties and intersection charting, relationship graphing, temporal events, geospatial proximities, and tabular views. 3: Link Analysis: With Centrifuge Link-Analysis you ask a graphical pattern search question and have Centrifuge highlight the exact matches for each search directly on the graph visualization. 4: Collaboration: Once a Centrifuge Analytics problem definition and visualizations have been finalized for exposing the nuances of the problem they can be saved as a template (model) and shared with other data analysts to reuse. http://www.centrifugesystems.com/product
Word Perfect Presentations Graphics	WordPerfect Presentations Grapics includes: Easy document creation; Built-in PDF forms; Flexible eBook publishing; Extensive compatibility, including Microsoft Office; Reveal Codes; Template Viewer; and Function key https://www.wordperfect.com/en/pages/old-brands/presentations-graphics/
Wynard Advanced Analytics	Wynyard Advanced Crime Analytics (ACA) is a powerful investigative analytics solution essential for intelligence and investigations teams in law enforcement and government agencies to prevent and solve crime faster by rapidly revealing actionable intelligence hidden in data. Deployed at organisations around the world, Wynyard ACA is powerful in preventing and solving a wide range of crimes including: Organised Crime, Transnational Crime, Violent Crime, Trafficking, New Generation Extremism and Gun Crime. https://www.wynyardgroup.com/crime_analytics.php

Customizable Solutions

During the past decade, an increasing number of law enforcement agencies are employing business intelligence (BI) software tools to fight crime. "many law enforcement agencies are facing the problem of being 'data rich but information poor'... these organizations have a great deal of potentially golden data that sits idle in silos because no one has solved the problem of how to integrate and harness it." (Hemsoth, 2012) An example of a law enforcement agency utilizing a BI solution occured in the State of Maryland in the U.S. They engaged the database software company Oracle to build a solution that would pull together data from a multitude of varied sources. The result of this collaboration "is called the 'Law Enforcement Dashboard' which the state says draws from 'more than 100 data sources across 22 agencies to access accurate, timely information that helps [users] make fast, well-informed decisions in the fight against violent crime.' They say that with the new system, one simple search will instantly allow users to access a person's offender status, criminal history, photos, warrant details, gun and license information and so on—all in a single view." (Hemsoth, 2012) Below is a list of a few BI software companies that have been selling customized products to the law enforcement community.

Application Name	Description
abmpegasus	"abmpegasus software incorporates management tools to make it easier to handle and disseminate evidence and intelligence obtained through covert techniques. Our continuous engagement with all levels of law enforcement ensures that abmpegasus remains at the forefront of covert intelligence technology. abmpegasus and its modules can be expanded to meet the operational needs if an individual agency or collaborative law enforcement requirements." www.abmsoftware.com/products/abmpegasus/
IBM- Fraud Detection/Intelligence Software Portfolio	**Cognos, i2, SPSS, Q1 Labs, Trusteer, and SoftLayer** - IBM has integrated multiple counter-fraud products in their software portfolio. They also gave them a single product ID number and a single licensing metric. "That alone will shave about three weeks off the ordering process for a large enterprise. Deployments on IBM's SoftLayer cloud will simplify the process of installing and operating the software, too.... IBM also unveiled Red Cell, a new group of about 500 Big Blue fraud-fighting super heroes whose goal is to help clients detect and put an end to fraud in their organizations. "It's just like X-Force, but it's applied to fraud intelligence rather than the security and malware space." https://www.ibm.com/analytics/us/en/technology/products/cognos-analytics
Microsoft Power BI and Azure	With Microsoft's advanced analytics capabilities such as Microsoft Power BI, Microsoft Azure Stream Analytics, and Microsoft Azure Machine Learning (Azure ML), police departments now have the capability to predict when and where crimes will happen in the future. By building a crime analytics and predictions Power BI dashboard, law enforcement agencies can take advantage of predictive policing approaches to bring about safer cities.... With Microsoft's data platform, law enforcement agencies now have the tools they need to turn vast amounts of data into powerful information that will bolster the fight against crime. " https://powerbi.microsoft.com/
MicroStrategy	MicroStrategy provides customized data management and analytic systems for many industries. "MicroStrategy empowers analysts to combine and correlate data from multiple systems – helping to maximize their insight into transactions that may include fraud, waste, or abuse. Analysts can apply sophisticated algorithms and leverage predictive tools to calculate the potential likelihood for fraudulent activity. By interacting with intuitive visualizations and threshold-based alerts, they can quickly spot behavior outside the realm of accepted benchmarks to promptly initiate an investigation." https://www.microstrategy.com/
QlikView	Quinn Analytics is a company specializing in delivering Qlik solutions to the public and private sectors, "With data volumes increasing exponentially, the need to turn data into useful and relevant information have never been greater. The solution is…agile applications with low life-cycle cost that can be easily repurposed as needs change. QlikView gives investigators and technicians unlimited ability to analyze large volumes of constantly changing data as well as connect to other sources to fuse information to address the multiple issues for law enforcement in analyzing call traffic and cell phone forensics."

	www.qlik.com/
SAS - Criminal Justice Data Integration and Analytics	"SAS (pronounced 'sass') offers "an integrated suite of solutions for homeland security and criminal justice professionals – including executives, border agents, analysts and officers. They deliver solutions that provide critical information for: 1. **Law enforcement**. Improve intelligence, support policing best practices, reduce crime and protect citizens by providing access to secure, accurate, real-time information at every stage of the intelligence life cycle. 2. **Fusion centers**. Process and corroborate information from multiple data sources, and give law enforcement and security agency personnel – analysts, investigators, officers and commanders – fast, secure access to intelligence they can use to act on threats to the public. 3. **Border management**. Enable border agents to determine which travelers and cargos are most likely to be high-risk or illegal – as well as which should be unimpeded – based on all available, relevant information sources, including social network linkages. 4. **Intelligence management**. Quickly and securely collect, process, evaluate, grade, analyze and disseminate intelligence garnered from big data. 5. **Insider threats**. Identify the precursors of malicious acts, and know which technical and nontechnical countermeasures will improve your organization's survivability and resiliency." https://www.sas.com
SAS - Memex	In 2010, "SAS, the leader in business analytics software and services, ... acquired Memex, a worldwide leader in intelligence management solutions that help improve intelligence processes, enhance public safety, and prevent and deter crime, terrorism and other threats. The company has a strong presence in the law enforcement and homeland security markets.... Since 1979, Memex has delivered innovative technology solutions and services around the world. More than 100 commercial and intelligence organizations rely on Memex to support and develop their intelligence-led operations, significantly improving their decision-making capabilities and operational effectiveness." https://www.sas.com
Teradata	Teradata provides customized solutions for government agencies that "leverage all their data to know more about their citizens, answer new questions, drive deeper insights and make better decisions to improve agency outcomes. As government agencies work to adapt data capture practices now standardized by the private sector, new data types—specifically, big data—are not waiting for them to catch up. Big data refers to data sets (both structured and multi-structured) whose size and complexity are beyond the ability of commonly used software tools for capturing, managing, and processing in a timely manner. Teradata solutions leverage data—such as legacy transactional systems, ERP systems, sensors, web data, cyber data, cloud-computing, Hadoop/Map-Reduce environments, text and other data types—so you can

	gain a single, integrated view of your operations and make faster, better decisions that enhance operational efficiency." www.teradata.com
Voyager Analytics	Voyager Analytics uses sophisticated artificial intelligence and cognitive computing algorithms to analyze relevant data, identify relationships, document interactions, assess risks, and identify potential insider threats. http://www.voyagerlabs.co

Freeware

Google has a web page containing a Law Enforcement Intelligence Digital Library: https://sites.google.com/site/lawenforcementintelligence/home . Included on this site are sections on: Academic Programs, Agency Contact Information, Associations (Professional), Books (Amazon.Com), Documents, Language & Culture, Literature Links, Portals and Networks, Software (Freeware), Training (On-Line), Web-Links and Index and a Sitemap. (https://sites.google.com/site/lawenforcementintelligence/system/app/pages/sitemap/hierarchy)

Below is information taken from the section on software that is available free of charge.

Application Name	Description
CARVER2	Target Analysis Software - Is "a non-technical method of comparing and ranking critical infrastructure and key resources." http://www.ni2cie.org/CARVER2.asp
Computer Security Evaluation Tool (CSET)	Computer Security Evaluation Tool - http://www.us-cert.gov/control_systems/satool.html. Is a cyber system assessment tool available to the U.S. Critical Infrastructure/Key Resources (CI/KR) community. https://ics-cert.us-cert.gov/Assessments
CrimeStat IV	CrimeStat IV (version 4.02) is the most recent version of CrimeStat, a spatial statistics program for the analysis of crime incident locations. CrimeStat was funded by grants from NIJ. CrimeStat is Windows-based and interfaces with most desktop GIS programs. It provides statistical tools to aid law enforcement agencies and criminal justice researchers in their crime mapping efforts. The program includes more than 100 statistical routines for the spatial analysis of crime and other incidents. CrimeStat inputs incident locations (e.g., robbery locations) in dbf, point shp or ASCII formats using either spherical or projected coordinates. It calculates various spatial statistics and writes graphical objects to ArcGIS, MapInfo, Surfer for Windows and other GIS packages. https://nij.gov/topics/technology/maps/pages/crimestat.aspx

Encryption Wizard (EW)	Encryption Wizard (EW) DoD Software Protection Initiative -- EW is a program used for protecting sensitive (but not classified) documents, and for protecting files before transmission via email. https://www.spi.dod.mil/ewizard.htm
Comprehensive R Archive Network	Comprehensive R Archive Network - Is a statistical computing and graphics program. http://cran.r-project.org/
Decrypto 8.5	Decrypto 8.5 - Is an automated cryptogram solver. http://www.blisstonia.com/software/WebDecrypto/
Environmental Protection Agency | VSAT	Environmental Protection Agency | VSAT - VSAT is a risk assessment software tool for water, wastewater, and combined utilities of all sizes. http://yosemite.epa.gov/ow/SReg.nsf/description/VSAT
SAS - Criminal Justice Data Integration and Analytics	Epi Info 7 - Is free from the CDC, intended for public health practitioners and epidemiologists, but it includes many statistical techniques that crime analysts use too. http://www.cdc.gov/Epiinfo
Gephi	Gephi is a tool for data analysts and scientists keen to explore and understand graphs. Like Photoshop™ but for graph data, the user interacts with the representation, manipulates the structures, shapes and colors to reveal hidden patterns. The goal is to help data analysts to make hypothesis, intuitively discover patterns, isolate structure singularities or faults during data sourcing. It is a complementary tool to traditional statistics, as visual thinking with interactive interfaces is now recognized to facilitate reasoning. This is a software for Exploratory Data Analysis, a paradigm in the Visual Analytics field of research. http://gephi.org/features
Microsoft COFEE	Computer Online Forensic Evidence Extractor - Is only available to individuals employed by law enforcement agencies within the United States and Canada. https://cofee.nw3c.org/
Near Repeat Calculator	Near Repeat Calculator - "This software originates with the relatively recent discovery of the near repeat phenomenon in burglary patterns, a discovery that has highlighted the communicability of crime events that affect the risk level at nearby locations." http://www.temple.edu/cj/misc/nr/
Pajek XXL	**Pajek-XXL** is used for analysis of huge networks - networks that cannot be loaded into physical memory using 'ordinary' Pajek. It is supposed that Pajek-XXL could be used to extract some smaller, interesting parts of a huge network that can be later further analysed (and visualized) with more sophisticated methods available in Pajek. The other possible use of Pajek-XXL is analysis of huge networks where identity of vertices is not important. Such examples are simulation studies on random networks, where we are interested in general properties, like distributions (e.g. degrees, triads,...). Using Repeat Last Command can generate some thousands of large random networks and compute mean values, variances and other statistics of interesting properties. http://mvar.fdv.uni-lj.si/pajek/PajekXXL.htm#Pajek3XL
Problem Analysis Module	Problem Analysis Module -- - Provides a framework for analyzing any persistent crime and public safety problem.

	http://www.popcenter.org/learning/pam/
Quantum GIS	Quantum GIS -- - "Open Source Geographic Information System (GIS) that runs on Linux, Unix, Mac OSX, Windows and Android." http://www.qgis.org/
RAIDS On-Line Public Crime Map	RAIDS On-Line Public Crime Map -- - Is a "free public crime map, RAIDS Online, connects law enforcement with the community to reduce crime and improve public safety." http://bairanalytics.com/raidsonline
RFFlow 5	RFFlow 5 -- Is a tool for drawing flowcharts, organization charts, and many other kinds of diagrams. http://www.rff.com/index.htm
R Project for Statistical Computing	"R is a language and environment for statistical computing and graphics.... It provides a wide variety of statistical (linear and nonlinear modeling, classical statistical tests, time-series analysis, classification, and clustering)". R is available for download without charge. https://www.r-project.org/
Risk Self-Assessment Tool for Commercial Facilities	Risk Self-Assessment Tool for Commercial Facilities - - Is a "web-based tool that delivers an all-hazard analysis of a facility's current risk level and offers options for consideration on reducing and managing potential vulnerabilities." http://www.dhs.gov/files/programs/gc_1259861625248.shtm
Social Network Visualizer	Social Network Visualizer (SocNetV) is a cross-platform, user-friendly free software application for social network analysis and visualization. With SocNetV you can: draw social networks with a few clicks on a virtual canvas, load field data from a file in a supported format (*GraphML*, *GraphViz*, *Adjacency*, EdgeList, GML, *Pajek*, *UCINET*, etc) or crawl the internet to create a social network of connected webpages. http://www.socnetv.org
Squidmat	Squidmat (courses of action evaluation program) - "The program compares two or more courses of action based on two or more evaluation criteria." http://faculty.tamu-commerce.edu/jmstauffer/Squidmat/
Statistical Software	Statistical Software (Links to several free programs) - http://www.freestatistics.altervista.org
TrueCrypt	TrueCrypt - Is a software system that encrypts data automatically. http://www.truecrypt.org/

Cyber Software

There is a range of cyber software available, from forensic to intrusion detection programs.

Application Name	Description
Digital Forensics Framework	Digital Forensics Framework is open source and comes under GPL License. It can be used either by professionals or non-experts without any trouble. It can be used for digital chain of custody, to access the remote or local devices, forensics of Windows or Linux OS, recovery hidden or deleted files, quick search for files' meta data, and various other things. http://www.digitalforensics.com

EnCase Forensic 8	EnCase Forensic 8 supports all smartphone operating systems and over 26,000 device profiles. You can logically or physically acquire data including text messages, pictures, applications data, deleted data, etc. to gather the critical evidence needed in your case. https://www.guidancesoftware.com/encase-forensic
Forensic Tool Kit	The Forensic Tool Kit processes and indexes up front so you don't waste time waiting for searches to execute, helping you to zero in on relevant evidence faster, and dramatically increasing analysis speed. It leverages one shared case database, allowing teams to use the same data, reducing cost and complexity of creating multiple case datasets. FTK is database driven, providing the stability necessary to handle large data. Its visualization technology displays your data in timelines, cluster graphs, pie charts, geolocation and more. http://accessdata.com/products-services/forensic-toolkit-ftk
The Sleuth Kit	The Sleuth Kit is a Unix and Windows based tool which helps in forensic analysis of computers. It comes with various tools which help in digital forensics. These tools help analyze disk images and perform in-depth analysis of file systems http://www.sleuthkit.org .
Cellebrite UFED	Cellebrite's UFED solutions present a unified workflow to allow examiners, investigators and first responders to collect, protect and act decisively on mobile data with the speed and accuracy a situation demands – without ever compromising one for the other. The UFED Pro Series is designed for forensic examiners and investigators who require the most comprehensive, up-to-date mobile data extraction and decoding support available to handle the influx of new data sources. Platform agnostic, the UFED Field Series is designed to unify workflows between the field and lab, making it possible to view, access and share mobile data via in-car workstations, laptops, tablets or a secure, self-service kiosk located at a station. http://www.cellebrite.com/Mobile Forensics
Tripwire	Tripwire is a wormhole mapping system that allows you to detect system activity (jumps, kills), static wormholes, wormhole effects, security and local pirates. It is secured with an A+ rated e-commerce SSL certificate and the latest internet security standards, you can be sure your intel is safe and secure. https://tripwire.eve-apps.com/
Bro	Bro is an intrusion detection system that targets high-performance networks. It comprehensively logs what it sees and provides a high-level archive of a network's activity. It enables high-level semantic analysis and keeps extensive records about the network it monitors. It interfaces with other applications for real-time exchange of information. https://www.bro.org
Suricata	Suricata is a free and open source, mature, fast and robust network threat detection engine. The Suricata engine is capable of real time intrusion detection (IDS), inline intrusion prevention (IPS), network security monitoring (NSM) and offline pcap processing. Suricata inspects the network traffic using a powerful and extensive rules and signature language, and has powerful Lua scripting support for detection of complex threats. With standard input and output formats like YAML and JSON, integrations with tools like existing SIEMs, Splunk, Logstash/Elasticsearch,

	Kibana, and other databases become effortless. https://suricata-ids.org/
Sguil	Sguil (pronounced sgweel) is built by network security analysts for network security analysts. Sguil's main component is an intuitive GUI that provides access to realtime events, session data, and raw packet captures. Sguil facilitates the practice of Network Security Monitoring and event driven analysis. The Sguil client is written in tcl/tk and can be run on any operating system that supports tcl/tk (including Linux, *BSD, Solaris, MacOS, and Win32) http://bammv.github.io/sguil/index.html

Content Analysis/Web Search Software

Below are some examples of computerized content analysis software now in use.

Application Name	Description
Authentic8 Silo	A virtual browser in the cloud for secure and mis-attributed analysis of data on the open and dark webs. (http://www.authentic8.com)
Crawdad Desktop 2.0	(http://www.crawdadtech.com/html/01_software.html) **Transana** (http://www.transana.org/) (for digital or audio data) http://www.digitalforensics.com
Lexalytics	Lexalytics (http://groovy.lexalytics.com/TextAnalytics
MCCA Lite	**Minnesota Contextual Content Analysis** (http://www.clres.com/)
Media Sonar	**Turns big data into smart data. (http://mediasonar.com)**
NetAbstraction/ Cutting Edge	**Deliver specialized, protected non-attributable access to the Internet. (http://www.cuttingedgeca.com)**
TABARI	**TABARI (Text Analysis By Augmented Replacement Instructions)** (http://www.eventdata.parusanalytics.com/software.dir/tabari.info.html
TextAnalyst	TextAnalyst (http://www.megaputer.com/index.php3)
Veritone	Content integration, indexing, and monitoring. (https;//veritone.com)

Source: (http://academic.csuohio.edu/neuendorf_ka/content/cata.html) and vendors

Author/Editor Biographies

Karen L. Aumond
Karen Aumond retired as the Executive Director of the Western States Information Network (WSIN) in 2016. She started her career in intelligence as a WSIN analyst in 1982 and became the Executive Director in 2005. Under the leadership of Ms. Aumond, the RISSafe application and associated policies and procedures were developed and deployed by WSIN in July 2008. WSIN operates a 24/7 RISSafe Watch Center, which supports the nationwide RISSafe program.

Ms. Aumond has long been an advocate of analyzing information contained in legacy intelligence databases. In November 2002, she was awarded a fellowship from the federal Counterdrug Intelligence Executive Secretariat to complete a research project on the "Analysis of Disparate Databases." The Master Telephone Index and the RISSLinks application are results of Ms. Aumond's work. Ms. Aumond has instructed many law enforcement and intelligence training classes. From 1991 to 2001, she taught quarterly at the Federal Law Enforcement Training Center Criminal Intelligence Training Program. Ms. Aumond has also taught classes for the California Department of Justice Advanced Training Center, the Border Patrol, and the Financial Crimes Enforcement Network, as well as to various High Intensity Drug Trafficking Areas.

Ms. Aumond is a member of the Advisory Board, International Association of Law Enforcement Intelligence Analysts (IALEIA). The holds the title of Lifetime Criminal Intelligence Certified Analyst (CICA) and in 2002 received the Society of Certified Criminal Analysts Lifetime Achievement Award. Ms. Aumond is a Lifetime Member of the California Narcotic Officers' Association. She has been recognized by the Federal Bureau of Investigation for her analytical work on a major nationwide case, "Operation CACUS," which resulted in the arrest of 52 members of the Hells Angels outlaw motorcycle gang. In 2016, she received the One Step Ahead Award from LexisNexis Risk Solutions, in conjunction with the Law Enforcement Intelligence Units (LEIU). This award is presented to groups or individuals who have made a significant contribution to the law enforcement criminal intelligence community.

Ms. Aumond received a Bachelor of Science degree in criminal justice (forensic science) from California State University-Sacramento, graduating with honors. She received a Master of Public Administration degree from Golden Gate University in 1999.

Alison Callery
Alison Callery is an Investigator and Certified Fraud Examiner currently working for the State of New Jersey. She previously spent 13 years as an Analyst with the NJ Division of Criminal Justice participating in numerous criminal investigations. While at DCJ, Alison worked in the Official Corruption Bureau for seven years before transferring to the Financial and Computer Crimes Bureau where she assisted in financial fraud investigations. She also contributed to the creation of the NJ Attorney General's Sandy Fraud Task Force, a multi-agency organization tasked with the investigation and prosecution of grant fraud and other types of fraud relating to Superstorm Sandy. She teaches Bank Records Analysis and Money Laundering for law enforcement throughout New Jersey and is also a Certified FIAT Instructor through IALEIA.

Paula Carter

Paula Carter is a lifetime Certified Intelligence Criminal Analyst with over thirty-five years of experience in intelligence and investigative analysis, fraud investigations, supervision of analytic projects and staff, database design, presentation of evidence, report preparation and the presentation of complex data utilizing visualization software. She is also the first non-Federal employee to be designated as a Certified Computer Analysis Response Team technician by the Federal Bureau of Investigation (FBI).

Ms. Carter began her career as an Organized Crime Intelligence Analyst with the New Jersey State Police Intelligence Bureau, and remained with the State of NJ for over thirty years with analytic assignments in the State Commission of Investigation and the Office of Insurance Fraud Prosecutor (OIFP) within the NJ Attorney General's Office. While with OIFP, Ms. Carter supervised the Case Litigation and Analytic Support Section; while there, she was selected to participate in the task force at the computer analysis laboratory administered by the FBI.ng, examination, and analysis of seized computer systems.

After retiring from the State of NJ in 2012, Ms. Carter joined the UnitedHealthcare Special Investigations Unit as an Investigations Consultant. Here she has managed the receipt, investigation and referral of allegations of fraud, waste and abuse. She also conducts proactive studies and prepares comprehensive investigative and regulatory reports and data visualizations. Ms. Carter has a B.S. in Business Administration from Rider University.

David Creagh

David Creagh has served in the U.S., Intelligence Community for 18 years. Currently, he is an intelligence analyst for the Federal Bureau of Investigation where he specializes in gangs and violent crime for the Baltimore Division. From 1998 to 2008, David served in the U.S. Air Force as an intelligence analyst for the National Security Agency. Following his department from the Air Force, David was an intelligence analysts and reports officer for the Department of Homeland Security. David earned his Associate's Degree in Telecommunications from the Community College of the Air Force, his Bachelor's Degree in Criminal Justice from the University of Maryland University College, and his Master's Degree in Intelligence Analysis from the Johns Hopkins University. The views expressed in this publication solely belong to the author and not that of the Federal Bureau of Investigation.

Robert C. Fahlman, O.O.M., Lifetime C.I.C.A.

Robert retired from the Royal Canadian Mounted Police (RCMP) in 2011 as Director General, Criminal Intelligence after 35 years of distinguished service. He served as Deputy Director General, Criminal Intelligence Service Canada (CISC) from 2002 – 2008, where he was responsible for launching the CISC National Threat Assessment, Sentinel Strategic Early Warning methodology, National Intelligence Requirements and the Canadian Criminal Intelligence Model (CCIM). He was seconded to Interpol General Secretariat in Lyon, France from 1999 – 2002 as Assistant Director, responsible for Interpol's global Criminal Intelligence Program. He is a member of the Advisory Board, International Association of Law Enforcement Intelligence Analysts (IALEIA), and was Executive Director, IALEIA from 2002 – 2004. He has served as the Chancellor, Society of Certified Criminal Analysts (SCCA) from 1995 – 1999 and holds the title of Lifetime Criminal Intelligence Certified Analyst (CICA) and was a founding member of the Board of Governors of the SCCA and the recipient of the 1997 SCCA Lifetime Achievement Award.

Robert is currently President, R & D Fahlman Consulting, Inc. He has extensive experience working with over 30 countries as an advisor in the field of intelligence systems, with a focus on intelligence governance, doctrine, threat-risk assessment, early warning and intelligence program development, and has written numerous research papers and conducted training seminars for both practitioners and executives. Robert has a Bachelor of Applied Arts (Journalism) from Ryerson University, Toronto and has completed additional studies at Carleton University and the Canadian Police College, Ottawa; the RCMP Training Academy, Regina; Queen's University, Kingston; and, Georgetown University, Washington, D.C. In 1992, Robert was awarded the Canada 125 Medal in recognition of his distinguished service to the Government of Canada and in 2011 was appointed an Officer of the Order of Merit of the Police Forces (O.O.M.) by the Governor General of Canada. The Order of Merit is the centrepiece of Canada's honours system and recognizes a lifetime of outstanding achievement, dedication to the community and service to the nation in the police sector.

David Gervais

Major David Gervais is a Military Intelligence Officer in the U.S. Army with 20 years of service. His assignments include Battalion Deputy Intelligence Officer, Battalion Intelligence Officer, Counter Proliferation Operations Officer, Signals Intelligence Company Commander, Senior Intelligence Analyst, Intelligence Advisor to Iraqi Security Forces and Intelligence Advisor to Afghanistan Security Forces. He currently serves as the Analysis and Control Element (ACE) Chief for the 21st Theater Sustainment Command in Germany. MAJ Gervais received a BS in Criminal Justice from Bowie State University, MS in Strategic Intelligence from National Intelligence University and an MS in Law Enforcement Intelligence and Analysis from Michigan State University. He is a member of the International Association of Law Enforcement Intelligence Analysts, International Association of Crime Analysts, and the Military Intelligence Corps Association.

Lt. (N) Lee Heard

Lt. Lee Heard has spent over 25 years in the Canadian Armed Forces Regular and Reserve Forces in the Infantry and Intelligence Corps completing three NATO deployments in Bosnia and currently serves as a Naval Intelligence Officer for HMCS York. He has spent the last 12 years in law enforcement intelligence as well as completing two NATO civilian deployments as an Intelligence Analyst in Afghanistan and Kosovo. Most notably, he has served as a Strategic Intelligence Analyst with the Ontario Provincial Police and the Criminal Intelligence Service of Ontario. In 2014, he became a Criminal Intelligence Certified Analyst (CICA) with IALEIA and currently serves as a civilian consultant with NATO in the UK.

Jennifer Johnstone

Jenny Johnstone's career in Law Enforcement began almost 30 years ago as a sworn Customs Inspector with Canada Customs. In 1993 she became an Intelligence Analyst with Canada Customs and during that time worked as part of a joint task Force with the RCMP focusing on contraband smuggling. In 2001 she joined the RCMP as a civilian intelligence analyst and has worked on Eastern European Organized crime as part of a team conducting an intelligence probe, Border related issues as part of an Integrated Border Intelligence Team with officers and analysts from several agencies in both Canada and the United States, as a tactical analyst as part of a newly created Integrated Gang Task Force and as part of the Coordinated Forces Special Enforcement Unit Outlaw Motorcycle Gang section. She served as a Strategic Briefing Analyst assigned to the office of the (RCMP) Deputy Commissioner West.

Jenny retired from the RCMP in 2016 and has since that time has worked overseas in Ukraine, South East Asia and Central America where she was responsible for developing and delivering training about such topics as structured analytical techniques, strategic analysis, ethics, intelligence led policing and the intelligence cycle.

Jenny is currently completing a MSc in Intelligence Studies and is a Lifetime Criminal Intelligence Certified Analyst, the Immediate Past President of the International Association of Law Enforcement Intelligence Analysts (IALEIA), the largest professional organization in the world representing law enforcement analysts, and currently serves on the Executive Advisory Board.

Jonathan Larkin. Th.D.

Dr. Jonathan Larkin has built up an 8-year career in Intelligence with Surrey Police (UK), predominately working as a Higher Intelligence Analyst from 2012 onwards. Jonathan has worked across both specialist and volume crime areas and is particularly experienced in using intelligence analysis to support proactive investigations. This has resulted in Jonathan acting as a professional witness, presenting his analyst at court, on multiple occasions as a professional witness, presenting his analysis at court, on multiple occasions. Jonathan's expert contribution has been recognised at a senior level on a number of occasions, one particular highlight involved Jonathan being awarded a Command Commendation for analysis he conducted during a lengthy and large scale operation that resulted in the successful investigation and prosecution of fraudulent conspirators who had targeted vulnerable, elderly victims.

Jonathan holds a number of professional qualifications and certifications, in addition to a Doctorate in Theology (obtained by original research), a Masters of Divinity Degree and a PDC in Terrorism Studies.

Clement de Maillard, Ph.D.

Dr. Clément de Maillard is seconded to INTERPOL's General Secretariat, Lyon as Criminal Intelligence Officer since 2014, by the French Gendarmerie. Before joining INTERPOL, his work with French Gendarmerie spans over period of 09 years and he had been working as the head of a tactical surveillance unit specialized in serious and organized crimes and terrorism for the South-West area of France. Dr. de Maillard received his doctorate from the School of Criminal Justice in Lausanne (Switzerland); he has written several contributions in criminology, especially on the model of intelligence-led policing, and he is specialized in criminal intelligence matters.

Patrick Perrot, Ph.D.

Dr. Patrick Perrot is a gendarmerie officer working for the criminal intelligence service in France. Over his career, he has combined both operational and scientific activities. After 8 years in charge of the Signal, Speech and Image processing department in a forensic field, his activities are currently dedicated to the development of criminal intelligence. He holds a PhD in modelling science from Telecom Paris Tech. His research interests include artificial intelligence, information extraction, machine learning, and knowledge engineering dedicated to the fight against crime. He is the author of several publications in these fields, and has been awarded with the ENFSI (European Network of Forensic Science Institutes) Referenced Best Articles Award by the European Academy of Forensic Sciences.

Marilyn B. Peterson
For the last 37 years, Ms. Peterson has played an active role in the law enforcement intelligence community. She was the first non-charter member of IALEIA in 1981, starting her career as Senior Analyst for the RISS project, MAGLOCLEN.

She has written dozens of articles and book chapters, with her most notable book being *Applications in Criminal Analysis* (1994, 1998 pb). She co-founded the Society of Certified Criminal Analysts in 1990 and was president of IALEIA from 1996 to 2000. After 25 years as an intelligence analyst, she went on to teach intelligence at the Federal level for 11 years. She is now the principal of Peterson Analytic Associates, LLC and continues to teach at the university graduate and undergraduate levels. She remains on the IALEIA Advisory Board. She has won several writing awards and three lifetime achievement awards. She was co-editor of *Criminal Intelligence Analysis* (1990), Managing Editor of the *Basic Elements of Intelligence Revised* (2000), and contributing editor *to Criminal Intelligence in the 21st Century* (2011). She has an undergraduate degree in criminal justice and a Master of Arts in Education.

Linda Randby, J.D.
Linda J. Randby is the senior legal counsel and Privacy Officer for the Pennsylvania State Police Bureau of Criminal Investigation ("PSP"). She has served in this capacity since July 2012. In this role, Ms. Randby handles legal issues related to the work of the Bureau of Criminal Investigation including matters related to drug investigations, gathering and dissemination of intelligence information, participation on task forces and privacy, civil liberties and civil rights. She has developed and implemented a nationally known privacy, civil liberties and civil rights program at PSP.

Prior to her appointment to PSP, she was with the Pennsylvania Board of Probation & Parole ("PBPP") from 2000 to 2012. During her time at the PBPP, she served as Chief Counsel, Deputy Chief Counsel and Assistant Counsel. Before her appointment to the PBPP, she worked as Deputy General Counsel at the Pennsylvania Higher Education Assistance Agency and as an Associate Attorney at the law firm, McNees, Wallace & Nurick. Ms. Randby is a member of the Pennsylvania Bar Association, Dauphin County Bar Association, and the James Bowman Inns of Court. Ms. Randby is admitted to practice before the Supreme Court of Pennsylvania, the Third Circuit Court of Appeals, the District of Columbia Court of Appeals and the United States District Court for the Middle District of Pennsylvania. She received her bachelor degree from Ashland University and her juris doctorate degree from Widener University School of Law. She was admitted to the Pennsylvania bar in 1993.

Alyssa Ryder
Alyssa Ryder has worked as a Crime & Intelligence Analyst with the Duluth Police Department since 2009, supporting departmental units, the multi-jurisdictional Lake Superior Drug & Violent Crime Task Force, Lake Superior Child Abduction Response Team (CART), and other partner agencies. She is a Certified Crime & Intelligence Analyst through the California Department of Justice and California State University-Sacramento and is working towards additional certifications in the field. Ryder received an MA in Criminology from the University of Minnesota-Duluth focusing her thesis practicum work on the utilization of analyst support for cold case investigations. She also earned BAs in Psychology (Law Concentration) and Theatre Arts (Performance Concentration) from Augsburg College. Ryder is a member of IALEIA, IACA, and MACIA (Minnesota Association of Criminal Intelligence Analysts) and co-facilitates the Arrowhead Cross Infrastructure Public Safety Group meetings. Ryder conducts training

and presentations for courses at the University of Minnesota-Duluth, the Arrowhead Public Safety Group meeting, Narcotics Investigation Training, and co-presented at a MACIA Training Symposium.

Kerri Salata, J.D.
Kerri A. Salata began her legal career as an Associate at an insurance defence firm in Hamilton, Canada, and was then recruited to the international law firm of Gowlings as an Associate to litigate on behalf of large banks. Kerri joined the Legal and Compliance group at Bank of Montreal (BMO) in 2009 as Counsel where she managed litigation dispute resolutions and quickly gained legal experience in fraud investigation, anti-money laundering issues, class actions, employment-related issues and privacy. Her experience with criminal risk and fraud-related issues led her to manage the Business Intelligence group beginning in 2014. Her intelligence team worked with law enforcement, internal investigators and business partners across BMO to gain a better understanding of emerging fraud trends and physical security threats to the bank, its employees and customers – all with a focus on detection and prevention. Kerri's role required an excellent understanding and application of privacy laws and case law. She is currently a Director in BMO's Wealth Compliance group. She has a Juris Doctor from the University of Windsor and was admitted to the Law Society of Upper Canada as a lawyer in 2006.

Navid Sobbi
Navid Sobbi is the Managing Director of National Surveillance and Intelligence Pty Ltd, and Group CEO of Praesidium Corp Group of Companies, Australia's leading Global Geopolitical Risk and Counter Intelligence Advisory firm, specialising in Technical Surveillance Counter Measures (TSCM), Digital Forensics, and Geopolitical Risk Advisory. He has a Bachelors degree in Law and a Masters in International Security Studies. He is currently completing a Masters in Cyber Security with a specialty in Digital Forensics. His expertise is regularly sought after by the likes of Channel 7, 60 Minutes, Channel 9, ABC Radio, Sky News, The Sydney Morning Herald, and The Daily Telegraph. He is also heavily involved in the Geopolitical Risk arena. He directs a team of specialists that have conducted TSCM audits for numerous government departments throughout Australia, South East Asia, and multinational organisations throughout the world.

Gregory Thomas, Ph.D.
Dr. Gregory Thomas is the assistant director of geospatial intelligence programs in the John A. Dutton e-Education Institute in the College of Earth and Mineral Sciences with the Pennsylvania State University. In this capacity, he is the geospatial intelligence option coordinator for the intercollege Masters of Professional Studies in Homeland Security. Prior to this appointment, Dr. Thomas taught in the geospatial intelligence program for several years.

Dr. Thomas brings to the program 26 years of intelligence and analytical experience in the law enforcement field. He previously worked for investigative agencies in the Commonwealth, including the Pennsylvania Crime Commission, the Pennsylvania Office of Inspector General, and most recently, the Pennsylvania State Police. In his position at the State Police as an intelligence analyst supervisor, Dr. Thomas selected, trained, and managed analysts as they provided support to criminal investigators and law enforcement personnel. Analysts under his supervision examined criminal intelligence information using techniques including geospatial intelligence applications, communications analysis, network analysis, and event analysis. With the State Police, he assisted with intelligence-led policing functions, complex conspiratorial investigations, as well as homeland security and anti-terrorism initiatives.

He obtained a Bachelor of Science degree in Criminal Justice with a minor in Sociology from Shippensburg University of Pennsylvania, a Master's of Public Administration from the Pennsylvania State University, and a doctorate in Administration and Leadership Studies from Indiana University of Pennsylvania. His dissertation work focused on the role of local law enforcement in homeland security.Dr. Thomas assisted in developing analytical training for criminal analysts. He is a lifetime Criminal Intelligence Certified Analyst through the International Association of Law Enforcement Intelligence Analysts. He has published articles relating to organized crime, criminal intelligence analysis, and terrorism.

Melissa Vives, Ph.D.

Dr. Melissa Vives obtained her Doctor of Philosophy in Public Service Leadership in 2016 with a concentration in Emergency Management from Capella University focusing her dissertation on cyber security concerns. She also has an undergraduate degree from Edinboro University and Master's degree in Criminal Justice from Tiffin University. She has a background in commercial/white collar crimes investigations as well as a history of anti-money laundering investigations. She is currently employed with the U.S. Federal Government conducting investigations for individuals who had exposures during the making of the Atomic Bomb. She also currently teaches at Colorado Technical University and Georgia Military College focusing on criminal justice and homeland security courses. She also finds time to be an avid world traveler.

Anne Walton

Anne Walton is a director at K2 Intelligence and an adjunct professor at John Jay College of Criminal Justice. In her role at K2 Anne helps financial institutions manage risk, focusing on anti-money laundering (AML), counterterrorism financing, and sanctions investigations. Prior to joining K2 Intelligence, Anne worked as an independent consultant, completing an investigation into the role of shell companies in a criminal activity as well as performing physical and cybersecurity threat assessments. Before that, Anne was also a senior intelligence analyst for Helios Global, where she produced intelligence reports and dynamic threat assessments for the Department of Homeland Security. She also worked as a research fellow for the Center on Global Counterterrorism Cooperation and the John Jay College Center on Terrorism, where she focused on the terror financing techniques of Al Shabaab and the Horn of Africa. Anne authored the article "Financial Intelligence: Uses and Teaching Methods," published in the *Journal of Strategic Security* (Vol. 6, Fall 2013). Prior to this Anne was an intelligence analyst with the NY/NJ High Intensity Financial Crimes Area (HIFCA) and was deployed to the El Dorado Money Laundering Task Force, where she provided analytical support to criminal investigations in the NY/NJ metro area. Anne holds an M.A. in criminal justice from John Jay College and a B.A. in justice from American University. She is a certified anti-money laundering specialist (CAMS).

Andrew Wright

Andrew Wright was a Strategic Criminal Intelligence Analyst with Criminal Intelligence Service Alberta, a serious and organized crime unit based in Alberta, Canada, but recently joined Interpol to work in Zimbawe. His current work assesses criminal organization dynamics, their criminal market involvement, and the threat posed to public safety. Prior to this, Andrew was a Tactical Anti-Money Laundering Intelligence Analyst with Canada's Financial Intelligence Unit (FINTRAC) in Ottawa. With his current work on criminal organizations, past work in anti-money laundering, and having worked earlier in his career abroad on conflict diamond issues, Andrew has a in depth grasp of organized crime issues. He holds a master's degree in international and intercultural communications and an undergraduate degree in political science.

Bibliography

Abadinsky. Howard (2010). *Organized Crime* (9th edition). Boston, MA: Wadsworth

abmpegasus (n.d.). Retrieved from http://www.abmsoftware.com/wp-content/uploads/2015/09/abm-a4-pegasus-overview.pdf

Accurint for Government (n.d.) Retrieved from http://www.lexisnexis.com/risk/products/government/accurint-government.aspx

Accurint for Law Enforcement (n.d.) Retrieved from http://www.lexisnexis.com/risk/products/government/accurint-le.aspx

Agnovi REX (2017). Retrieved from https://www.agnovi.com/investigation-software-for-small-teams/

AICPA (2007) *Standard Auditing Statements*. Association of International Certified Public Accountants.

Alexander, Keith., & Hermann, P. (2014, May 5). *Gang activity behind shooting near D.C. zoo, police say.* Retrieved from The Washington Post: https://www.washingtonpost.com/local/crime/2014/05/05/890f4902-d48f-11e3-aae8-c2d44bd79778_story.html

Alkaabi, Ali O.S (2010) "Combating Computer Crime: AnInternational Perspective" (PhD Thesis) Queensland University of Technology, Queensland, Australia.

American Civil Liberties Association. (2015).ACLU – Obtained Documents Reveal Breadth of Secrecitive stingray Use in Florida. Retrieved from http://www.aclu.or/blog/free-future/aclu-obtained-documents-reveal-breadth-secretive-stingray-use-florida

Analyse-it (n.d.). Retrieved from https://analyse-it.com/products/standard/

Analyst's Notebook (n.d.). Retrieved from http://www-03.ibm.com/software/products/en/analysts-notebook

ArcGIS for Law Enforcement (n.d.). Retrieved from http://solutions.arcgis.com/local-government/law-enforcement/

Anderson, Jessica. (2015) "Former gang leader at center of jail scandal sentenced." RetrievedfromCNN; http://www.baltimoresun.com/news/maryland/crime/bs-d-ci-tavon-white-sentencing-20150209-story.html (February 9).

Anderson, Richard. (1997). "Intelligence-led policing: a British perspective." In A. Smith (ed) *International Perspectives on Policing in the 21st Century* , 5-9. Lawrenceville, NJ: IALEIA.

Andress, Jason, & Winterfeld, S. (2014). *Cyber warfare: Techniques, tactics, and tools for security practitioners* (2nd ed.). Waltham, MA: Elsevier.

Ariely, Dan. (2009). *Predictably Irrational*. Harper Collins.

Armed Forces Communications and Electronics Association. (2007). *The Need to Share: The U.S. Intelligence Community and Law Enforcement*. Fairfax, VA: AFCEA International.

Assemblée nationale. (2013). *Rapport d'information en conclusion des travaux d'une mission d'information sur l'évaluation du cadre juridique applicable aux services de renseignement*. Assemblée nationale. Jean-Jacques Urvoas; Patrice Verchère.

Association of Certified Fraud Examiners (2002). *Encyclopedia of Fraud*. Austin, TX: Obsidian Publishing.

---------------- (2008) *Fraud Examiners' Manual*. Austin, TX: Association of Fraud Examiners.

---------------- (2015). Report to the Nations. Accessed January 18, 2016 at http://www.acfe.com/rttn-summary.aspx

---------------- (2016). *Report to the Nations on Occupational Fraud and Abuse*. Austin, TX: Association of Certified Fraud Examiners.

Australian Attorney-General's Department (2013). *National Plan to Combat Cybercrime.*

Ayres,D. (1994). "In a city of graffiti, gangs turn to violence to protect their art." Retrieved from New York Times: http://www.nytimes.co/1994/03/13/us/in-a-city-of-graffiti-gangs-turn-to-violence-to-protect-their-art.hhtml?pagewanted=all (March 13)

Babel Street (n.d.). Retrieved from http://www.babelstreet.com/Product_About.aspx

Babel X (n.d.). Retrieved from http://www.babelstreet.com/Product_Babel_X.aspx

Barciz, David (2014) *An ounce of prevention is worth a pound of suppression: a collaborative framework for comprehensive gang reduction.* www.lulu.com

Barker, Thomas (2010) *Biker Gangs as Organized Crime Groups.* New York: Routledge.

Bayer, Michael D. (2010). *The Blue Planet: Informal International Police Networks and National Intelligence.* Washington DC: National Defense Intelligence College.

BehrmanM. (2015) "When gangs go viral: using social media and surveillance cameras to enhance gang databases". *Harvard Journal of Law and Tecnology,29 (1), 315-338.*

Bellman, Richard. (1961). *Adaptative control processes: a guided tour.* Princeton University Press.

Bengio, Yoshua. (2013). Deep learning of representation: looking forward. In Spingler (Ed.), *Statistical Language and Speech Processing* (Vol. 7978). lectures notes in Computer Science.

--------------- Goodfellow, I., & Courville, A. (2015). *Learning deep architecture for AI.* MIT Press.

Bennett, T. B. (2002). *Applying the center of gravity concept to the war on drugs.* Carlisle Barracks, PA: U.S. Army War College.

Besson, Jean-Louis. (2004). *Les cartes du crime.* Presses universitaires de France.

Black's Law Dictionary Online Free Dictionary 2nd edition. Accessed at http://thelawdictionary.org/letter/f/page/82/, June 19, 2016.

Blakes Bulletin. (2015). *Digital privacy act receives royal assent, but breach notification provisions lag behind.* Retrieved from: http://www.blakes.com/English/Resources/Bulletins/Pages/Details.aspx?BulletinID=2148

Bodnar, John (2003) *Warning Analysis for the Information Age.* Washington, DC: Joint Military Intelligence College.

Bouchard, Martin. and Konarski, R. (2014). "Assessing the core membership of a youth gang from its co-offending network" in *Crime and Networks,* C. Morselli, ed. London: Routledge.

Bouchard, Martin and Amirault, J. (2013). "Advances in research on illicit networks". *Global Crime,* Volume 12.

Bouza, Anthony V. (1976) *Police Intelligence: The Operations of an Investigative Unit.* New York: MS Press.

Bradford, W.C. (2004) Revaching the Visual Learner: Teaching Proerly through Art Retrieved from Social Science Research etwork, http://ssrn.com/abstract=587201 (June)

Brantingham, Paul, & Patricia Brantingham. (1993). *Environment, routine and situation : toward a pattern theory of crime* (Transaction Publishers ed.). (R. Clarke, & M. Felson, Eds.) Routine activity and and rational Black choice : advances in criminological theory.

Broadhurst, Roderic. (2006). "Developments in the global law enforcement of cyber-crime". *Policing: An International Journal of Police Strategies & Mangement.* 29(3), 408-433.

Bronitt, Simon & Gani, M. (2003). "Shifting Boundaries of Cybercrime: From Computer Hacking to Cyber-terrorism." *Criminal Law Journal,* 27(6), 303-321.

Brookover, Barbara (2016) *"Exploring Crime Analysis: Key Readings on Essential Skills* (second edition)." International Association of Crime Analysts, April..

Bureau of Justice Assistance. (2008). *Fusion center guidelines: developing and sharing information and intelligence in a new era.* Washington: U.S. Department of Justice.

California State University, Northridge. (n.d.). *The problems of definitions.* Retrieved from CSUN.edu: http://www.csun.edu/~hcchs006/6.html

Calvani, Sandro. (2010). "Transnational organized crime: emerging trends of global concern". NATO Defense College, lecture in Rome Italy.

Canadian Charter of Rights and Freedoms. 1982. Canada Act 1982.

Carey v. Population Services, Intern., 431 U.S. 678 (1977)

Cariens, David. (2011) "Report Writing Principles: A Guide for Intelligence Professionals", in *Criminal Intelligence Analysis for the 21st Century,* Wright, Morehouse, Peterson and Palmieri, eds.. Sacramento, CA: LEIU and IALEIA.

Carter, David (2004). *Law enforcement intelligence: a guide for state, local, and tribal law enforcement agencies.* Washington, DC: U.S. Department of Justice.

--------------- (2009). *Law enforcement intelligence: A Guide for state, local, and tribal law enforcement agencies (2nd edition).* Washington, DC: U.S. Department of Justice

---------------- (2012). Law Enforcement Intelligence and National Security Intelligence: Exploring the Differences. *IALEIA Journal, 21(1), 1-14.*

Cassara, John and Avi Jorisch (2010) *On the Trail of Terror Finance: What Law Enforcement and Intelligence Officials Need to Know.* Arlington, VA: Red Cell Publishing.

Castree, Sam. (2012). "Cyber-plagiarism for sale. The growing problem of blatant copyright infringement in online digital media stores". *Texas Review of Entertainment and Sports Law*, 14(1), 25-45.

CBC News (2016) "Stingray surveillance device questions prompt federal privacy complaint". Retrieved from http://www.cbs.canews/technology/stingray-open-media-1.3533417

Chapman, Chip. (2014). An Independent Review of the Police Disciplinary System in ... Retrieved June 01, 2016, from https://www.gov.uk/government/uploads/system/uploads/attachment_data/file/385911/An_Independent_Review_of_the_Police_Disciplinary_System_-_Report_-_Final....pdf

Chen, M., S. Mao and Y. Liu (2014) "Big Data Analysis in Smart Manufacturing A Survey". *Scientific Research.* Retrieved June 30, 2017 from http://www.scirp.org/(S(vtj3fa45qm1ean45vvffcz55))/reference/ReferencesPapers.aspx?ReferenceID=2019784

Chermak, Stephen, Jeremy Carter, David Carter, Edmund F. McGarrell and Jack Drew (2013) "Law enforcement's Information Sharing Infrastructure A National Assessment" in *Police Quarterly* 2013 16: 211 originally published online 19 February 2013 http://pqx.sagepub.com/content/16/2/211

Clark v. Community for Creative Non-violence, 468 U.S. 288, 293, 1984

CLEAR Investigation Software (n.d.) Retrieved My 17, 2017 from http://legalsolutions.thomsonreuters.com/law-products/solutions/clear-investigation-software

Consumer Sentinel (n.d.) Retrieved March 5, 2017 from https://www.ftc.gov/enforcement/consumer-sentinel-network

CNN (2017) "What is MS-13? The transnational street gang on the FBI's radar". Retrieved May 2, 2017 from CNN Wire Service: http://fox6now.com/2017/03/03/what-is-ms-13-the-transnational-street-gang-on the fbis-radar/ (March 3).

Coderre, David (2004) *Computer-Aided Fraud Prevention and Detection.* New York: Wiley and Sons.

Cohen, Lawrence and Marcus Felson (1979). "Social Change and Crime Rate Trends: A Routine Activity Approach", in *American Sociological Review*, 52:170-83.

Cole, J. (2012). Target Identification - Arthur D. Simons Center for ... Retrieved June 27, 2016, from http://thesimonscenter.org/wp-content/uploads/2012/12/IAJ-3-4-pg49-59.pdf

Coambs, Paul (2011) "Collection", in *Criminal Intelligence for the 21st Century*, Wright, Morehouse, Peterson and Palmieri, eds. Sacramento, CA: LEIU and IALEIA.

Conley, Courtney (2017) ABC News, (April 28), "Violent Gang MS-13 believed linked to 11 recent killings," accessed 4/30/17 at http://www.abcnews.go.com/US/violent-gang-MS-13-believed-linked-11-recent/story/ID/48703080

Cook, John and Marilyn P. Sommers (1987) "From Gaming to Tax Evasion: Going After the Distributors" in *Police Chief Magazine* (January).

Cope, Nicholas (2004). "Intelligence-led policing or policing-led intellligence". *British Journal of Criminology* , 191, 194.

Coyne, John and Bell, Peter (2015). *The Role of Strategic Intelligence in Law Enforcement: Policing Transnational Organized Crime in Canada, the United Kingdom, and Australia.* Basingstoke, UK: Palgrave Macmillan.

Crime Tech Solutions (2015) Retrieved July 2, 2017 from http://crimetechsolutions.com

CrimeView Desktop (n.d.). Retrieved from http://www.theomegagroup.com/police/crimeview_desktop.html

Criminal Intelligence Service Canada. (2007) *Integrated Threat Assessment Methodology* Version 1.0, Ottawa, Canada: Criminal Intelligence Service Canada.

-------------- (2014) "About Us". Retrieved from http://www.cisc.gc.a/about-ausujet/index-eng.htm

Criminal Procedures Investigations Act 1996

Cumming, Alfred, & Masse, T. (2004). *FBI intelligence reform since September 11, 2001: issues and options for Congress*. Washington, D.C.: Congressional Research Service.

Cunliffe, Rachel (2017) "The Leap 100 understand the importance of cyber security" *City A.M. Newsletters*, retrieved June 14, 2017 from http://www.cityam.com/266587/leap-100-understand-importance-cyber-security

Cush, A. (2016). "Social media surveillance probably played a role in sparking the Freddie Gray Riot." Retrieved July 6, 2017from Spin: http://www.spoin.com/2016.10/scial-media-surveillance-probably-played-a-role-in-sparking-the-freddie-gray-riot.

CyberCop Brochure (n.d.) Retrieved June 14, 2017 from https://www.opsecprofessionals.org/articles/CyberCopbrochure.pdf

Dagg *v*. Canada (Minister of Finance), (1997). 2 *S.C.R.* 403

Dataminr (n.d.). Retrieved June 8, 2017 from https://www.dataminr.com/about/

dBASE PLUS 11 (2017). Retrieved June 8, 2017 from http://www.dbase.com/dbasesql/overview/

Department of Homeland Security (2010) *Intermdiate Fusion Center Analyst Training Manual*. Washington, DC: Department of Homeland Security

---------------- (n.d.) "National Cybersecurity Protection System" . Retrieved from https://www.dhs.gov/national-cyberecurity-protection=spstem-ncps June 15, 2017.

Department of Justice (2007). *Analyst toolbox: a toolbox for the intelligence analyst*. Global Justice Information Sharing Initiative.

Department of Legislative Services. (2009). *Criminal gangs in Maryland*. Annapolis: Office of Policy Analysis.

Desai, Sumbul. (2016). "Study of online cyber crimes in India". *American Journal of Computer Science & Engineering Survey, 4*(2).

Digital Privacy Act. (2015). Statutes of Canada, 2015, c. 32.

DigitalStakeout Public Safety Intelligence (n.d.). Retrieved from http://www.digitalstakeout.com/public-safety-intelligence

Dintino, Justin J. and Frederick T. Martens (1983). *Police intelligence systems in crime control*. Springfield: Charles C. Thomas.

Docketerman, E. (2016). *Your identity is worth $5 on the black market*. Time Magazine. Retrieved June 16, 2017 from http://newsfeed.time.com/2013/08/26/your-identity-is-worth-5-on-the-black-market/

Drinkwater, Doug. (2014, May 15). "Cyber-attacks on Lockheed Martin quadruple". *SC Magazine*. Retrieved from http://www.scmagazineuk.com/cyber-attacks-on-lockheed-martin-quadruple/article/347140/

Drug Enforcement Administration. (2015). *2015 National Drug Threat Assessment Summary*. Washington DC: U.S. Government Printing Office.

Dunbar, Laura. (2012) *Gang Cohesion and Intervention Strategies: A Review of the Literature*. Research Report R292. Ottawa, ON: Correctional Service of Canada

Echosec (n.d.). Retrieved May 17, 2016 from https://www.echosec.net/faq/

Echosec Public Safety Intelligence (n.d.). Retrieved May 17, 2016 from https://www.echosec.net/public-safety-intelligence/

Edelhertz, Herbert and Charles H. Rogovin, editors (1980) *A National Strategy for Containing White-Collar Crime*. Lexington, MA: Lexington Books.

Eikmeier, Dale C. (2013). Addressing the Fog of COG - Combined Arms Center. Retrieved June 27, 2016, from http://usacac.army.mil/cac2/cgsc/carl/download/csipubs/COG.pdf

---------------- (2007) "A Logical Method for Center-of-Gravity Analysis." *Military Review,* Vol. 87, No. 5, September-October.

---------------- (2014). "After the Divorce: Clausewitz and the Center of Gravity". Retrieved June 27, 2016, from http://smallwarsjournal.com/printpdf/15355

El Paso Intelligence Center (EPIC) (n.d.). Retrieved June 1, 2017 from: https://sites.google.com/site/lawenforcementintelligence/web-links-and-index

ESRI for Law Enforcement (2011). Retrieved July 6, 2017 from http://www.esri.com/industries/law-enforcement

Federal Bureau of Investigation. (2016). *New FBI academy program integrates agents and intelligence analysts*. Retrieved from FBI.gov: https://www.fbi.gov/news/stories/new-fbi-academy-program-integrates-agents-and-intelligence-analysts. January 28.

---------------- (2016) "Integrating Intelligence and Investigations" Retrieved from https://www.fbi.gov/about-us/nsb/integrating_intel. January 4, 2016.

---------------- (2011) "35 alleged members and associates of SSB Blood gang indicted on federal racketeering, drug, and gun charges." Retrieved June 3, 2017 from FBI.gov: https://archives.fbi.gov/archives/baltimore/press-releases/2011-alleged-members-and-asociates-of-ssb-bloods-gang-indicted-on-federal-racketeering-drug-and-gun-charges (October13).

------------------ (2012) "Member of 18th Street Gang sentenced to over 24 years in prison for a racketeering conspiracy related to gang activities." Retrieved June 3, 2017from Federal Bureau of Investigation: https://archives.fbi.gov/archives/baltimore/press-releases/2012/member-of-18th-street-gang-sentenced-to-over-24-years-in-prison-for=a-racketeering-conspiracy-related-to-gang-activities (August 6).

Felson, Marcus, and Ronald Clarke (1998). Opportunity Makes the Thief. London: *Home Office* .

Fenton, Justin. (2016) "Tayvon White, center of Baltimore jail corruptionscandal, returns as a urder trial witness". Retrieved February 18, 2017 from *Baltimore Sun*: http://www.baltimoresun.com/news/maryland/crime/bs-md-ci-tavon-white-returns-20160309-story.html (March 9)

Ferguson, Andrew. (2015, January). "Big Data and Predictive Reasonable Suspicion". *University of Pennsylvania Law Review , 163* (2), pp. 327-410.

---------------- (2012, May). "Predictive Policing and Reasonable Suspicion". *Emory Law Journal , 259.*

FinCEN website. (2017) Retrieved May 4, 2017 from http://www.fincen.org.

FileMaker Pro (n.d.). Retrieved May 17, 2017 from http://download.cnet.com/FileMaker-Pro/3000-2065_4-10720179.html

Fishman, Clifford S. (2006) "Recordings, Transcripts and Translations as Evidence" in *Washington Law Review.* Retrieved June 22, 2017 from https://digital.law.washington.edu/dspace-law/bitstream/handle/1773.1/272/81washlrev473.pdf?sequence=1

Foreign Military Studies Office (FMSO) (2017, March 10). Retrieved June 3, 2017 from http://fmso.leavenworth.army.mil/

Fowler, C. W. (2002). *Center of gravity: Still relevant after all these years*. Carlisle Barracks, PA: U.S. Army War College

Fox News (2015) "Organized crime filed against 170 motorcycle gang members after Texas shootout". Retrieved May 7, 2017 from Fox News: http://www.foxnews.com/us/2015/19/police-report-multiple-fatalities-after-shooting-in-texas.html (May 19).

Fuchs, Erin (2015) "A confrontation between cops and teenagers kicked off the horrifying Baltimore riots". Business Insider, accessed June 11, 2017 at http://www.businessinsider.com/confrontation-at-mondawmin-mall-led-2015-4 (April 28).

Geis, Gilbert, Robert F. Meier and Lawrence M. Salinger (1995) *White-Collar Crime Classic and Contemporary Views, 3rd ed*. New York: The Free Press.

Geofeedia (2016) Retrieved June 8, 2017https://www.geofeedia.com/company/about.

---------------- (n.d.). Retrieved June 8, 2017 from https://geofeedia.com/products/geolocation-social-media-monitoring/

---------------- (n.d.). Retrieved June 8, 2017 from https://geofeedia.com/products/how-it-works/

Giraud, Chrisstophe. (2014). *Introduction to high dimension statistics*. Chapman and Hall, CRC Press.

Gladyshev, Pavel., & James, JI. (2016). "A survey of mutual legal assistance involving digital evidence. *Digital Investigation*, 18, 23-32. C

Global Intelligence Working Group (2007) "Minimum Criminal Intelligence Training Standards" version 2. Washington, DC: Bureau of Justice Assistance (October).

Global Intelligence Working Group (2012) "Law Enforcement Analytic Standards", version 2. Washington, DC: Bureau of Justice Assistance, Global Intelligence Working Group and International Association of Law Enforcement Intelligence Analysts

Godfrey, E. Drexel and Don R. Harris (1971). *Basic elements of intelligence; a manural of theory, structure and procedure for use by law enforcement agencies against organized crime.* Washington: Department of Justice.

Godson, Roy and Wirtz, James J. (2000). "Strategic Denial and Deception". *International Journal of Intelligence and Counterintelligence, 13(4), 424-437.*

Gordnier, John. (2011). "Legal issues in U.S. criminal intelligence: An overview". In R. Wright, B. Morehouse, M. B. Peterson, & L. Palmieri (Eds.), *Criminal intelligence for the 21st century* (pp. 16-27). Law Enforcement Intelligence Unit and International Association of Law Enforcement Intelligence Analysts.

Gorilla Convict. (2015) "Inside the history of the Black Guerrilla Family". Retrieved May 13, 2017 from Gorilla Convict: http://www.gorillaconvict.com/2015/05/inside-the-history-of-the-black-guerrilla-family. (May 15).

Govtech (2017) " 5 Steps to Cyber-Security Risk Assessment" Retrieved June 15, 2017 from http://www.govtech.com/security/5-Steps-to-Cyber-Security.html

Granovetter, Mark. (1973). "The strength of weak ties". *The American Journal of Sociology*, Volume 78, 1360-1380.

Griswold v. Connecticut, 381 U.S. 479 (1965)

Hanneman, Robert. and M. Riddle. (2005) *Introduction to Social Network Methods.* Department of Sociology, University of California.

Harris, Don. (1976). *Basic elements of intelligence; a manual for police department intelligence units.* Washington: U.S. Department of Justice.

Hashimi, Sadaf., M. Bouchard,C. Morselli, and M. Ouellet. (2016). "A method to detect criminal organizations from police data". *Methodological Innovations*, Volume 9, 1-14.

Hashimi, Sadaf. and Bouchard, M. (2016). "On to the next? Using social network data to inform police target prioritization". *Policing,* June.

Heatherington, Cynthia and M.K. Sankey (2008) *The Manual to Online Public Records.* Tempe, AZ: BRB Publications.

Hemsoth, Nicole. (2012, February 2). How BI is Becoming Crime's Biggest Enemy. Retrieved from https://www.datanami.com/2012/02/02/how_bi_is_becoming_crimes_biggest_enemy/

Heurer, Jr., Richard J. and Randolph Pherson. (2015) *Structured Analytic Techniques for Intelligence Analysts.* Los Angeles: Sage.

Hines, M. (2006). "Helping Law Enforcement Fight Cyber-Crime". *PC Mag.* Retrieved 10 May 2016 from http://www.pcmag.com/article2/0,2817,1962273,00.asp.

History Learning Site. Accessed February 7, 2016 at http://www.historylearningsite.co.uk/medieval-england/the-bayeux-tapestry/.

Holder, Eric. (2012). Attorney General Eric Holder Speaks at the Singapore Academy of Law. *Justice Department Releases.*

Homeland Security Information Network (HSIN) (2017, February 22). Retrieved June 5, 2017 from https://www.dhs.gov/homeland-security-information-network-hsin

Howard, Sally (2015). "The terrifying rise of the all-girl gang." *The Telegraph.* Accessed 4/30/17 at www.telegraph.co.uk/women/womens-life/111343706/terrifying-rise-of-the-all-girl-gang.html (posted 1/18/15)

Human Right program, Your guide to the Canadian Charter of Rights and Freedoms. Retrieved from http://Canada.pch.gc.ca/eng/1468851006026

Hunter et al. v Southam, Inc., (1984) 2 scR 145, 1984 CanLII 33 (SCC),p. 159-160.

Hunton, Paul. (2010). Cyber Crime and Security: A New Model of Law Enforcement Investigation. *Policing, 4(4),* 385-394.

--------------- (2011) "The stages of cybercrime investigations. Bridging the gap between tehnology examination and law enforcement investigation". *Computer Law and Society Review, 27 (1), 61-67.*

IALEIA (2004) "Law Enforcement Analytic Standards." (2004 and 2012) Washington, DC: U.S. Department of Justice, Office of Justice Programs.

IBM DB2 (2016, June 23). Retrieved from http://www-03.ibm.com/press/us/en/pressrelease/50023.wss

IBM Informix (n.d.). Retrieved from https://www.ibm.com/analytics/us/en/technology/informix/#what-is-db2-for-zos

IBM Netezza (n.d.). Retrieved from https://www-01.ibm.com/software/data/netezza/

IBM Watson (n.d.). Retrieved from https://www.ibm.com/us-en/marketplace/watson-analytics?S_PKG=AW&cm_mmc=Search_Bing-_-IBM+Analytics_AP+Horizontal+Watson+Analytics-_-WW_US-_-statistics+software_Exact_AW&cm_mmca1=000000WB&cm_mmca2=10000752&mkwid=37ec2017-f265-47d9-a3b2-8d2db761e703|510|259960&cvosrc=ppc.bing.statistics%20software&cvo_campaign=IBM%20Analytics_AP%20Horizontal%20Watson%20Analytics-WW_US&cvo_crid=15863227495&Matchtype=e

IBM-Woodie, Alex. (2014, March 21). IBM Flushes Out Fraud with Big Data Analytics. Retrieved from https://www.datanami.com/2014/03/21/ibm_flushes_out_fraud_with_big_data_analytics/

Infobright (n.d.). Retrieved from https://en.wikipedia.org/wiki/Infobright

Information Sharing Environment (ISE) (n.d.). Retrieved from https://www.ise.gov/about-ise/what-ise

Infragard (n.d.). Retrieved from https://www.infragard.org

Intelink (n.d.). Retrieved from: https://sites.google.com/site/lawenforcementintelligence/web-links-and-index

Interbase (2017). Retrieved from https://www.embarcadero.com/products/interbase

International Association of Law Enforcement Intelligence Analysts. (2001). *Starting an analytic unit for intelligence led policing.* Lawrenceville: International Association of Law Enforcement Intelligence Analysts.

Internal Revenue Service web site. Retrieved from http://ww.irs.gov/irm/part4/irm_04-026-010.html

Internet Safety Campaign Africa. (2015). *News updates for Africa at large.* Retrieved May 17, 2017 from www.cybercrime.org.za

Internet World Stats (2017) "Internet Usage Statistics" (March 2017) accessed June 14, 017 at http://www.internetworldstats.com/stats.htm

Jabara v. Webster, 691 F.2d 272 (6th Cir. 1982) *cert. den.* 464 U.S. 863, 1983

Jobard, F., & Maillard, J. d. (2015). *Sociologie de la police. Politiques, organisations, réformes.* Paris: A. Colin.

Johannson, Frans. (2006). *The Medici effect: what you can learn from elephants and epidemics.* Boston: Harvard Business School.

Johnston, D. (2001). "Cyber Cops – Law enforcement goes high tech to battle cyber crime". *ServerWorld.* 15(11).

Johnson, Jeffrey A., Reitzel, J.D., Norwood, B.F., McCoy, D.M., Cummings, D.B., and Tate, R.R. (2013). "Social Network Analysis: A Systematic Approach for Investigating". *FBI Law Enforcement Bulletin.*

Katos, Vassilios and Peter Bednar. (2008) "A Cyber-Crime Investigation Framework". *Semantic Scholar.* Retrieved June 30, 2017 from https://pdfs.semanticscholar.org/a2a6/f862c737dc687fb04e04effbf37b525ec316.pdf

Katz v. U.S., 389 U.S. 347 (1967)

Keeley-Townsend, K., Sullivan, J., Monahan, T., & Donnelly, J. (2010). Intelligence-led mitigation. *Journal of Homeland Security and Emergency Management , 7* (1).

Kent Policing Authority. (2012). *Policing Kent.* Retrieved from Kent Police: http://www.kent.police.uk/about_us/attachments/policing_plan_2012.pdf

Kessler, G. C., & Ramsay, J. D. (2013). Paradigms for cybersecurity education in a homeland security program. *Journal of Homeland Security Education*, 2, 35–44.

Khimm, Suzy. (2015) "We're going to protect our community ourselves." Retrieved May 10, 2017 from *New Republic*: https://nwrepublic.com/article/121703/baltiore-gang-truce-over-freddie-gray-can-it-last (May 3)

Khullar, Ritu. (2010) "Conceptualizing the Right to Privacy in Canada." Canadian Bar Association

King, H. (2016) "Top 5 social media scams to avoid". CNN. Retrieved from http://money.cnn.com/2016/04/22/technology/facebook-twitter-phishing-scams/. April 22.

Klug, Jonathan P. (2012). *Behind the mosaic: Insurgent centers of gravity and counterinsurgency.* S.l.: Biblioscholar.Counterinsurgency. (2007). Retrieved June 01, 2016, from https://netwar.wordpress.com/2007/08/30/counterinsurgency

Krayniak, John and Marilyn B. Peterson (2000) "Blood Money: Lab Case Highlights Nationwide Medicaid Fraud Units", in *The White Paper,* Vol. 14, No. 2, (March/April)

Krippendorff, Klaus. (1989). "Content analysis". In E. Barnouw, G. Gerbner, W. Schramm, T. L. Worth, & L. Gross (Eds.), *International encyclopedia of communication* (Vol. 1, pp. 403-407). New York, NY: Oxford University Press. Retrieved May 17, 2017 from http://repository.upenn.edu/asc_papers/226

Lanzarote Committee. (2016) "Child Abuse". Retrieved May 17, 2017 from https://rm.cooe.int/CoERMPPublicCommonSearchServices/DisplayDCTMContent?documentId=090000168058cdfd

Law Enforcement Enterprise Portal (LEEP) (n.d.). Retrieved from https://www.fbi.gov/services/cjis/leep

Law Enforcement Intelligence Units. (2008). *Criminal intelligence file guidelines.* Sacramento, CA: LEIU. Retrieved June 15, 2017 from https://it.ojp.gov/documents/LEIU_Crim_Intell_File_Guidelines.pdf

le Carre', John (1977) *The Honourable School Boy.*Victoria, Australia: Bolinda Publishing

Le, Vy. (2012). "Organized crime typologies: structure, activities, and conditions". *International Journal of Criminology and Sociology,* Volume 1, 121-131.

Lee, Seung. (2016). "Your money or your data: Ransomware Viruses Reach Epidemic Proportions". *Newsweek,* 166(19).

Lemieux, Frederic (2012) and B. Bales. "Cyber Crime and Intelligence-led Policing. In Search of a Proactive Investigation Model". In S. Leman-Langlois (Ed.) *Technocrime 2.* Routledge: 65-78

Lewin, Esther and Albert Lewin (1989) *The Random House Thesaurus of Slang.* New York: Random House.

Lindsey, R. (1985) "They're behind bars, but not out of business." Retrieved May 12, 2017 from *The New York Times:* http://www.nytimes.com/198506/02/weekinreview/they-re-behind-bars-but-not-out-of-business-html. (June 2)

Lipton, Eric, David Sanger and Scott Shane (2016) "The Perfect Weapon: How Russian Cyberpower Invaded the U.S." *New York Times* (December 13). Retrieved June 17, 2017 from https://www.nytimes.com/2016/12/13/us/politics/russia-hack-election-dnc.html?_r=0

Loh, Stanley. (2015) "A Proactive Approach for BI". In A. Acevedo & M. Santos (eds.),*Integration of Data Mining in Business Intelligence Systems* (pp. 83—97), Hershey, PA: IGI Global

Madden, Sam. (2012, May)." From Databases to Big Data". *IEEE Internet comupting journal , 16* (3).

Maillard, Clement. d. (2014, Février 17). "La France et le renseignement criminel: entre volonté et réalité, une ambition à écrire". *Sécurité et stratégie ,* pp. 49-59.

---------------- (2014, July). "Le délinquant est-il vraiment si rationnel? De l'influence économique dans la pensée criminologique à l'étude de la prévisibilité de la délinquance". *Les Cahiers de la sécurité et de la justice* (29).

---------------- (2014, Janvier). "Sécurité et renseignement". *Le Débat ,* pp. 75-84.

Martens, Frederick T. (2000). "Uses, abuses and misuses of intelligence". In M. B. Peterson, B. Morehouse, & R. Wright (Eds.), *Intelligence 2000: Revising the basic elements* (pp. 37-47). Lawrenceville, NJ: Law Enforcement Intelligence Unit and International Association of Law Enforcement Intelligence Analysts

MediaSonar (n.d.) Retrieved from https://www.mediasonar.com/solution/

Mena Report. (2016). Belgium, Netherlands: results from JHA Council Day 2: more cooperation on cyber crime and forensic investigation. *Mena Report, Expanded Academic ASAP.*

Mcillwain, Jeffrey. (1999) "Organized Crime: A Social Network Approach" in *Crime, Law and Social Change,* Volume 32,

Microsoft Power BI (n.d.) Retrieved June 8, 2017 from https://powerbi.microsoft.com/en-us/

Microsoft Power BI and Azure (2017). Bhandari, Parul (2016, March 3). Predictive policing: The future of law enforcement. Retrieved June 8 2017 from https://enterprise.microsoft.com/en-us/articles/industries/government/predictive-policing-the-future-of-law-enforcement/

Microsoft SQL Server (2016, March). Technical White Paper. Retrieved June 8, 2017 from https://www.microsoft.com/en-us/sql-server/sql-server-2016

Microsoft Visio (n.d.). Retrieved June 14, 2017 from https://en.wikipedia.org/wiki/Microsoft_Visio

MicroStrategy (2017). Retrieved June 8, 2017 from https://www.microstrategy.com/us/solutions/by-industry/federal-government

Morehouse, Bob (2011) "The Role of Criminal Intelligence in Law Enforcement" in *Criminal Intelligence for the 21st Century*, Wright, Morehouse, Peterson and Palmieri, eds. Sacramento, CA: LEIU and IALEIA.

Muckin, Michael and Scott Fitch (2016) "A Threat Driven Approach to Cyber Security" (white paper). Retrieved June 14, 2017 from http://lockheedmartin.com/content/dam/lockheed/data/isgs/documents/Threat-Driven%20Approach%20whitepaper.pdf

MySQL (n.d.). Oracle MySQL Datasheet. Retrieved from https://www.mysql.com/products/enterprise

Memheld, Pierre (2015) "Intelligence Analysis and Cognitive Biases: An Illustrative Case" In *Journal of Intelligence and Analysis*,22(1).

NAACP v. Alabama, 357 U.S. 449, 462, 1958

National Gang Intelligence Center. (2015) *2015 National Gang Report*. Washington, DC: National Gang Intelligence Center.

National Geospatial Intelligence Agency (n.d.) Retrieved July 7, 2017 from https://www.nga.mil/pages/default.aspx.

National Institute of Justice. (n.d.) "What is a gang definition?" Retrieved May 15, 2017 from the National Institute of Justice https://www.nij.gov/topics/crime/gangs/pages/definitions.aspx.

National Institute of Security Technology (2012) *Guide for Conducting Risk Assessments*. (September) Retrieved June 14, 2017 from http://nvlpubs.nist.gov/nistpubs/Legacy/SP/nistspecialpublication800-30r1.pdf

National White Collar Crime Center (NW3C) (2017). Retrieved June 8, 2017 from http://www.nw3c.org/member-benefits/law-enforcement-tools

NCSS (2015). Retrieved June 6, 2017 from https://www.ncss.com/software/ncss/?gclid=CKiD5YPA49ICFZOGaQodYOwJ0g

Netmap (2017). Retrieved June 6, 2017 from http://www.netmap.com

Open Source Center (n.d.). Retrieved from https://sites.google.com/site/lawenforcementintelligence/web-links-and-index

Oracle (n.d.). Retrieved from https://en.wikipedia.org/wiki/Oracle_Database

National Centre for Policing Excellence (2005) *Guidance on the National Intelligence Model* 2005 Produced on behalf of the Association of Chief Police Officers. Retrieved 31/01/16 at 14:11 https://whereismydata.files.wordpress.com/2009/01/national-intelligence-model-20051.pdf

National Crime Information Center (NCIC) (n.d.). Retrieved from https://www.fbi.gov/services/cjis/ncic

National Data Exchange (N-DEx) System (n.d.). Retrieved from https://www.fbi.gov/services/cjis/ndex

National Gang Intelligence Center. (2011). *2011 national gang threat assessment -emerging trends*. Retrieved from Federal Bureau of Investigation: https://www.fbi.gov/stats-services/publications/2011-national-gang-threat-assessment

----------------. (2009). *National Gang Threat Assessment*.

---------------- (2013) *National Gang Threat Assessment*.

---------------- (2015) *2015 National Gang Report*. Washington, DC: National Gang IntelligenceCenter.

---------------- (2015, December). *Highlights of gang-related legislation*. Retrieved from National Gang Center: https://www.nationalgangcenter.gov/legislation/Highlights

National Institute of Justice (2017) "What is a gang definition?" Retrieved June 30, 2017 from National Institute of Justice at https://www.nij.gov/topics/crime/gangs/pages/definitions.aspx.

National Intelligence Model (2000) Retrieved June 23, 2017 from https://ict.police.uk/national-standards/intel

National Policing Improvement Agency (2008). *Practice Advice on Analysis* 2008 Produced on behalf of the Association of Chief Police Officers.) Retrieved February 15, 2016 at http://library.college.police.uk/docs/npia/practice_advice_on_analysis_interactive.pdf

National White Collar Crime Center (2011) *Financial Records Examination and Analysis – Course Manual, Version 4.3.* Richmond, VA: National White Collar Crime Center.

Nebraska Department of Insurance (nd) "Insurance Fraud Hints", accessed April 3, 2016 at www.doi.nebraska.gov/fraud/hints.

Newman, Lily H. (2016) "Hacker Lexicon: What's the Attribution Issue?" Wired Magazine (December 24)..Retrieved June 17, 2017, from https://www.wired.com/2016/12/hacker-lexicon-attribution-problem/

Newman,M.(2008) "The mathematics of networks". *The New Palgrave Encyclopedia of Economics.*

Nix.J, M.Smith, M. Petrocelli, J.Rojek,andV.Manjarrez (2016) "The use of social media by alleged members of Mexican cartels and affiliated drug trafficking organizations". *Journal of Homeland Security and Emergency Management*, 13(3).

North Atlantic Treaty Organization (NATO). (2012). *National cyber security framework manual.* Retrieved from https://ccdcoe.org/publications/books/NationalCyberSecurityFrameworkManual.pdf

Nossen, Richard and Joan Norvelle (1993) *The Detection, Investigation and Prosecution of Financial Crimes, 2nd ed.* Richmond, VA: Thoth Books.

Office of the Attorney General of Florida. (2009) "How do gangs recruit their members?" Retrieved May 17, 2017 from Florida Gang Reduction. http://www.floridagangreduction.com/figangs.nsf/pages/Recruiting

Office of the Privacy Commissioner of Canada. (2014). *Overview of privacy legislation in Canada.* Retrieved from https://www.priv.gc.ca/en/privacy-topics/privacy-laws-in-canada/02_05_d_15/

Office of the Privacy Commissioner of Canada. (2017). "Applying Sections &(3)(d1) and 7(3)(d2) of PIPEDA". Retrieved from *https://www.priv.gc.ca/en/privacy-topics/privacy-laws-in-canada/the-personal-information-protection-and-electronic-documents-act-pipeda/pipeda-compliance-help/gd-d1_d2_2017703/*

--------------- *(2014) Special Report to Parliament, Checks and Controls: Reinforcing Privacy Protection and Oversight for the Canadian Intelligence Community in an Era of Cyber Surveillance.*

---------------- (2013) *Drones in Canada Will the proliferation of domestic drone use in Canada raise new concerns for privacy?* Retrieved from https://www.priv.go.ca/media/1760/drones_2-1303_e.pdf

O'Neill, Ann (2015) "Tsarnaev trial: Timeline of the bombings, manhunt and aftermath. CNN (May 15, 2015) Accessed May31,2017 at CNN http://www.cnn.com/2015/03/04/us/tsarnaev-trial-timeline/

Organization for Economic Co-operation and Development (2013) *The OECD privacy framework.* OECD Publishing. Retrieved July 4, 2017 from http://www.oecd.org/sti/ieconomy/oecdguidelinesontheprotectionofprivacyandtransborderflowsofpersonaldata.htm#part2

Oxford Dictionary (2014) http://www.oxforddictionaries.com/definition/english/analysis Retrieved 10/02/14 at 20:10.

Palantir Law Enforcement (2017). Retrieved from https://www.palantir.com/solutions/law-enforcement/

Parker, Donn B. (1976). *Crime by Computer.* New York City, NY: Charles Scribner's Sons.

Papachristos, Andrew V., Hureau, D. M., Braga, A.A. (2013). "The corner and the crew: The influence of geography and social networks on gang violence." *American Sociological Review, 78*, 417-447.

Patton, D., J. Lane, J. Macbeth, J. Smith-Lee. (2016) "Gang violence on the digital street: cases study of a south side Chicago gang member's Twitter communication." *New Media and Society.*

Pell, Stephanie K. and Soghoian, Christopher. (2014) "Your Secret Stingray's No Secret Anymore: The Vanishing Government Monopoly over Cell Phone Surveillance and its Impact on National Security and Consumer Privacy". *Harvard Journal of Law and Technology*, Volume 28, Number 1 14-155.

Permanent Subcommittee on Investigations. (2012). *Federal support for and involvement in state and local fusion centers*, Washington DC: United States Senate.

Perrot, Patrick. (2014). "L'analyse du risque criminel: l'émergence d'une nouvelle approche". *Revue de l'Electricité et de l'Electronique .* Decembre.

---------------- & Kader, T. (2015). Forecasting analysis in a criminal intelligence context. *Proceedings International Crime and Intelligence Analysis Conference.* Great-Britain.

Peterson, Marilyn B. (1985) "Financial/Corporate Analysis with Computerized Applications" in *Law Enforcement Intelligence Analysis Digest*, Volume 1, No. 1.

---------------- *(1990) "Telephone Record Analysis" in Criminal Intelligence Analysis*, Paul P. Andrews, Jr. and Marilyn B. Peterson, eds. 1990, Loomis, CA: Palmer Enterprises, pp. 85 – 115.

-------------- (1994 and 1998a) *Applications in Criminal Analysis: A Sourcebook.* Westport, CT: Greenwood Press and Praeger (pb)

--------------- (1998b) "Joining the Debate: Product vs. Process," by Marilyn B. Peterson, in *IALEIA Journal*, Vol. 11, No. 1, Winter.

---------------- (1998c) *A Guide to the Financial Analysis of Personal and Corporate Bank Records* Richmond, VA: National White Collar Crime Center.

---------------- (2005). *Intelligence-led policing: the new intelligence architucture.* Washington, DC: Bureau of Justice Administration , 5.

--------------- (2006) "Analyze This and That", in *Fraud Magazine*, March/April.

---------------- (2007). "Developments in Law Enforcement Intelligence Analysis". In *Can't We All Just Get Along: Improving the Law Enforcement Intelligence Community Relationship* (pp. 3-20). Washington DC: National Defense Intelligence College.

----------------(2009a) *A Guide to Counter Threat Finance Intelligence.* Springfield, VA:self-published.

----------------(2009b) "Follow the Money" in *INTERSEC,The Journal of International Security* (July).

---------------- (2011) "Analysis and Synthesis" in *Criminal Intelligence for the 21st Century*, Richard Wright, Bob Morehouse, Marilyn Peterson and Lisa Palmieri, editors. Richmond, VA : IALEIA and LEIU.

---------------- and R. Fahlman, G. Ridgeway, P. Erwin, and M. Kuzniar (1996) *Successful Law Enforcement Using Analytic Methods.* Lawrenceville, NJ: IALEIA.

Phillips, B. (2015) "How Does Leadership Decapitation Affect Violence? The Case of Drug Trafficking Organizations in Mexico". *The Journal of Politics*, Volume 77.

Phillips, Scott W. (2012, September). The attitiudes of police managers toward intelligence-led policing. *FBI Law Enforcement Bulletin , 81* (9), pp. 13-16.

----------------(2012) "Police Supervisors' Attitude Toward Analysis in Policing: A Force-Field Analysis". *IALEIA Journal*,21(1).

Pot, J. (2016). *Ransomware attackers refuse to decrypt hospital's files after being paid off.* Retrieved from https://www.yahoo.com/tech/kansas-hospital-pays-ransomware demand-235824773.html

Privacy Act. (1985). Revised Statutes of Canada, 1985, c. P-21.

ProMonitor for Law Enforcement (n.d.). Retrieved May 21, 2017 from http://www.lexisnexis.com/risk/products/government/promonitor.aspx

QlikView (2016, March 24). Retrieved from: http://www.greatlakesbisummit.com/2016/sessions/quinnanalyticstopic/

Quattro Pro (n.d.). Retrieved from https://fileinfo.com/software/corel/quattro_pro

R Project for Statistical Computing (n.d.). Retrieved from https://www.r-project.org/about.html

RCMP – Lower Sackville (re) 2015 CanLII35478 (NS SIRT)

R. v. Cole, (2012) 3 SCR 34.R. v. Grant, 2009 SCC 32, [2009] 2 S.C.R. 353

R. v. Dyment, (1988) 2 SCR 417, 1988 CanLII 10 (SCC), para. 15.

R. v. Edwards (1966), 104 C.C.C. (3d) 136 (SCC)

R. v. Elliott (2016) ONCJ 35 (CanLII)

R.v. Fearon (2014) SCC 77 (CanLII)

R. v. Jones (2011) ONCA 632 (CANLII)

R. v. Kwok (2007) CanLII 2942

R. v. Little (2009) CanLII 41212 (ON SC)

R. v. Morelli, (2010) SCC 8, para. 106.

R. *v.* Spencer, 2014 SCC 43, [2014] 2 S.C.R. 212

R. v. Tessling (2004) SCC67 (Can LII)

R. v. Tuduce (2014) ONCA 547 (CanLII)

R. v. Vu(2011) BCCA 536 (CanLII)

R. v. Vye (2014) BCSC 93

R. v. Ward, 2012 ONCA 660 (CanLII)

R. v. Wills (1992) CanLII 2780

Radcliff, D. (2008). "Portrait of a Hacker". *SC Magazine*. 19(10), 40-41.

Ratcliffe, J. (2008). *Intelligence-Led Policing.* Cullompton: Willan Publishing.

---------------- (2016). *Intelligence-led policing.* New York: Routledge.

---------------- (2011) "Intelligence-led Policing: Anticipating Risk and influencing Action," in *Criminal Intelligence for the 21st Century*, Wright, Morehouse, Peterson and Palmieri, eds. Sacramento, CA: LEIU and IALEIA

---------------- & Guidetti, R. (2008). State police investigative structure and the adoption of intelligence-led policing. *Policing: An International Journal of Police Strategies and Management* , 109-128.

Regional Information Sharing Systems (RISS) (n.d.). Retrieved from https://www.ise.gov/mission-stories/state-and-regional

Riley v. California, 134 S. Ct. 2473 (2014)

Robbins, Liz. (2017) "MS-13 gang members arrested in girls/ killings on Long Island, police say". Retrieved May 22, 2017 from *New York Times*: https://wwww.nytimes.com/2017/02/02/nyregion/ms-13-gang-kilings-long-islland.html?_r=0

Roberts v. United States Jaycees, 468 U.S. 609, 622, 1984, as quoted in Boy Scouts of America v. Dale, 530 U.S. 640, 647, 2000

Roe v. Wade, 410 U.S. 113 (1973)

Rohard, A., & Perrot, P. (2015). "Géomatique et renseignement criminel". *La revue Géomatique expert* . (Abril)

Ronczkowski, Michael R. (2007). *Terrorism and Organized Hate Crime: Intelligence Gathering, Analysis, and Investigating, 2nd Ed.* Boca Raton, FL: CRC Press, Taylor and Francis.

Rossmo, Kim (2000) *Geographic Profiling.* Boca Raton: CRC Press.

Royal Canadian Mounted Police. (2007). *Using Intelligence Led Policing as a Model to Prioritize Organized Crime Investigations – A Canadian Perspective* [Power Point Presentation]. Retrieved from https://www.scm.oas.org/pdfs/2007/DPT00005T.ppt.

Runyon v. McCrary, 427 U.S. 160 (1976)

Sanchez, Boris and Kevin Conlon (2017), "Ft Lauderdale Shooter Claims He Carried Out Attack for ISIS, Says FBI", on CNN, accessed February 19 at http://www.cnn.com/2017/01/17/us/fort-lauderdale-shooter-isis-claim/.

Sanger, David E. and Broad, W.J. (2017) "Trump Inherits a Secret Cyberwar Against North Korean Missiles". *The New York Times.* Retrieved from https://www.nytimes.como/2017/03/04/world/asia/north-korea-missile-program-sabatoge.html. (March 4)

Santos, Rachel B. (2014) "The Effectiveness of Crime Analysis for Crime Reduction: Cure or Diagnosis?"*Journal of Contemporary Criminal Justice*, 30(2).

SAP Hana (n.d.). Retrieved from http://www.sapphiresystems.com/en-us/solutions/sap/sap-hana/

SAP Sybase (n.d.) Retrieved from https://www.sap.com/product/data-mgmt/sybase-ase.html#

SAS - Criminal Justice Data Integration and Analytics

SAS - Memex (2010, June 23). Retrieved from http://www.businesswire.com/news/home/20100623005207/en/SAS-Acquires-UK-Software-Firm-Memex

SAS (2016). Retrieved from https://www.sas.com/en_us/company-information.html#history and https://www.sas.com/en_us/industry/government.html#homeland-security-criminal-justice

Schmidt, Michael and Perez-Pena, Richard (2015) "F.B.I. treating San Bernardino attack as terrorism". *New York Times* (Dec.4) accessed May 31, 2017, at https://www.nytimes.com/2015/12/05/us/tashfeen-malik-islamic-state.html?_r=0

Schmitz, C. (2017) "Supreme Court set to tackle privacy of phone text messages". *The Lawyers Weekly*, Vol. 36, No. 33.

Schneider, Steven. (2009). *Iced: The Story of Organized Crime in Canada.* New York: John Wiley & Sons.

Schwartz, Dan. and Rouselle, Tony. (2009). "Using social network analysis to target criminal networks". *Trends in Organized Crime,* Volume 12, 188-207.

----------------. (2008). "Targeting Criminal Networks: Using Social Network Analysis to Develop Enforcement and Intelligence Priorities". *IALEIA Journal, 18 (1), 18-43.*

Schussler, Bethany (2011) "Financial Intelligence" in *Criminal Intelligence for the 21stCentury,* Wright, Morehouse, Peterson and Palmieri, eds. Sacramento, CA: LEIU and IALEIA.

Senate Select Committee on Intelligence (1994*) An Assessment of the Aldrich H. Ames Espionage Case and Its Implications for U.S. Intelligence.* Washington, DC: U.S. Government , November. Accessed May 29, 2016, at http://fas.org/irp/congress/1994_rpt/ssci_ames.htm

Shuy, Roger (1990) "Tape Recorded Conversations"in *Criminal Intelligence Analysis,* Paul P. Andrews and Marilyn B. Peterson, eds. Loomis, CA: Palmer Press.

---------------- (2004) "Language Crimes The Use and Abuse of Language Evidence in the Courtroom" Accessed 17 February 2017 at http://scholar.google.com/scholar_url?url=http://vohkoohe.ingyenweb.hu/%40Angolos%2520cuccok/2004-2005-1/Applied/shuy.doc&hl=en&sa=X&scisig=AAGBfm2OqZqKbu6Vc_LZs-DkHGJ_OFG6JQ&nossl=1&oi=scholar

---------------- (2015) "Discourse Analysis in a Legal Setting" in *Handbook of Discourse Analysis, 2nd edition,* Deborah Tannen, Heidi Hamilton and Deborah Shiffren, eds. New York: John Wiley.

Simon, Jeffrey D. (2013) *Lone Wolf Terrorism Understanding the G rowing Threat.* Amherst, NY: Prometheus Books.

Singleton, T.W. (2010) "Mitigating IT risks for logical access". Retrieved from http:///www.isaca.org/Jurnal/archives/2010/Volume-5/Pages/Mitigating-IT-Risks-for-Logical-Access.aspx

Smith, Mitch, Richard Perez-Pena and Adam Goldman (2016) "Suspect is killed in attack at Ohio State University that injured 11:, *New York Times* (October 28, 2016) accessed February 19, 2017 at https://www.nytimes.com/2016/11/28/us/active-shooter-ohio-state-university.html?_r=0

SmartDraw (2017) Retrieved From https://www.smartdraw.com/features/

Snaptrends (n.d.). Retrieved from http://snaptrends.com/about/

Social Network Analysis, www.orgnet.com/sna/html, accessed 1/7/06

Software (Freeware). (n.d.) Retrieved from https://sites.google.com/site/lawenforcementintelligence/software-freeware

Sokmensuer, Harriett (2017) "Two suspected MS-13 members accused of killing Houston teen in 'Satanic Ritual'". Accessed 4/30/17 at http://people.com/crime/ms-13-satanic-alleged-killing-teen-houston/ (posted3/3/17)

Southeastern Public Safety Institute (2008) *Financial Investigative Techniques: Follow the Money – Training Manual.* St Petersburg, F: St. Petersburg College (August).

Sparrow, Malcolm (1991). "The application of network analysis to criminal intelligence: an assessment of the prospects". in *Social Networks,* Volume 13, 251-274.

Spann, Delena (2014) "Fraud Prognostications" in *Fraud Magazine* (October/November).

---------------- (2014) *Fraud Analytics Strategies and Methods for Detection and Prevention.* New York: John Wiley.

Snaptrends for Law Enforcement (n.d.). Retrieved from http://snaptrends.com/social-media-for/law-enforcement/#Snaptrends-for-Law-Enforcement

Spencer, David W. (2007). "Predictive Intelligence: What the Drug Enforcement Administration Can Glean From the Intelligence Community". In *Can't We All Just Get Along: Improving the Law Enforcement Intelligence Community Relationship* (pp. 93- 116). Washington DC: National Defense Intelligence College.

Stelfox, Peter (2009). *Criminal Investigation, An Introduction to Principles and Practice.* Devon, UK: Cullompton Willan Publishing.

Steve M. Solomon, Jr., Inc. v. Edgar

Strang, Steven. (2014). "Network Analysis in Criminal Intelligence*" in Network and Network Analysis for Defence and Security.* A.J. Masys, ed. London: Springer.

Sullivan, Erin. (2011, June 4). *New intelligence-led policing strategy strives to stop crime before it happens, not react after*. Retrieved from Tampa Bay Times: http://www.tampabay.com/news/publicsafety/new-intelligence-led-policing-strategy-strives-to-stop-crime-before-it/1173615

Tableau (2017). Retrieved from https://www.tableau.com/trial/tableau-10?utm_campaign=Prospecting-CORE-ALL-ALL&utm_medium=Paid+Search&utm_source=Bing&utm_language=EN&utm_country=USCA&kw=tableau%20software&adgroup=CTX-Brand-Tableau+Software-P&adused={creative}&matchtype=p&placement={placement}

Technopedia.com (2017) "Doxing". Retrieved June 17, 2017 from https://www.techopedia.com/definition/29025/doxing

Tech Target, retrieved June 19, 2016 from http://searchcloudcomputing.techtarget.com/definition/big-data-Big-Data.

Teradata (2017) Retrieved from http://www.teradata.com/solutions-and-industries/government/?LangType=1033&LangSelect=true

Telelink. (2013). *Data Interception and Theft*. Retrieved from http://itsecurity.telelink.com/data-interception-and-theft .

The White House (2016) "Presidential Policy Directive -- United States Cyber Incident Coordination" Retrieved June 14, 2017 from https://obamawhitehouse.archives.gov/the-press-office/2016/07/26/presidential-policy-directive-united-states-cyber-incident (June 26)

Thompson Reuters World-Check (n.d.). Retrieved from http://thomsonreuters.com/en/products-services/risk-management-solutions/relationship-risk-management/thomson-reuters-world-check.html

Toch, Hans. (2012). Police officers as change agents in police reform. In M. Marks, & D. Sklanksy, *Police reform from the bottom up: officers and their unions as agents of change* (p. 27). New York: Routledge.

Toobin, Jeffrey. (2014) "This is my jail where gang members and their female guards set the rules." Retrieved May 15, 2017 from *The New Yorker*: http://www.newyorker.com/magazine/2014/04/14/this-s-my-jail

Townsend, K., Sullivan, J., Monahan, T., & Donnelly , J. (2010, Oct). Intelligence-led mitigation. *Journal of Homeland Security and Emergency Management , 7* (1), pp. 1-2.

Tufte, Edward (1983) *The Visual Display of Quantitative Information.* New Haven, CT: Graphic Press

Urbas, G. (2012). Cybercrime, Jurisdiction and Extradition: The Extended Reach of Cross-Border Law Enforcement. *Journal of Internet Law*. 16(1), 7-17.

United Nations. (1948) *Universal Declaration of Human Rights.* United Nations General Assembly resolution 217 A. Retrieved from http://www.un.org/en/universal-declaration-hman-rights/

United Nations Office on Drugs and Crime (UNODC).. (2011). *Criminal Intelligence Manual for Analysts*. Vienna, Austria: United Nations.

---------------- "Results of a pilot survey of forty selected organized criminal groups in sixteen countries" (2002).

U.S. Army. (2015). *Techniques for Document and Media Exploitation, ATP 2-91.8*. Washington, DC: U.S. Government Printing Office.

U.S. Department of Homeland Security. (2013). *National response framework.* Retrieved from http://www.fema.gov/media-library-data/20130726-1914-25045-1246/final_national_response_framework_20130501.pdf

U.S. Department of Homeland Security, (2015) *Intellectual Property Rights Seizures Statistics, Fiscal Year 2014.* Retrieved June 18, 2016 from http://www.cbp.gov/sites/default/files/documents/2014%20IPR%20Stats.pdf .

U.S. Department of Justice. (2003). *National criminal intelligence sharing plan.* Washington, DC: U.S. Department of Justice.

U.S. Department of Justice. (2008). *Privacy, civil rights and civil liberties: Policy and templates for justice information systems.* Washington, DC: Author.

---------------- (2016) Criminal RICO: 18 U.S.C. §§1961-1968 A Manual For Federal Prosecutors, 6th Revised Edition. Washington, DC: US Department of Justice (May).

U.S. Office of Personnel Management. (2015, June 4). *Information about the latest cybersecurity incident.* Retrieved from https://www.dhs.gov/how-do-i/report-cyber-incidents

U.S. Treasury (2015) *National Money Laundering Risk Assessment.* Washington, DC: U.S. Treasury.

United States v. Allen, 106 F.3d 695, 6th Cir. 1997

United States v. Jacobsen, 466 U.S. 109, 1984

United States v. Jones, 132 S. Ct. 945 (2012)

United States v. Young, 350 F.3d 1302, 11th Cir. 2003

University of Southern California (2015). "Disparities in the criminal justice system. Gang injunctions and sentencing enhancements". Accessed 4/30/17 at http://safeandjust.uscmediacurator.com/gang-injunctions/

Van der Hurst, R. (2009). "Introduction to social network analysis as an investigative tool". *Trends in Organized Crime*, Volume 12, 101-121.

Virginia Department of Criminal Justice Services. (2013). *Review of the intelligence-led policing model.* Richmond, VA: State of Virginia.

Walton, Ann (2013) "Financial Intelligence: Uses and Teaching Methods" in *Journal of Strategic Security.*

Ward, P. and .A Horne (2015) "Interception of Communications" Retrieved from www.nontic.org/online-security.html.

Waxman, Matthew C. (2010). Police and National Security: American Local Law Enforcement and Counterterrorism After 9/11. *Journal of National Security and Policy, 3(2), 377-407.*

Weidman, G. (2014). *Penetration testing: A hands-on introduction to hacking.* San Francisco, CA: No Starch Press, Inc.

Wells, Ian. (2011). "Staffing the Intelligence Unit". In R. Wright, B. Morehouse, M.B. Peterson, and L. Palmieri (Eds.), *Criminal Intelligence for the 21st Century: A Guide for Intelligence Professionals* (pp. 28-43). Richmond, VA: LEIU and IALEIA.

Wentzel, John. (2016) "Anticipating Surprise: Using Indications, Indicators and Evidence for Attack Preparation" retrieved from https://www.recordedfuture.com/cyber-attack-preparation

Williams, Phil. (2001). "Transnational Criminal Networks" - RAND Corporation. Retrieved June 01, 2016, from http://www.rand.org/content/dam/rand/pubs/monograph_reports/MR1382/MR1382.ch3.pdf

Wright, Richard E., B. Morehouse, M.B. Peterson and L. Palmieri, eds. (2011). *Criminal intelligence for the 21st Century: A Guide for Intelligence Professionals.* Richmond, VA: LEIU and IALEIA.

Zalma, Barry. (2012) "Red Flags of Insurance Fraud" posted on http://www.Zalma.com/blog/red-flags-of-insurance-fraud accessed March 27,2015.

Index

13 Rebels, 164
2014 Report to the Nations on Occupational Fraud and Abuse, 111
28 C.F.R. 23, 68
5WHs, 48
9/11 Commission, 18, 178
Abadinsky, 78, 229
Accurint, 201, 229
AFCEA, 178, 179, 229
AICPA, 113, 229
Alkaabi, 136, 229
American Civil Liberties Association, 73, 229
Analysis of Competing Hypothesis, 189
Analyst's Notebook, 116, 209, 229
anarchy, 64
Anderson, 9, 11, 229
Andress, 127, 129, 229
anomalies, 34, 114, 118, 120, 186
ArcGIS, 206, 209, 210, 216, 229
Ariely, 34, 229
artificial intelligence, 28, 30, 32, 34, 216, 224
Aryan Nation, 159
Association of Certified Fraud Examiners, 111, 151, 229
attribution, 133, 196, 238
Australian Attorney-General's Department, 133, 229
Ayres, 162, 229
Babel X, 201, 229
Bandidos, 159, 164
Bank Secrecy Act, 138, 140, 141
bankruptcy fraud, 112, 114
Barciz, 160, 230
Basic Principles of National Application, 61
Bayer, 177, 178, 230
Behavioral Economics, 34
Bellman, 33, 230
Bengio, 33, 230
Bennett, 99, 230
Big data, 25, 30, 233,236
Bitcoin, 137
Black Guerrilla Family, 159, 163, 165, 234
Bouchard, 79, 80, 86, 230, 234
Bouza, 11, 230
Bradford, 145, 230

Brantingham, 24, 34, 230
Bribery, 111
Broadhurst, 133, 230
Brookover, 47, 230
burglaries, 22, 24, 29, 30, 32, 42
burglary, 32
business intelligence, 33
Business Watch International, 201
Calvani, 78, 230
Canadian Charter of Rights and Freedoms, 69, 230
car robberies, 29
car theft, 30
CarFax for Police, 201
Cariens, 156, 230
Carter, 1, 6, 16, 176, 177, 178, 180, 190, 192, 222, 230, 231
Case Analysis, 39, 195
Cassara, 139, 231
Cell Hawk, 210
Cellebrite, 132, 219
Center of Gravity Analysis, 77, 191
Central Intelligence Agency, 177
centrality, 80, 82, 83, 84, 85, 86, 87, 89, 91, 183
Centres of Gravity, 98, 101, 105, 106
centres of gravity analysis, 100, 104, 105
Chapman, 52, 100, 231, 233
Chen, 30
Chernak, 15
Child pornography, 131
civil liberties, 12, 14, 59, 60, 62, 64, 65, 67, 68, 177, 225, 242
Clarke, 24, 34, 230, 233
Coambs, 141, 231
Coderre, 113, 125
Cohen, 24, 34
cohesion, 19, 82, 84
Cole, 69, 70, 100, 104, 231, 239
Collection Plan, 42, 43, 196
Commodity flow analysis, 149, 192
Commodity Flow Analysis, 120, 192, 196
commodity flow chart, 120, 121, 123, 149, 155, 192
communication, 50, 93, 94, 192, 195
Communication Analysis, 92
communications analysis, 134, 192, 226
Communications Analysis, 77, 107, 192, 196, 200
Comprehensive Financial Investigations Solution, 210
Conley, 162, 231

constitutional rights, 59, 66, 67, 68
Consumer Sentinel Network, 202
content analysis, 92, 96, 97, 98
Cook, 146, 231
Cope, 16, 231
corruption, 111
Cossacks, 159, 164
Counterdrug Intelligence Plan, 13
counter-terrorism, 27, 175, 193
CrimeNtel, 210
Criminal Business Analysis, 39
Criminal Information System Operating Policies. See 28CFR 23.20
Criminal Intelligence Coordinating Council, 15
Criminal Intelligence File Guidelines, 66
Criminal Intelligence Model Policy, 15
Criminal Intelligence Service Canada, 74, 231
Criminal Intelligence Sharing Summit, 14, 67
criminal market, 192, 199, 227
criminal network, 94, 99, 100, 101, 103, 104, 105
criminal networks, 24, 99, 100, 101, 102, 103, 104, 105, 106, 107, 183
criminal target modeling, 33
critical infrastructure, 131, 135, 186, 216
critical thinking, 149, 156
Cumming, 17, 232
Cunliffe, 127, 232
Cutting Edge, 202, 220
cyber crime, 111, 235, 236
Cyber-Crime, 127, 234
cybersecurity, 128, 227, 235, 242
data mining, 132, 144, 145
DataWalk, 210
degree,, 82, 83, 183
Demographical Analysis, 42
Denial and Deception, 191, 234
density, 24, 82, 84
Department of Homeland Security, 15
Department of Homeland Security's, 181
Dialed Number Recorder, 94
Digital Privacy Act, 232
Dintino, 59, 232
discourse analysis, 97
document exploitation, 187, 189
Doxing, 130
Drug Market Profiles, 38
drug trafficking, 22, 59, 101, 102

economic crimes, 29, See white collar crimes
edges, 80, 82, 83, 87
eigenvector, 82, 84, 89, 91
eigenvector),, 82
Eikmeier, 99, 195, 196, 197, 232
email, 93
embezzlement, 111, 124
Encase, 132
environmental criminology, 24, 25, 34
European Convention on Human Rights, 22
Event Flow Analysis, 117, 118
extremist groups, 59
Facebook, 28, 93
Federal Bureau of Investigation, 5, 6, 9, 17, 159, 162, 165, 222, 233, 237
Felson, 24, 34, 230, 233
Fenton, 163, 233
Ferguson, 29, 233
Fiduciary responsibility, 111
financial analysis, 113, 146, 148, 149, 150, 154, 156, 158, 179, 180, 192, 193
Financial analysis, 113, 192
Financial Crimes Enforcement Network, 179
financial intelligence, 186
First Amendment, 63, 64
Force Field Analysis, 39
Forecasting, 238
forensic linguistics, 97
Fourth Amendment, 62, 63
Fowler, 98
Fusion Center Guidelines, 15
Gang Crime, 159
Geofeedia, 132, 173, 203, 233
geographic tracking, 93
geospatial analysis, 186, 193, 201, 209
GeoTime CRT, 211
Gephi, 184, 217
Giraud, 33, 233
Global Intelligence Working Group, 14
Godfrey, 12, 59, 60, 234
Gordnier, 75, 234
Granovetter, 80, 234
Handling Code, 45
Hanneman, 82, 83, 84, 234
Harris, 12, 59, 60, 234
Hashimi, 79, 80, 234
Hells Angels, 159, 164

Hetherington, 141

High Intensity Drug Trafficking Areas, 179

Holder, 131, 133, 234

Homeland Security Information Network, 179

homicides, 30

hotspots, 29, 32

human trafficking, 59, 104

Hunton, 135, 136, 234

Hurst, 81, 243

hypotheses, 118, 120, 132, 189

IACP Intelligence Summit, 13

IALEIA. See International Association of Law Enforcement Intelligence Analysts

ID napping, 128, 129

Indications and Warnings, 191

Indicator analysis, 124, 185

indicators, 16, 93, 95, 112, 114, 124, 135, 138, 150, 151, 180, 191, 196, 200

insurance fraud, 111, 112, 113, 124

insurgencies, 99

Intelligence Evaluation, 45

Intelligence Reform and Terrorism Prevention Act, 178

intelligence-led policing, 9, 10, 12, 14, 15, 21, 23, 26, 35, 59, 105, 112, 113, 115, 125, 195, 239, 240, 243

International Association of Chiefs of Police, 12, 13

International Association of Law Enforcement Intelligence Analysts, 12, 234, 235

intrusion, 60, 62, 65, 128, 130, 140

James, 133, 225, 233, 234

Johannson, 19, 235

Johnston, 131, 235

Katos, 136

k-core,, 82, 84

Kent Constabulary, 9, 10, 11, 17, 20

Kent Policing Model, 11

Kessler, 128, 235

Khimm, 165, 235

Khullar, 68, 235

Klug, 99, 100, 101, 236

Knowledge management, 21

knowledge workers.", 25

Krayniak, 115, 236

Krippendorff, 96, 97, 236

Lanzarote Committee, 131, 236

Law Enforcement Analytic Standards, 15, 234

Law Enforcement Intelligence Unit, 11, 66, 234, 236

Le, 78, 236

le Carre, 55, 236

Lemieux, 135, 136
Lindsey, 163, 236
link chart, 120, 180
Loh, 132, 236
Lumen, 211
Madden, 30, 236
Maillard, 5, 21, 23, 24, 25, 224, 235, 236
Market Analysis, 39
Martens, 59, 75, 232, 236
matrix, 33, 94, 121, 184, 192
Mcillwain, 86, 236
Media Sonar, 204, 220
metadata analysis, 92
misuses of intelligence, 59, 236
MS-13, 159, 161, 162, 183, 231, 240, 241
muggings, 29
narcotics, 92, 101, 103, 104, 106, 175, 176, 193
National Advisory Commission on Criminal Justice Standards and Goals, 12
National Counterterrorism Center, 179, 181
National Criminal Intelligence Sharing Plan, 14
National Cybersecurity Protection System, 132, 232
National Gang Intelligence Center, 163, 165, 237
National Institute of Justice, 160, 161, 162, 237
National Institute of Standards and Technology, 134
National Insurance Crime Bureau, 113
National Intelligence Model, 13, 38, 45, 237, See NIM
National Media Exploitation Center, 189
National Policing Improvement Agency, 39, 41, 51, 237
National Security Intelligence, 176, 177, 178, 180, 231
Nebraska Department of Insurance, 124, 238
Nebraska DOI, 124
Netmap, 211, 237
network analysis, 80, 113, 124, 134, 181, 183, 184, 201, 218, 226, 241
Network analysis, 80, 81, 124
Network Analysis, 39, 42, 44, 47, 124, 183, 195, 199, 235, 241
network capital, 83
neural networks, 33
New York Police Department, 11
Newman, 134, 238
nodes, 80, 82, 83, 101, 183
Norvelle, 151, 153, 238
Nossen, 151, 153, 238
NY Times, 130
offender behavior, 33
Office of the Privacy Commissioner, 72, 73, 238

Office of the Privacy Commissioner of Canada, 238

online games, 96

Operation Intelligence Assessments, 39

Operational analysis, 23

Organisation for Economic Co-operation and Development, 60, 238

organized crime, 12, 22, 23, 28, 59, 99, 106, 124, 175, 227, 234

Organized crime, 77, 78, 92, 223, 236

Pagans, 159, 164

Pajek, 184, 217, 218

Palantir, 212, 238

Pattern Analysis, 39, 42, 114, 196

Pearson, 132

PENLINK, 212

Perrot, 5, 21, 25, 224, 238, 240

Peterson, 1, 5, 6, 7, 10, 12, 15, 20, 53, 55, 92, 93, 94, 111, 114, 115, 120, 128, 137, 138, 141, 146, 147, 148, 149, 150, 151, 154, 180, 181, 182, 183, 189, 191, 192, 193, 195, 196, 198, 199, 225, 230, 231, 234, 236, 237, 239, 240, 241, 243

Philips, 81

Phillips, 16, 17, 18, 137, 239

Phishing, 129

Posse Comitatus Act of 1867, 177

Pre crime observation system, 29

Predictive Analysis, 28

Predictive Analytics, 125

President's Commission on Law Enforcement and the Administration of Justice, 11

preventive solutions, 32

privacy, 12, 14, 33, 59, 60, 62, 63, 64, 65, 66, 67, 68, 177, 225, 230, 238

Privacy Act, 71, 74, 239

Problem Profiles, 39

Queen, 164

ransomware, 128

Ratcliffe, 9, 16, 23, 24, 158, 240

reasonable suspicion, 66

records management systems, 87

Regional Information Sharing System, 12, 179

regressive analysis, 32

relational database, 113, 144, 145, 207, 208, 209

Results Analysis, 39, 199

Riley v. California, 62, 240

risk analysis, 29

Risk Analysis, 39, 199

risk assessment, 33, 38

Robbins, 162, 240

Sanger, 135, 236, 240

Santos, 155, 236, 240

SAS - Memex, 215, 240

Schmitz, 70, 240

Schneider, 78, 241

Schussler, 138, 241

Schwarts, 83

search or seizure, 63, 69

Second Life, 131

sexual assaults, 29

Shareware, 130

Shuy, 97, 241

Simon, 97, 241

Sintelix, 208

Sleipnir Matrix, 184

SNA. See Social Network Analysis

social media, 93, 192

social media analysis, 173

social network analysis, 107, 160, 183, 184, 241, 243

Social Network Analysis, 77

Social Network Visualizer, 184, 218

Sokmensuer, 162, 241

Sommers, 146, 231

Source Evaluation, 44

South Side Brims, 165

Spann, 125, 241

Sparrow, 80, 82, 84, 241

Springer, 164, 241

stock manipulation, 111

Strang, 81, 241

strategic analysis, 23, 24, 191

Strategic Assessments, 39

Stuxnet, 135

Subject Analysis, 39

Sullivan, 17, 235, 242

Suspicious Activity Report, 140

tactical analysis, 23, 40

Tactical Assessments, 39

Tagging, 162

Target Profile Analysis, 190

Target Profiles, 39

technopedia, 130

telephone record analysis, 92

Temporal Analysis, 42, 53

Teradata, 215, 242

terms of reference, 42, 43

Terms of Reference, 40, 41, 43, 46, 48, 51, 52

texts, 93, 192
The White House, 127, 242
threat analysis, 180, 181, 184, 186, 193
threat assessment, 180, 181
time series analysis, 30, 31
Timeline Analysis, 115, 186, 200
timelines, 113, 116, 134, 146, 180, 181, 197, 211
Toobin, 164
Townsend, 9, 235, 242
Treasury, 137, 140, 179, 242
Trenton Times, 116
Tufte,, 115, 242
tweets, 93
U.S. Department of Justice, 5, 14, 15, 20, 59, 60, 65, 66, 67, 68, 230, 234, 235, 242
UCINet, 184, 212
United Nations, 68, 78, 136, 190, 242
United States v. Jones, 63, 243
University of Southern California, 166, 243
Urbas, 133, 242
Veritone, 220
Virginia Department of Criminal Justice Services, 9, 243
Visual Investigative Analysis, 189
Visualization programs, 145
Vulnerability analysis, 180, 181
vulnerability assessment, 181
Ward, 71, 129, 240, 243
Waxman, 179, 243
Weidman, 127, 243
Wentzel, 135, 243
West Coast Crips, 165
white collar crime, 111, 112, 124
White Collar Crime, 5, 111, 113, 151, 152, 153, 154, 186, 193, 205, 237, 238, 239
white supremacy, 64
Whooster.com, 206
wire intercept, 96
Zalma, 112, 243

Made in the USA
Lexington, KY
04 September 2018